TALE OF A LION

ELLEN
CUMBESS

outskirtspress
DENVER, COLORADO

Every lion needs a pride. This is for my family.

Contents

Preface

"LIFE IS NOT what you see, but what you've projected. It's not what you've felt, but what you've decided. It's not what you've experienced, but how you've remembered it. It's not what you've forged, but what you've allowed. And it's not who's appeared, but who you've summoned. And this should serve you well, beloved, until you find what you already have."

~MIKE DOOLEY, WWW.TUT.COM

Prologue

It's a Jungle Out There

The beginning of each and every day was, at this particular time, a whirlwind of chores: Getting everyone up and out of bed, refereeing arguments over who had the right to the bathroom, finding missing articles of clothing, walking dogs, and ensuring that this household of 8 (a husband and 6 children) each reached his or her intended destination. That included getting myself dressed and out the door to work. While I continually failed to reach *my* destination on time, it could not be helped. Regardless of my successful planning, an early start, or organizational skills, all timing hinged upon the arrival of the school bus that came each weekday morning to transport our mentally challenged daughter to school. Theirs was a total failure to keep to a schedule conducive to my own! By the time I would arrive at the office, I was most assuredly in a disheveled state. At times, my hair was even uncombed.

My life was exactly as it appeared—exhaustive! None-the-less, a family that size has to eat. My husband, Bobby, worked every day (ALL DAY), including weekends and holidays, trying to provide as best he could. Still, our financial needs exceeded his income level. So, I worked too.

I was fortunate to have found work locally at a manufacturing facility. One day it happened that I found myself on the invitee list for what was labeled a *team building* exercise. Although there was a certain amount of truth to that statement, categorizing this event as *team building* seemed inaccurate to me in that every person attending—including myself—was an administrative assistant from her own respective area. Therefore, none of us actually worked *together*. The ladies who belonged to this particular classification were all very friendly. We had been associated through our employment for several years and had all come to know and like each other—as much as that many different individuals can. We each knew of each other's family history and make-up, had met the others' family members at holiday celebrations. In a large part, we were extended family members to each other.

So entering the large conference room where the training was to be held created no anxiety among us, for we were all familiar with one another. It was not until the trainer, a local psychologist, Larry Little*, and his associate appeared did we began to sense any apprehension. They both introduced themselves with a brief statement of what their backgrounds were and what the intention of the training was. In essence, we were about to partake in a personality profile assessment.

Each of the participants was given a two-sided legal sheet of paper containing twenty lines of four words. Our initial task required us to circle the one word in each line that best described ourselves. We were cautioned that several of these words might be applicable, but we were limited to the one that "best" suited us or most strongly represented us. In a very quick few minutes, all pencils were down. We were then instructed to go to the "key" and grade (if you will) our answers. The end result of this was each person in the room finding herself classified as one of four animals: a Lion, a Camel, a Monkey, or a Turtle.

The discussion that followed was around the simple characteristics of each:

"When you think of a lion, what do you think of?"

People freely offered words—roaring, man-eating, king of the jungle.

"What about Monkeys?"

"Monkeys like to play." "They swing from tree to vine." "They jump around." "They eat bananas."

"Anyone have any thoughts about a camel?"

Again people commented randomly: "Camels move very

deliberately." "They can travel for long periods of time without stopping for a drink of water." "Yes, they are very consistent."

"Finally, we have the Turtle. What do you think of a turtle?"

"Turtles are S-L-O-W!!! Horribly slow."

"Are they lazy?"

"NO" was the quick response given.

"Why not?"

My first thought was, "If it took me all day to get from here to there and I did it, that would not be an indication of lazy; that would be an indication of never giving up."

"True," the facilitator commented. "But you don't want to get behind one on the road, right?"

"Oh, hell no!"

As we each in our own time came to realizations about the various traits of these animals, we were then asked to reveal our own identifying animal as arrived at by the profiling exercises. One by one, each of the participants stated, "Camel," "Camel," "Camel." Suddenly a woman at the end of the table shrugged her shoulders and said giggling, "Monkey," to which everyone laughed along with her—realizing that monkeys like to play. What the trainer was showing us was already coming to pass. Around the rest of the table more animals were unveiled: A few Turtles, another Monkey, and even more Camels.

By the time my turn came, I felt very conscious of the fact that no one had stated the same. *I was a Lion!*

The facilitator then said, "OK, we'll break into *like* groups at this point and discuss more traits that we find indicative of our own value and those traits we identify as being those of the others. Since I am a Lion also," he continued, addressing me, "I will work with you."

The break-out seemed to relax everyone even more, as discussions ensued and the volume in the room became louder and louder. There was much laughter. After only five or so minutes of discussion, although it seemed much longer, we remained in our groups, but returned to order. The facilitator then helped everyone identify those traits of each that were easy for the others to deal with and those which were not so easy. Monkeys want to play when everyone else has things to get done. Turtles are very slow and do not do well in groups. In some instances, it was easy for the individuals in that classification to identify with their traits. In others, it was not. My own lion identifier spawned conversation around the lion roaring at everyone and taking over a room—being pushy. People actually commented that, at times, they were afraid of me—not that I would hurt them physically, but in terms of what response they might get from me. I had heard this type of thing before, but dismissed it as nonsense. Now it was starting to make perfect sense! I could actually envision myself knuckles down on a desktop leaning over someone demanding that they do what I wanted. At times, even my stance was a roar.

In the next segment, we explored how one rewards the various animal personalities: Turtles need one-on-one attention. Monkeys need fun time.

Before even getting to the camels, the question came up, "How do you reward a lion?"

"Well, you certainly don't pet them." Everyone laughed! (Everyone but me, that is.)

"You would reward a lion with a big piece of meat—something they could sink their teeth into, right?"

Everyone agreed.

"Therefore, try to envision this: Lions like projects. Rather than complimenting a lion on doing a project well (patting them on the head), they would much rather you give them a bigger project—a piece of meat for them to sink their teeth into!"

Ahh—that makes sense.

Towards the end of the session, one woman (classified as a Monkey) asked me, "Is everyone in your family a lion?"

Without a moment's thought, I quickly responded, "No, I don't think so—but they had better act like one!" My mind flashed to Fridays in the office when I would sit and make a list of all that I wanted to accomplish over the weekend. This was no ordinary list. It would consist of such things as:

- Paint the house
- Mow the lawn
- Re-tile the bathroom
- Go through all the clothing and sort to box up winter/summer
- Grocery shop
- Laundry
- Ironing
- Repair fence in the back

Project after project would be planned on my list of things to do. I would then go home on Friday afternoon and announce to everyone, "We have a ton of things to do this weekend, so don't stay up too late tonight. We're all getting up early to get started on this." I would crack the whip all weekend long, insisting that everyone work non-stop to accomplish this unreasonable list of things to do. By Monday morning, had we not accomplished everything on the list—despite reasonable explanation—I found myself depressed.

In that instant, I had a very profound realization. If I was assessing accurately based on the training, NO ONE IN MY FAMILY WAS A LION! Could that be true? I was consumed with curiosity. Despite being instructed against it, I copied the test and brought it home to my family, insisting that every member (other than my non-communicative daughter) take this test. Within minutes, I had total confirmation of what I had suspected. Of the five children testing, the oldest and youngest (both boys) were Monkeys. Everyone else, including my husband—TURTLES!

In the days that followed, no conversation had around this training compared with the self-examination with which I scrutinized myself over the differences uncovered in my own family. I had, in fact, been roaring at them—for YEARS! Worse was the fact that they all hated it. It was one thing to be faced with the fact that people distance themselves from you. It was entirely another to have to face that EVERYONE, including those in your own family, do the same thing— and they do this as a means of survival. *Was I roaring at everyone?*

The answer to that question was a resounding roar of a *YES* that played over and over inside my head for the next several weeks. I vacillated between feeling totally empowered (king of the jungle) to feeling sad and alone (frightening people rather than befriending them). It was truly a difficult realization. However, it was the very starting point for the exploration into my life's history that took me down the road I always wanted to travel, the road I had been on my entire life—without a steering wheel. *Tales of a Lion* is the story of that journey.

* The Make a Difference Workshop, facilitated by scholar, author and entrepreneur Larry Little, PhD, LPC, is an interactive, relevant and powerful experience where participants gain tools and knowledge for more relevant and effective leadership. The basis of Dr. Little's approach is in the power of relationships and understanding your own personality and the personalities of those you lead, in order to more effectively speak their language. For more information about Dr. Little, the Make a Difference Workshop, or his work at The Enrichment Center Group, please visit www.theenrichment-center.org or call 256-341-0811.

Stage I

1. Queen for a Day

LIFE BEGAN FOR me in the Bronx. My father was a New York City police officer; my mother, a housewife. It was his second marriage; her
third. Among my father's extra-curricular activities were drinking and
gambling—neither of which were things he was good at. As I grew to
adulthood, I kept this simple in my head: My father couldn't pick a
horse, and my mother couldn't pick a husband.

My father would drink to excess. While accurate, that statement
doesn't quite capture the extent of his drinking. He drank himself into
a stumbling down rage. Sometimes my father would go out for a loaf
of bread—and come back with it three days later!

As a result of his drinking and gambling, my father squandered
every cent he earned before it ever hit the bank account. Thus my
mother was left to run the household and support the three children
in our family on a hope and a prayer. In desperation (I'm quite certain); she enrolled herself as an Avon representative and began selling
Avon products door-to-door.

My mother's assigned territory was a huge building complex
known in the area as Fordham Hill. The buildings in Fordham Hill
had many floors; as many as 17 not counting the roof. It was about
a 5-block walk from our apartment in one straight shot of a path. My
mother would take me (4 years old at the time), and we would walk to
Fordham Hill, where we would literally go door to door selling Avon.
She would sit and speak to the lady of the house, I to the children. In
looking back, I note that we were a terrific sales team. While Mom
enticed the ladies of the house into perfume, cosmetics, etc., I would
show the children the latest and greatest bubble bath toys.

It was a very big development and a profitable market. We were a
far cry from well-to-do, but we were making it. If we had a very successful night and sales were high, we would treat ourselves to a taxi

ride home. The guard of the Fordham Hill development would call us a cab from the guard house. That luxury of a ride cost $1.00, with a 25-cent tip.

After profitable sales milestones were achieved, my mother would invest in flyers and extra books to boost her clientele. Some of our outings were centered around her stamping the back of the books with her name and phone number, and then me running door to door hanging the books in plastic bags on the door knobs of the front doors, saving her the legwork.

Sales increased, as did profits. I am unclear as to whether my father actually knew my mother was selling Avon and didn't mind—or if he was completely in the dark about it. Suffice to say, this activity—or *any* activity—was NOT to interfere with anything that had to do with him. That I do remember.

After months of this door-to-door endeavor, my mother received a phone call from her district manager advising her that she had achieved a certain elite status of sales and, as a result, would be receiving recognition at the next monthly sales meeting. Avon made a pretty big deal of this. The recognition was not only a monetary bonus and gifts, but also the presentation of a crown (tiara). Their sales women were queens!

All month long, my mother and I were quite excited at the prospect of her being recognized by the other Avon representatives. We planned what we would wear, our hair-do's—everything. This was to be truly a special day!

In all of our anticipation, it should have come as no surprise that we were the only ones in our family who thought of this as a big occasion. My brother (ten years my elder) spent most of his time out of the house, and my sister (seven years my elder) wished she did. They did not participate in or have anything much to do with the sale of Avon. For that matter, they didn't have much of anything to do with my mother or me at that time. My father, oblivious to everything but the races and his beer, couldn't have cared less about my mother's achievement.

So the big day came. My mother was thrilled! She spent over an hour getting ready, selecting just the right shoes to go with her dress. I, too, got all dressed up and was very excited to be going out with her.

Meanwhile, this one time that my mother had something special to go to; my father arrived home from work late. Those of us who were home had already eaten dinner, and we were about ready to go. My sister, Genie, was sitting in the bedroom, listening to the radio and drawing. Dad—obviously late because he had been at the corner bar—was loud and obnoxious, screaming about his dinner. Mom quickly ran inside to fix his plate, rather than leave him on his own. No sooner had she put the plate down in front of Dad than he slammed his arm across the table knocking everything over and yelling, "This is ice cold!"

Mom stayed fairly calm, as this was not her first rodeo. "Yes, it's cold because we ate earlier. I have an appointment—remember?"

Whether or not he remembered is not relevant. My father's dinner was cold, and the proverbial shit was about to hit the fan. In seconds, he swung at Mom, knocking her to the ground. She held her face for a second and then went to get up, at which point he went at her again. I had seen him go into a rage before, but never at my mother. Prior incidents of him losing his temper involved his yelling about something my brother or sister had done. This time he was enraged and out of control. I ran into the bedroom and begged Genie, "Do something!" She grabbed the phone to call the police.

Since dear old Dad was a police officer, we were calling his coworkers to deal with him. My father was not going to have anyone from work come to handle him; that would have been humiliating! (Too bad slapping my mother around was not as humiliating to him as his buddies walking in and seeing it would be). At any rate, Dad realized that Genie was calling the police from the bedroom and snatched the phone off the hook in the living room. Once the extension was off the hook, a call could not be placed. We heard a dial tone and my mother's screaming. Thinking quickly, Genie instructed me to run to the living room and put the phone back on the hook.

"Run out and take the phone in the living room and hold it in your lap – NOW.

"Huh?"

"Go out there!"

"Do I have to?"

"Yeah . . . Go!"

I ran through the house and sat in the recliner next to the phone, holding it in my lap with the receiver in the cradle until my sister yelled, "OK!" This only took a few seconds, but it was horrible—my father hitting my mother, all the while yelling at me to leave the phone alone.

Within minutes, the police arrived and were banging on the door. Genie and I ran over each other trying to get it open quickly. As they walked in (and there were more than one), my father released his grip on my mother's arm—which he had been twisting up behind her back while he used his other hand to hit her. He smiled at the officers/coworkers as they approached him.

"Hey, Frank—how's it going?"

I was only five years old. I looked up at these people whom I equated with *The Cavalry* and realized that they had now been re-duced to just a few guys my father knew.

"Come on, Frank, let's walk it off."

To this day, I don't know where or how my mother regained her composure to think straight. But she looked up and said, "*Walk it off*—are you kidding? Genie, get me a pen and paper!" My sister quickly went to fulfill her request, and my mother walked up to the officer closest to her and said, "I'm taking down your badge numbers. Either you arrest him, or I'm calling your watch commander!"

I was impressed! Granted, my mother had just had the shit beat out of her, but she was making it clear that she was not going to have this happen again. She actually wrote down each of the officers' badge numbers and instructed them to take my father out of her house. She then went into the bathroom for a few minutes, redid her hair and make-up, and upon returning to the living room, said to me,

"Get your purse, we're going!" This incident was not going to prevent her from getting her award and receiving her crown!

My father was never allowed back into the house. We packed his belongings into boxes and had them placed outside the apartment door for him to pick up at the end of that week. This story—while not one of the better memories our family has—is retold from time to time. On every occasion, it is referred to as *The Night My Mother Got Crowned—Twice!*

2. First Impressions

ON MY FIRST day of school, at the tender age of five, my mother insisted that my hair be done especially for an event later that evening.

My mother was very old school when it came to getting hair done. She insisted on using the pin curl method, rather than curlers. For anyone out there who has no knowledge of this—pin curls were groupings of hair that would be twisted around your finger into a loop, which would then be flattened against your head and held still with a bobby pin; thus the term *pin curl*.

So on that day, my mother painstakingly wound strands of my hair into pin curls, which then covered my entire head. I was somewhat used to this practice. It was how she knew to do hair. But I was under the impression that this was something exclusive to *in the house*—and that I would never have to be seen in public this way!

I was only in kindergarten, and my day at school was, in fact, a half day. Still, my mother wanted so much to ensure that my hair would remain curled that evening that she insisted I wear these pin curls to school. "This doesn't look right! I don't want them in," I protested.

"It'll be fine," she insisted. "No one will notice."

"Oh sure–no one! My entire class is filled with blind kids . . . MOM!"

I begged and begged, but Mom wouldn't back down. She wanted my hair fixed for that evening and was not going to take no for an answer!

"Wait here. I've got something that will fix it," she insisted. I was thinking she was going to bring a scarf out to wrap around my hair, much in the same manner my sister, Genie, would cover up her curlers. Genie was a typical teen at that time. She constantly complained that her hair wasn't done and would set her hair in rollers TO GO OUT! Every time she went out, her hair was in rollers. That was not just Genie. All of her girlfriends went out that way. They spent YEARS in rollers. There must have been something cool about it or Genie wouldn't have been caught dead doing it!

This was different. This was pin curls. I looked like an alien! I waited to see what my mother was going to bring out that was going to fix this situation.

"Here we go!" she declared. I saw her reflection in the mirror coming up behind me and could not believe what I was looking at! In her hand was the very tiara she had been given the night she got crowned by Avon. It was made of rhinestones, with combs on each side that would hold the band to your head secure. "Let's put this on."

"Are you kidding?—MOM?"

"There now—that's much better. You will be the envy of everyone."

It was as if my mother had gone crazy—thinking that having my hair pinned down to my head secured with bobby pins would not be noticed because of a tiara on top of this hair-do! *Oh, God!*

I arrived at school and continued to ask my mother for a scarf— something to put on top of my head. "I look ridiculous!" I kept telling her, but she ignored my complaints. Leading me into the building, she asked, "Where do the students for Ms. Green's class go?"

There I was, headed for the auditorium of PS 86 with pin curls in my hair—topped by a tiara. I might as well have been naked! It couldn't have been any worse. As I entered the auditorium and walked down the aisle, I could feel the kids looking at me, thinking I was some sort of freak. I finally found my section and climbed over the seats to the center of the seating. The kid next to me just looked with his jaw dropping and said "W-O-W- -!" It wasn't a good wow. It was like a *Holy Cow!* wow or an *Oh My God* wow.

One by one, kids began looking at me. The silence grew in the auditorium. At the point when it seemed conversation had completely vacated the noisy room, I realized that I was now the main attraction—and not in a good way! I excused myself and ran to the restroom and began hurriedly removing the tiara and pin curls. I had no comb, no brush—nothing with which to fix my hair. I pulled the tiny combs off the sides of the tiara and used them to push the sides of my hair back and then returned to the auditorium, tiara in hand.

But the damage had been done! The image of my head in that tiara was indelibly marked into everyone's memory for all time. I tried my best to keep a stiff upper lip, but I couldn't stand it. No matter what anyone was talking about, I felt they were talking about *me*— and it wasn't positive. I cried most of that day and was hatefully angry when I returned home in the afternoon.

My mother never understood how awful that experience was for me, never acknowledged my embarrassment. In her mind, I was simply overreacting to something nice she was trying to do for me.

Seeing Olympic Skier Julia Mancuso wearing her tiara as she attacked the slopes so many years later was no comparison to my tiara-wearing back in kindergarten! After all, Julia was in the Olympics, and her hair was styled properly underneath—not rolled into little knots. As I watched the Olympics, I waited for my phone to ring with Mom on the other end saying, "See, that fashion sense finally caught on!"

3. The Muse

THERE WAS A strange dynamic or hierarchy in my family that became evident to me at a young age. My brother, the oldest (senior to me by ten years), was not necessarily pampered, but he was humored by both my mother and my grandmother. Perhaps it came from Mike being the firstborn. Perhaps it was because he was the son. Whatever the reason, the sun seemed to shine up his ass and out his nose.

Mike's father had been my mother's first husband. They weren't together very long. My mother always spoke fondly of him, telling stories of how every payday he would come home with a little gift for her. It was never anything expensive, but something that he would present her as a remembrance—something that obviously showed my mother that he thought she was special. I believe it was my grandmother that came between them, causing the separation and ultimate divorce. That was something I could never understand: How did my grandmother have such an influence over my mother that she caused the breakup of her marriage? After all, if she had been that influential, she should have been able to prevent it!

Anyway, the progeny of this marriage, my brother, never finished high school. For a while, Mike attended DeWitt Clinton; a public high school in the Bronx. But he left after two or three years.

Mike told everyone that he wanted to become a photographer. Instantly he was enrolled in the Famous Photographer's correspondence course. We had no money! How my mother came up with the money for that Famous Photographer's course was a mystery to me. How she justified it was an even bigger mystery. Mike had just demonstrated that he had no follow-through by dropping out of school!

In addition to the tuition and fees associated with this course, my brother was given camera equipment. One camera in particular was a Minnox. I remember this vividly because it was the smallest camera

I had ever seen. It was the type of camera seen in spy movies, which would be taken out of one's pocket and used to photograph secret documents! No bigger than a half pack of cigarettes, this silver spy camera was one of Mike's favorite toys. But he had others as well. The camera equipment he used to take photos of weddings was just the opposite of the Minnox; quite large. It contained those big film panels inserted and removed by a handle from the side. Talk about a production!

With all this, it must be conceded that Mike was a great photographer. He had a really good eye for framing a picture and was able to judge what would make a good shot. He took pictures of the Verrazano Bridge which are as good as any I have ever seen. One photo he took actually hung on display in a gallery in New York. Mike's knack for photography quickly earned him a place among the staff of a company called H&H Photography in the Bronx. Through this agency, he would get one assignment after another. He was well on his way to success.

Most weekends, Mike photographed weddings. This required him to dress in a tux, or at least a very nice dark suit. He seemed to like dressing up, being very particular about his appearance. But he had no ability to manage his own hair! In desperation, he would offer to pay me one dollar if I would style his hair with a hot comb before these commitments. First Mike would rant and rave, throwing combs and brushes around in the bathroom, like a child in the throes of a tantrum, until he would finally surrender and call for help. "Ellen, can you fix this for me? Damn this hair! Why should something so simple be so difficult?" I would then tell him to calm down, and I would fix it!

Mike very much needed to be managed. But at the same time, he was extremely difficult to manage. My mother loved and indulged him. My grandmother loved and indulged him. My sister and I found ourselves falling in line to serve in some capacity along these lines (though we didn't understand it). If there was a lucky star in our family, Mike landed on it!

Because he was the only male in the house, Mike was granted his own bedroom. This was quite a coup, considering that we lived in a two-bedroom apartment. That literally meant that he was the only person in the house afforded real privacy.

At one point, Mike decided to set up a darkroom in his bedroom so that he could develop his own pictures. This was not so uncommon among photographers at the time. Developing your own pictures was a part of the artistry. My grandmother provided Mike with all the darkroom equipment—developer, trays, solution, etc.

It should be mentioned that Nana had also paid to have the wood floors in the apartment sanded and refinished, giving them a rich golden glow. In terms of New York living, that was a true luxury! Any apartment with freshly refinished floors was a treasure. Now, developing solution and newly refinished flooring are not the best combination! Odds of using this room as a darkroom and not spilling any solution on the floor were 50/50 at best. When the inevitable occurred and Mike managed to spill the solution on the floor, the finish was eaten off as if it were hit with battery acid. The mark left on the floor was a huge white stain. I remember both my mother and grandmother commenting on the stain—how terrible it was and how unfortunate it was that this had happened. But nothing happened to Mike as a consequence. No trouble, no drama—nothing! Certainly no one asked him to stop using the bedroom as a darkroom.

As he became more and more serious about his photography, my brother would request that I dress up and model for him. As I was mostly confined to the house, this was somewhat of a treat for me. He would tell me what to put on, and then we would go to the Fort on Claflin Avenue to take pictures. I would have to jump off rocks or do cartwheels or spin around—anything that would translate to an action shot for Mike to practice on. After taking 20 or 30 shots, we would return to the house, where Mike would then develop the film. This was way before the age of digital photography, so every picture cost money—though this was of no concern to Mike.

I must admit, there was a part of this situation that was quite exciting for me! From my perspective, I was the center of attention, having all these pictures taken of myself and then having others scrutinize how they came out. I quickly became accustomed to being the little model in the house.

My brother got paid weekly. He always appeared at the house with cash on payday. His salary was considerable (unlike my mother's). At age 17, Mike was earning over $200 per week. He would come home with his paycheck in a stack of $20 bills, which he would then divide into two piles of $100 each. Next I would be called into his bedroom where—after Mike had taught me how—we played poker for money. I would place a bet; my brother would call it or raise it. We would play until I had lost all the money in front of me—that is, until Mike had won all his money back. Regardless, it was all Mike's money anyway; we were just using it to play with.

Even at a young age, I became tired of losing $100 each week playing cards. I struggled to learn to get better at the game. On one occasion, I managed to win Mike's $100 from him by bidding and betting wisely. I was elated! However, my happiness was not going to remain. This was only a game, and now Mike wanted his money back. *Not this time,* I thought to myself. *I'm keeping it.* A struggle ensued, with Mike grabbing at the cash trying to recapture it. In the struggle, I managed to get punched in the mouth. (I actually think it was from my own hand springing back from resisting Mike). Whatever the cause, it was a hard enough blow that it caused my top front teeth to be knocked out!

Blood was everywhere! Mike laughed, running to get a facecloth to wipe me off. No sooner was I wiped clean of the blood, than he jumped up and grabbed his camera. "Photo Op!" he yelled. I was still crying as he clicked away shot after shot.

"This is great," he exclaimed. "Such emotion!"

I was furious! Not only was I missing my two front teeth, but this idiot was turning my pain into his own art form.

It was at that moment that a realization hit me: As far as Mike was concerned, I was only here for his amusement.

4. Break On Through to the Other Side

BEING A SINGLE parent is a daunting undertaking. It is typically not done by choice, but rather is endured by a conscious decision not to give up. My mother found herself raising three children in the Bronx—alone. Her income level was meager. She worked as a clerk in an office in Manhattan for most of my childhood. When the salary awarded her proved to be insufficient, she took a second job working at Alexander's Department Store on Fordham Road. Her schedule was grueling—working from 9-5 downtown, taking the New York Central Railroad home to Marble Hill Station and then a bus to Alexander's, where she remained until 9:30 pm. To ensure my safety, my mother instructed my older sister, Genie (age 13 or 14 at this time) to stay at home with me every afternoon.

My grandmother worked at a dry cleaner's in Manhattan. She was a crackerjack seamstress as well as a real people-person. Despite a very modest income, she always made clothing for us with the finest fabrics. In doing so, she would create matching outfits for my sister and me, and, at times, even a coordinating outfit for my mother. Now, my mother loved this idea. I too found this to elevate me to that of equal status with them. However, my sister HATED it! Barely a teen, she found herself more times than not wearing matching clothing to her mother and her sister, who was seven years her junior. To Genie, it was humiliating!

With Genie and I, it was never a question of love. Sure, my sister loved me as an older sister loves her kid sister. But the novelty wore off before it began. We were not together in the house but rather, trapped in the same space, each trying to entertain ourselves.

My sister's social life often consisted of being with her boyfriend. I cannot remember a time when I saw the two of them together that they were not attached at the lips! In fact, making out was an art form—and Genie was an artist!

On one particular afternoon—much like any other—Genie was going to have her way, and she invited her boyfriend up to the apartment, despite my mother's strict instructions not to do this. Genie and her beau were fixed on the couch in the living room, kissing. They kissed and kissed and kissed!

Although quite able to entertain myself, my ability to make the best of the time I spent alone was dwindling, and I found myself peaking around the corner of the room watching them. It seemed to go on forever! I remember giggling and saying, "Jeez, come up for air already!"

Genie jumped off the couch and yelled, "Get back in the bedroom, you little brat!"

Instantly I ran back into the bedroom we both shared and slammed the door in anger.

Our bedroom was large enough to have been a master bedroom. Its entrance was marked by two French doors flanked by sheer curtains—which diminished the view, but did not block it. Our beds were unique. I have never seen anything like this before or since: A king-size caned headboard with two single beds protruding from it. The beds themselves were on wheels and could easily be parted to the side to enable them to be made up each day—which is not to say we ever made them, but we could have if we had wanted to! There were also a dresser with a mirror, a chest of drawers, an art table for my sister to draw on, stacks of books and art supplies, a hamper, and posters everywhere.

There was plenty to do that evening, but no television. After listening to the radio for a while, I felt banished—almost imprisoned in the bedroom. I decided that I had just as much right to sit in the living room as anyone! *The heck with what my sister says—I'm going out there!* I approached the bedroom door, only to be faced with the reality that the door was stuck.

"I can't get out!" I exclaimed.

"Good!" my sister yelled from the next room.

"But I want to get out! The door is stuck. Help me!"

At this point, my sister must have succumbed to the fact that I was not going to be quiet. She rose from the couch and dismissed her boyfriend, telling him she would see him later on. He left the apartment.

Genie took her time, but eventually came to open the door for me. She pushed a few times, but it wouldn't budge.

"The paint is sticking. It's stuck!"

"Try again. Please! I hate it in here, and I want to get out!"

Genie pushed and pushed, making no progress other than adding to frustration for both of us. "Damn it!" she exclaimed. "What the hell?"

Before I knew what was happening, Genie had pushed through the pane of glass just above the handle. It scared her, and it happened so quickly that she didn't have time to think. In the blink of an eye, Genie pulled her arm back through the jagged edges of the glass. "*AHHHH!*" she began screaming. The door was open, but now Genie's arm was badly cut. Blood was literally spraying out of her wrist onto the walls, the door, the floor, and us.

"Look what you made me do!" She shoved the bloody wrist in my face.

"I didn't do it."

Genie continued to scream and cry. I was scared to death! In a panic, I ran next door to the neighbors' apartments, banging on doors for anyone who was at home.

"Help us! Help us, please!!!"

The apartment door across from ours opened, and a young man stood looking at me in my bloody shirt and pants.

"My sister cut her arm open. Help us!"

He called to his family to tell them he was going across the hall.

"Call for help—call the police," he told me.

I quickly dialed Zero and all but hysterically asked the Operator to send an ambulance.

"My sister is bleeding to death!"

Little did I know it, but she actually was! Genie had managed to sever every vein and artery in her right arm, and the blood was drain-ing from her quickly.

Hearing the commotion coming from our apartment, neighbors came one by one, and each assumed a role in this emergency. The first neighbor who had come happened to have been a long-time boy scout, all the way from Cub to Eagle, and had training in tying tour-niquets. He snatched his belt off in one swift pull, directing me, "Go get every towel you can find."

I ran back into the apartment and grabbed towels, dish towels, facecloths—everything I could find. As soon as I brought them back out, the neighbor began wrapping my sister's arm with the towels. Then, taking his belt, the neighbor pulled it around her toweled arm tight and said, "This is supposed to stop the bleeding."

By this time, the neighbors had my sister sitting on a wooden chair with her arm hanging over the opening of the staircase, blood continuing to drip. Neighbor women came into the apartment with mops, bleach and other cleaning supplies to get the blood cleaned up before my mother came home from work. The doctor who lived in the building came up the stairs and examined my sister's arm and the situation. He shook his head in disbelief and said, "I can't do enough for her here. We have to get her to a hospital."

The ambulance seemed to take forever, but eventually it did show up. The EMT's carried my sister down four flights of stairs on that same wooden chair she had been sitting on all the while. I wanted to go with her, but was not allowed. Instead, I remained behind with the neighbors who cleaned for hours!

By the time my mother returned from work, the apartment was a faint rendition of the slaughter house image that had preceded her return. Mom grabbed my hand and said, "Come, we're going to the hospital."

We took a taxi to the hospital, sitting there for what seemed like all night, waiting to hear the news. Genie's injury was so extensive that she required over 1,000 stitches, both inside and out, to close the wound. There was also a significant blood loss. She remained in the hospital for several days, her arm in a huge cast up to above the elbow. Weeks of healing ensued, along with multiple surgeries to make reparations.

When all that could be done had been done, Genie's hand was significantly thinner than before. Her fingers curled closed, increasing in tightness from the index finger to the pinky. She could pull them open, but they would spring back closed as soon as she let go. She was also in a cast for such a long period that she taught herself to write with her left hand. It wasn't the same; but eventually she became quite skilled at writing and drawing with her left hand.

In my sister's eyes, the largest setback resulted from the number of days she had missed from school. Genie's grandmother had scheduled a cruise to Paris and had every intention of taking Genie with her. (We had different fathers and therefore, different paternal grandmothers). At this time, Genie was in the eighth grade in a Parochial school. Students graduate from the elementary program in their eighth year and must have completed a certain number of days to do so. When looking at how very many days she had already missed from school because of the injury, taking a trip that would have resulted in a three-week absence from school would have translated to Genie being required to repeat the eighth grade. There seemed to be no choice for her but to cancel going to France.

Missing that trip really hurt my sister. As it turned out, Genie would never have another opportunity to travel overseas. In addition, although healed, her hand was never the same. The doctors had restored it to full use, but it was always distorted, with her fingers curled.

Genie never again mentioned or blamed me for her accident. However, whenever we crossed a large street where she had to hold my hand, Genie would take that curled-up pinky and dig her nail into the side of my hand as she held on. While I always hated her doing that—I was glad that she had the strength in that hand to do it!

5. Crowning Glory

MY FIRST COMMUNION was as memorable an occasion in my life as I can remember. For a young girl being raised Catholic, fantasies of growing up, falling in love, and being proposed to are pre-empted by dreaming of that magical day when you will make your First Communion. On that day, you are able to receive the Eucharist for the first time. While that in and of itself should be the enticement of the occasion, it is not. What is, however, is the thought of selecting and wearing your first white dress and veil! Yes, First Communion requires the attire of a mini-bride at the tender age of 7. And we wonder why we grow up dreaming of becoming brides!

For the occasion, flowers were delivered to the apartment—the first floral delivery had I ever received *just for me!* They were white gardenias, smelling even better than they were beautiful. There was white silky ribbon streaming from the bouquet. Even the box seemed special, containing that wonderful fragrance!

By virtue of the attire, a girl appears special—dressed all in white from head to toe. But this makes you also *feel* special, and one feeds off the other. I spent the better part of an entire hour that day primping in front of the mirror, admiring my brand new white dress, white knee socks, white patent leather shoes, white gloves, and the veil— also special, although my least favorite of all parts of the attire. I loved the *idea* of the veil. But I wanted very much to have the privilege of selecting the veil I wanted—not one of the identical veils the school nuns had chosen for all of us to wear. The dresses were unique; why not the veils?

Still, it was my day. As I marched out the door and down the four flights of stairs to exit the building, neighbors were coming to their doors to get a peek at the girl making her First Communion—ME! Continuing out into the courtyard, I could see neighbors looking out their windows to catch a glimpse. Some even threw cards to me containing money. It was raining money! What a great day! It was the best day ever!

Even my sister, Genie, paid attention to me that day. She was 14 then. A 14-year-old and a 7-year-old have literally nothing in common—except perhaps the same mother. But on that day my sister was standing right by my side, as if showing me off. She even took a photo of me posing with her friends.

I completely missed the focus of the purpose behind the day, instead capturing the highlights as being primary: the dress, the flowers, being the center of attention—and certainly being the focus of my sister's attention! It was a great day. It was May 1ˢᵗ. I will forever remember the date.

Following my First Communion came the day commemorating the Feast of Mary. It was not a holy day of obligation, but rather a day of religious observance, complete with ceremony and the entire garb that goes with it. One of the significant details of this occasion was that one girl who had made her First Communion most recently would have the privilege of crowning the statue of the Blessed Virgin Mary in the church—the highlight of the ceremony.

We members of the previous Communion class were told the day before the ceremony to bring our Communion attire to school with us, so that we could change for the ceremony (thus ensuring that we would keep the white articles white). The principal came to the classroom, and a drawing was announced to make the selection of the girl who would do the crowning totally unbiased.

The girls were lined up around the classroom and told to select one piece of paper each from the box. I remember trying to pick up one certain piece, which seemed to be sticking to the bottom. For a quick second I thought, *Oh, just reach for another one.* But something told me to stick with the one I had, so I picked and picked at the edge until I got hold of it. Oddly, when I finally did pick it out and got a good look at it, there was scribbling on it: circles around and around in the shape of a larger circle. I showed my friend, "Look, this one is scribbled on."

With that, people began to exclaim, "You got it!!"

The Sister smiled and said, "Ellen got the paper; she will crown."

There were a few disappointed looks from other girls, but the majority of the room accepted the situation and went on about their day. We were then told to go to lunch and then in the afternoon, we would go to the church for the ceremony.

I was so excited, I couldn't wait! I ran to the bathroom and began to put on my outfit. Why I started with the socks and shoes, I do not know. But as I changed, other girls came in and told me to stop. "You'll get in trouble if they see you in your white clothes!" So I stopped. But I didn't change the white socks and shoes.

Lunch lasted about 30 minutes, followed by a recess period, when we all went to the park to play. There I was; half in my school uniform and half in my Communion outfit—the white knee socks and white patent leather shoes. As always, we played punch ball in the playground. I loved playing and could run fairly fast, even in the patent leather shoes. Between the excitement of winning the drawing and being out in the playground, I completely lost sight of the fact that as I was playing, I was getting black smudges of dirt on the socks. After 20 minutes, I was hot, sweaty and filthy. Now I had to get dressed and ready for the ceremony!

My dress was on me in an instant! I returned to the classroom to the sneering looks of the Sister in charge: "You weren't supposed to get your white socks dirty. Just look at you!"

OK, I messed up—but maybe Mary won't look at my socks, I thought.

Two-by-two, we marched in line to the church and prepared for the ceremony to begin. Since I was in the ceremony, I remained at the back of the church, while everyone else sat in the pews. I was surrounded by the teachers and nuns who were orchestrating the event. I felt very important to be in the middle of all the commotion.

I became overwhelmed when my escort walked in. Neal was one of the most handsome older boys I had ever seen. He was to walk me down the aisle! *Can this be happening to me?* I was thinking. *Nothing this good ever happens to me! Oh God—I think I'm going to faint!*

The music began, and we were nudged to walk. Neal winked at me, which I think was just supposed to assure me that this was all going to be fine—but I couldn't breathe! My heart was pounding, and I was shaking. I carried a crown of flowers on a pillow up the aisle, staring more at Neal than the statue of Mary.

When I got to the altar, I realized that I was to climb a ladder to be able to reach the top of the statue. *Oh, dear!* I climbed up one step after another, shaking furiously all the while. When I got to the top, I reached out to put the flowers on Mary's head, but my nerves were shot. Rather than placing the flowers atop her head, I knocked into the statue and it began to tip over. Now I was at the top of the ladder, shaking as if I might fall—and the statue of the Blessed Virgin Mary was falling over!

My hero, Neal, reached out and grabbed the statue, standing it back up. All in one move, he grabbed my hand and helped me place the flowers where they belonged, then kept his arm out to provide me a brace so I could get down without killing myself!

That day, Neal saved me from the humiliation of knocking the statue of the Blessed Virgin Mary over, breaking it into what surely would have been a hundred pieces. I hadn't thought I could be any more taken by Neal that I already was, but he was my hero then—and he would be forever!

With my friends, I drifted down all four blocks of the walk home in my Holy Communion outfit. My sister was in the street in front of our house with her friends. They said hello even before she did—and asked the big question, "Who crowned?"

I couldn't stop smiling. I was beaming with delight. "*I* did—with Neal!"

"WHAT?" my sister screamed. "*You* did? Oh, great—the little princess crowned."

Suddenly I realized that the bonding I had thought Genie and I shared earlier when I made my Communion was only her "behaving" in front of my mother. We were now back to our old relationship; she as the cool older sister, with me as the pain-in-the-ass kid sister she had to watch.

*Oh, well. S*till numb from all the events and varying emotions of the day, I decided it didn't matter.

6. The Gift that Keeps on Giving

DAYS WERE HOT during the summers in New York City. The buildings tended to block wind, and the concrete absorbed the heat, radiating it back. Although hot, summer in the city was also good. Time was free for doing whatever you could think of to do.

My sister would babysit me after school during the year, but summer break would have had us together on our own all day long. To my mother, that was not a viable plan. Instead, she opted to send me to a day camp program offered by a neighboring parish.

Visitation Day Camp took campers from all over the Bronx to well thought-out activities all summer long, five days per week, for the bargain price of $15 per week. Looking back, I realize how fortunate I was to have the world at my feet, as I went from place to place all summer long. But back then, I took this for granted and resented being corralled into any type of structure.

The camp was divided into groups—boys separate from girls and all divided by age: 6-8 were Midgets; 9-11 were Juniors; and 12-14, Seniors. Every Friday, a printed schedule was handed out announcing the intended destinations for the upcoming week. Sometimes Midget girls and Senior Boys would go to the same place. I never understood exactly how they decided which groups would go together, although I suspected it was based a great deal upon the counselors and which ones were friends with whom. Regardless, we went and did almost everything. As campers, we visited pools, beaches, and amusement parks. If the weather was uncooperative, plans changed instantly, and we were taken to a museum in Manhattan, or shown a movie in the cafeteria of the school, where we all opened our beach towels like blankets and ate snacks in the dark—all of which was great fun!

Though not so much when taken to the beach or a pool, when going to an amusement park—such as Palisades or Rye Beach—we were told we had to be in a group of four. So everyone got themselves into a group. Then group by group, the counselors would hand us tickets to go on rides. As soon as they verified that there were four in each group and we all had our tickets, they sent us on our way with instructions to "Meet back here at the big clock at 2:30, so we can board the bus." Boom—we were free to do as we pleased! Likewise, when we were taken to a museum downtown, the same rules applied. "Be back here at such and such a time. Bye for now." It was like heaven! At a very young age, I was virtually turned loose to enjoy and explore each day with three of my closest camp friends.

The attraction for many in going to the beach was jumping over the waves in the water. Places like Rockaway or Jones Beach had pretty decent sized waves (bigger on stormy days), and that made for an exciting time in the water. In order to be allowed to venture into this deep water, a camper would have to have taken and passed the swimming test. This test required a camper to be able to swim across and back the distance of a large public pool in Yonkers: Tibbett's Brook Pool. Either you made it across and back, or you didn't party with the big kids, so to speak.

I liked swimming, but I didn't *love* it. I certainly didn't love the idea of being in water over my head. *What's the attraction?* I used to wonder. *I can lie on the beach towel and get a tan, or I can throw myself into deep water. Those are the only choices?* Actually, I would have been quite content to sit. But—I would have been sitting alone. My friends wanted to swim. They craved the excitement that the waves, the diving boards, and the freedom afforded them. I wanted to be with them. So they dragged me, and I pushed myself; it was a little of both.

My weeks were quite full of activities, going far and near and being entertained with all that New York had to offer in the summertime. Conversely, my weekends were spent in those hot city streets, limited to the front of my apartment building, where my mother could find me if she looked out the window. God couldn't help you if she would whistle and you failed to come running! On the very rare occasion

I would venture away from the front of the building, I would alert someone who stayed behind to come and get me quickly if they heard my mother whistle for me.

My father, having been put out of the house by court order when I was five, somehow managed to get permission for visitation. On Saturdays, he would come around to see me. From a very young age, I had a love of horses. Sometimes for a treat, my father would take me to Van Cortlandt Park where, among other things, they had pony rides. The rides were along a trail barricaded on either side with wood post fencing. The ponies were kept in a barn stall with saddles already on them. As potential riders came, they would be led to a pony in a stall, helped up on the pony, belted in to secure the rider to the saddle, and then led to the track. When the stable hands got you to the beginning of the ride, they would place clothespins on the saddle blanket, one for each ride that was paid for. Then every time you would go around, they would remove a clothespin. Dad would put me on the pony rides and I would remain quite content. In fact, it was not long before I learned the system well enough to snag a handful of clothespins so as to extend my riding time!

I remember riding those ponies on many a Saturday. But I didn't realize until the last one that while I rode, my father drank in a bar across the street from the park entrance. On that particular day, when I could no longer provide my own handful of clothespins and was removed from the pony, I realized that I was alone. I looked everywhere, but my father was gone. As I wandered through the park, getting closer to the street, I saw him in the doorway of the bar. He was, let's say, in an altered state. I was disgusted and practically in tears. I had no money. All I wanted to do was to go home!

The city busses ran along this very busy street. I knew that the bus to take me home ran close to where I was. I went to the bus stop to catch the #20. When the bus came, I boarded the bus as if I belonged. The bus driver quickly stopped me and asked for my token or change in payment. I remember whispering in his ear, "My father's drunk, and I have no way to get home. Please let me ride." He gave me a look I will never forget. Then this very nice bus driver said, "Sit down, kid!" And before I knew it, I was home.

The following Saturday, my father appeared at the front of the apartment building very apologetic. He said he had wanted so much to take me home, but he couldn't find me! *Yeah, sure you did*, I thought to myself. *I'm young—not stupid!*

"Here, honey. Here's something for you. Buy yourself a treat." I looked down and realized I had been handed a five dollar bill. Five dollars was a good bit back then. I was rich! I ran to get my friend, Rachel, who lived on the other side of the building. "Hey, I've got $5. Want to come with me to the toy store?"

"Sure, El." (Rachel never called me by my full name, as if two syllables were one too many). We ran around the corner to the toy store, where I am certain I was the first girl in the neighborhood to purchase a Barbie doll with bendable legs. This was a great day! With the change, Rachel and I went to the candy store where we sat at the counter and had egg creams and pretzels. Life was great!

The euphoria quickly left me upon returning to the apartment building. While we had been shopping, my father had been drinking. He had hit his own level of euphoria and was now stumbling down drunk. Now, I don't mean staggering—I mean literally falling down. My father fell and hit his head on a parked car. There he lay in the street, head bleeding, calling my name. I thought I would die!

Rachel grabbed my hand and said, "Come on, just keep walking." We walked as close to the building as we could without becoming part of the wall.

Still my father continued to call my name – louder as we walked: "Ellen! Come over here, Ellen! Now!" We reached the stairs to the entrance of the building and I couldn't continue. This was never going to end. He was always going to do this. He would come and get me, say he wanted to visit, and then race to a bar. He was always going to be drunk!

Rachel stayed on the stairs and I walked over to my father. I remember looking down at him as he laid there—a mess. He slurred out, "I'm sorry." I told him, "All my friends are here. Everyone I know can see you in this condition. I don't know what to do. I hate this! If you can't come to see me and not do this—then don't come back!"

I wasn't crying; I was numb. I just walked over to the stairs where Rachel was waiting and told her to come on. We went upstairs to my apartment to play with the new Barbie, and I told my mother what had happened.

From that day forward, my father gave me exactly what I asked for—his absence.

7. What a Zoo!

WHILE OUR FAMILY did not have any money to speak of—and often less than was needed—my mother always managed to find a way to go places and do things. Movies were a favorite. Of course, there was no such thing as cable television back then, but New York City residents were granted the luxury of eight television stations—some of which were public broadcasting networks, but all of which offered a variety of entertainment.

Television, however, did not compare with the experience of viewing a movie on the big screen. "Some movies are just meant to be seen larger than life," my mother used to insist. We would ride the bus to the theatre, and she would grab my hand and lean over to whisper in my ear as we approached the ticket window, "Now I have candy in my purse, so don't ask for anything at the candy counter. Maybe later on, we can get some popcorn—if you're good." I always thought this was how everyone handled snacks, so I never questioned her when she would say this.

On the rare but big treat occasions, we would go to Radio City Music Hall downtown, where the audience was shown the latest family movie followed by a very elaborate stage show. During the Holiday season, that show included a live Nativity scene and several routines danced by the Radio City Rockettes. "Your sister could have been a Rockette," mom would always tell me. The thought of that possibility impressed her more than it did me!

More than once, I was taken to the Bronx Zoo. Though certainly not the largest in the world, the Bronx Zoo contained quite a variety of attractions. Mom and I would spend the day just walking and talking, looking at all the animals and exhibits and wondering if they were happy living there, or whether they were just accustomed to it.

What I particularly liked about the zoo was its ability to distract me. All else in my mind would disappear. There were no school obligations nagging at me, no real life drama haunting me. I was simply fascinated with seeing one creature after another of many different colors, shapes and sizes. I would sometimes try to imagine what it must be like for them—walking one minute on the Serengeti plains freely, the next, caged in the middle of the Bronx.

The Bronx Zoo had a very interesting way of presenting each animal display to the viewers: As you entered the park, you could purchase a key. This key was not just an ordinary key. It was a plastic elephant key. The trunk of this key, when inserted into the various boxes posted in front of the animal cages, would then unlock a recording that would describe the animal contained therein, its natural habitat, what the animal liked to eat, etc. Children often wore these keys on lanyards around their necks. It wasn't until I had reached an adult age that I realized how ingenious this plan was. For a nominal fee, you could unlock the secrets of the zoo with this key—and the kids were the ones who held that power. The downside, of course, was arriving at a cage display where another child had already unlocked the audio for the crowd!

Such was the case when we found ourselves at the giraffe exhibit one time. It was a typically crowded day at the zoo—a beautiful Saturday afternoon. The sun was shining. Not too hot, not too cold. "Pleasant," as my mother would say. I felt calm, happy to be outside on a beautiful day. We walked from one area to the next, looking for new things to interest us. Mom would comment, pointing out behaviors that she observed in the animals.

As we stood letting our minds wander, staring at the magnificent giraffes, I couldn't help but to be awestruck at their size. This animal is huge! Giraffes stand significantly taller than the fencing that contains them.

So there we stood on this very sunny day, looking at the giraffes in the cage. They didn't walk, they sauntered, swaying from side to side as if showing off for their audience. There were two in particular that approached the very edge of the cage, so as to be able to reach the greenery in the tree tops. The one nibbled on leaves, very disinterested in the crowd beneath. But the other, much taller giraffe seemed to be looking around outside the cage, as interested in the crowd as the crowd was in him.

My mother and I began to look around elsewhere, thinking of where we would walk next. Suddenly the crowd responded to something with a gasp. As I turned my head, I felt a gritty, wet sensation up the right side of my face. The giraffe had stretched his head over the top of the fence, and leaning down into the crowd, he LICKED MY FACE!!!!!

I was stunned, as was the crowd—in awe of what they had just witnessed. My mother laughed and said, "He kissed you! I don't think I've ever seen anything like that," she declared.

"Neither have I," commented others in the crowd.

As strange as this was, I couldn't help but continue to look the animal right in the eyes. I was left feeling confused, wondering if I were incredibly lucky to be singled out in such a fashion or was I somehow a victim?

8. The Night the Lights Went Out

AT PRECISELY 5:16 p.m. on November 9, 1965, the Northeastern United States suffered a major electrical blackout. I was 8 years old at the time. My sister, Genie, was 15.

To set the stage: It was Genie's responsibility (or *job,* as I would say) to watch me after school until my mother came home from work. Mom worked in the Pan Am Building (now the MetLife Building), located on 42nd Street and Park Avenue. My grandmother (Nana), who lived on the other side of the same apartment building, also worked in Manhattan, at a dry cleaning establishment in the 80's on the East Side.

A large woman—and by large, I mean overweight—Nana was diminutive in stature, but husky. Nana also had her quirks. She would ride buses, but she had no interest in riding the subway—or in flying. As a child growing up, I heard countless renditions of the story of how my grandma was given an airline ticket from her son (my uncle) to visit him and his family in California, but was sickened at the thought—so she rode the bus to California instead! Nana normally rode the bus to and from work—a 45-minute ride from the Bronx, one of the four boroughs adjacent to Manhattan.

The shift from Daylight Savings to Standard Time had already occurred. At 5:15 in November in New York, it is pitch black dark outside. City lights are all illuminated, as are hallway lights in the buildings and store front signs above doorways. At dusk, New York City comes to full life—excitement!—with all its lights and glory.

On this particular evening, the excitement was only just beginning. Genie and I were sitting in the apartment four stories above the ground. The record player was playing one of her albums, and we were in the adjoining room (the kitchen) investigating what there was to eat. Mom usually prepared dinner when she got home, but we were both hungry for a snack. While looking for goodies, we came upon a box of frozen fish sticks. Now my sister was no cook—but she could handle placing frozen items on a baking pan and turning on the oven!

As we waited for our snack, the lights began to flicker. There's a sound one hears with a power failure. It's almost a sigh that accompanies the ceasing of the electric current and the void that follows. It's a very strange sound, one I had never heard before. The record speed was disrupted, and the words of the song became garbled. Then the lights were gone, and the room went black. Genie exclaimed, "Oh crap! What's going on?" Quickly she opened up the window and looked out into the street, only to observe that there was no light anywhere! The entire street, the apartment building, everything was dark, except for the headlights of cars and busses. You could hear the anxiety in people's voices carrying up towards the window of the apartment. Traffic stopped in its tracks.

Our only option was to turn on the transistor radio that we had in the bedroom. Transistors were great little devices run by 9-volt batteries. They came equipped with an earpiece for listening quietly, so as not to disturb anyone. However, there was no need for the earpiece tonight! We both wanted to hear. The news was basic, lacking much description or reason. It repeated this message over and over: "The entire New York Metropolitan area is in darkness!"

My sister, being the opportunistic teen-ager that she was, decided that this unscheduled interruption in the power supply was cause to celebrate! Rules were only to be adhered to when life remained the status quo. Now, with the apartment in darkness (as was everything around it), there was certainly no cause to remain inside, especially with one's little sister. "C'mon," she hollered, throwing me a jacket to put on. "We're going downstairs!"

Leaving the apartment always signified the start of a race. Whoever was last out would slam shut the door, which would lock itself automatically. Then the race was on! Jumping over steps two-by-two or sometimes more, we would bounce down the stairs, giggling frantically. Running down the apartment stairs was a skill requiring the same type of agility as running hurdles. We were used to it, however, as we did this every day, several times each day—four flights down in a matter of seconds.

Instantly Genie and I were in the courtyard and about to enter the street. Commotion was everywhere. People were all walking about trying to figure out what had happened and how long this would last.

There is truly nothing more annoying than to have unscheduled freedom at 15 years of age, only to have your younger sister in tow! It wasn't but a few minutes before Genie had run into her boyfriend and others who were making plans for the evening. I most definitely was not part of those plans! I could see them all deliberating about what to do with me. Again Genie looked down at me and said, "C'mon, we're going!" She grabbed my hand and dragged me across what was now a very congested city street to the stores on the other side. There were a candy store, a laundry, a liquor store, and a pharmacy. All the stores were locked from the inside to prevent looting. (Remember, no power—no alarms).

Genie knocked on the door of the pharmacy. The owner opened the door. "My mother isn't home yet, and we were in the apartment in the dark. We were scared! Can my sister stay here with you until my mother gets home?"

"Certainly. Come on in, Ellen."

"What?" She was ditching me!

I entered the store owned by Irving Bean and his wife, to be greeted by several customers who had stopped in on their way home from work, only to be caught by the timing of the power failure. It was a very mixed group of older people, middle-aged people—and I—waiting out the situation together in a pharmacy, with the door locked.

There is only so much you can do in a pharmacy to entertain yourself—at any age. I weighed myself a few times. Put a penny in a machine and got my horoscope. Looked over greeting cards. I even offered to clean up a bit. But the minutes dragged!

It was 6 p.m. when Genie dropped me off at the store. For her, the night was young. For me, the night was dragging on. We all listened to news updates on Mr. Bean's transistor radio, but the news wasn't good; the end was nowhere in sight.

Until that occasion, I had never realized the impact electricity has on a city the size of New York. I had never given any thought to how the subway was powered, what governed traffic lights and store alarms. It's one thing walking around in the dark—with the lights and power on. But it is something entirely different when there is *no* power—anywhere! Flashlights are really valuable. Even more valuable are batteries. No batteries—no radio and no flashlight!

After several hours of sitting, I was getting not only bored but hungry. Further, I was also still dressed in my leotard and fishnet stockings, having come from dancing lessons before this happened. I was told to always change immediately when I got home. But with my mother not there to enforce her own rules—who listened? Now, among other things, I was going to be caught in my tights! My mother was going to be pissed, especially after spending the evening underground in a subway car. *With any luck, she had a seat,* I kept thinking to myself. *At least if she's sitting down, she won't be so angry. But if she has spent the evening standing in the subway car and then comes home to find me in my leotard—I'm toast!*

By 9:30 p.m., there was still no sign of either my mother or my grandmother. Occasionally as I looked out through the plate glass window of the shop, I could see my sister or one of her friends parading around in the street, smoking cigarettes, eating an ice cream, laughing and having fun. I wasn't having much fun at all! I felt like a caged rat, or an unwanted pet dropped off at a kennel.

Oh, no—the dog! We had left poor Cinnamon in the apartment by herself.

Cinnamon was an adorable mutt of a dog that had followed my sister home one day, and Genie had begged until my mother agreed to let her stay. But Cinnamon had had no training of any kind. She chewed on the rug, the leg of the recliner—anything she could find to amuse herself. Also she would get so excited when anyone picked up her leash to walk her, that she would instantly lose control of her bladder and begin to pee! Countless times, Cinnamon would see the leash, begin wagging her tail in excitement, and begin to pee. Meanwhile, whoever was going to walk her would quickly jerk the leash into the hook on her collar and begin dragging her down four flights of stairs to get her to ground level as fast as possible; never quite fast enough, though! Poor Cinnamon - being dragged by her neck, would pee all the way down four flights of stairs! Returning back to the apartment, both the walker and the dog would have to climb through the trail of urine to get back home. And, without fail, the Superintendent of the building—having seen you walking Cinnamon in the courtyard—would know that she had peed all the way down the stairs and would be on his way to hand you a mop to clean it up! So there was no simply walking the dog. You would drag her down, watch her go, bring her back, and then mop the hallway!

I could only imagine what the scene would be at the conclusion of *this* evening: Me in my leotards, getting yelled at for that; the dog getting scolded for having torn up the apartment. Ah, but the silver lining in the cloud: My sister was going to get her butt beaten when they realized she had ditched me. Justice was about to be served!

At 9:45 p.m., my grandmother rounded the corner on foot. She was just getting home from work! I began banging on the window to get her attention.

Mr. Bean came out from behind the counter, "Stop, Ellen—I see her. I'll go tell her you're here!" Even for his age, Mr. Bean moved quickly across the street to tell my Nana I was in the store. He waved for me to come out.

Nana didn't even comment on my leotards or fishnet tights. She was tired, glad to be home, and glad to see me. As we got closer to the entrance of the building and she realized that Genie had ditched me, her face grimaced and she became audibly angry. "Just wait till
I get ahold of your sister!"

Yeah—just wait! I thought to myself.

When we got back to the apartment, Cinnamon, though scared, was fine—and so was the apartment.

The blackout lasted about 13 hours—well into the early morning hours. My mother made it home at about midnight. She had been rescued from the subway, after being led out by firemen, who walked the passengers along the tracks to safety and into the street. There she could board a bus to get home. My sister was grounded for what seemed like the rest of her life! And my life returned to normal.

I will never forget the evening the power failed in New York City. To this day, I am never without a stockpile of candles, matches, flashlights, an emergency radio—and batteries!

9. Cold Hands, Warm Heart

AT THE AGE of 6, my request for Christmas was to be given ice skates. I had seen skating on the Wide World of Sports and instantly became obsessed with it! Santa (via my mother) granted my request and brought me my very first pair of figure skates. They were the generic kind—not purchased from a pro shop, but rather from a local department store.

The nearest skating rink was located in Riverdale, 20 minutes away by City Bus #38. Every Sunday, my mother would take me to skate during a public session. I learned how to go around with the flow of traffic as others did, and with the help of some very kind guards at the rink, learned some basics about recovering after a fall safely.

Riverdale Rink was essentially an outdoor rink shielded from the winds by canvas tarp-like curtains that surrounded the exterior opening of the facility. Because of this exposure to weather (and therefore warming), the rink would shut down sometime during the spring— usually in the first or second week of April. The ice would be melted away, and the concrete flooring would be exposed until fall, when the ice would be restored and the use of the facility would resume as a rink. The wait during the summer seemed long, as I had become very attached to the idea of skating every week!

My mother did some investigating and learned that lessons were offered through a skating school affiliated with the rink, though not run by it. She signed me up for group lessons, which were scheduled weekly before the public session that I attended. Now my skating began at noon on Sundays. I would take my group lesson and then remain at the rink from 1 until 4, skating in a public session. In short, I was skating five hours every Sunday—and loving every minute of it!

When Christmas break arrived, I begged to spend every waking moment at the rink. There were several public sessions held each day: 10 a.m. - noon; 1-5; and 7-11 p.m. Some days my begging was more successful than others, and I was allowed to spend the entire day into the evening—which meant I was skating from 10:00 in the morning until 11:00 in the evening! The more I skated, the more I wanted to skate. I was learning quickly and progressing in what tricks I was able to perform. My instructor recommended to my mother that I begin taking private lessons, which would afford me more individual attention and, ultimately, the ability to progress more rapidly.

This was no longer a mere activity; I was in training! Now back in the day, serious competitive figure skating consisted of compulsory figures as well as free-style skating. To optimize a private lesson, it was also suggested that I attend what were called patch sessions, which translated to renting a portioned-off section of the ice. This was offered very early in the morning. So my schedule changed again. Beginning at 5:45 a.m., I would enter the rink and begin my lesson, doing compulsory figures for the first hour and 30 minutes, take a fifteen minute break, and then resume skating free-style for an additional hour and a half. This rigorous schedule did not serve to diminish my desire! In fact, just the opposite became true. The more I skated, the more I wanted to skate. Before too long, I was skating every day. My mother approached my elementary school and made arrangements for me to arrive late in order to accommodate my skating schedule.

Over time, the skates I wore got better and more expensive, as did the lessons and ice time. I had one skating dress that was made especially for me by a dressmaker. This was my official attire for competition: one dress for all seasons. I had a skirt and various sweaters that I would wear to practice. To this day, I do not know how my mother managed this financially. She was a single parent working full time to support her three children, and my skating was getting quite expensive. Gifts from relatives were often checks in cards offered expressly to cover expenses incurred from skating lessons and competitions.

When I was 8 years old, my mother's kid brother—my Uncle Butch—sent airline tickets for my mother, my sister and me to come to his home and visit for Christmas break. We had never taken a vacation, much less a plane ride as a family!

At first the news was exciting. Then I realized exactly what that would mean: No skating for the entire Christmas break! I did want to fly and travel, as well as to visit my cousins. But I did *not* want to forego the opportunity to spend hours on end skating! My mother was unwavering in her decision. "We have been invited—and we are going!"

I was unable to conceal my disappointment. I was visibly sad, almost to the point of moping. We packed, dressed and left for the airport, but try as I might; I was unable to get myself into the spirit of travelling. All I wanted to do was to skate.

Uncle Butch lived in Peoria, Illinois. He had a very good job working for Prudential Insurance Company. His home was a two-story private house with a huge yard. He came by himself to pick us up at the airport, the rest of his family staying at home so there was sufficient room in his car for all of us. He looked so happy to see us all! I remember giving him a hug when we saw him—but it was half-hearted. I wanted to be back at home, and he knew it!

As we drove to my uncle's house, he mentioned that my mother had made him aware of my preference to remain at home, rather than coming to visit. He kept looking in the rear-view mirror at me while he spoke, and I thought I was in some sort of trouble. "We wanted to be able to treat you to this trip—to have you visit our home, play with your cousins. We have a great deal in store for you while you stay here!" He sounded really sure that it was going to be a good time for me. But still, I could not imagine what would be so wonderful as to take the place of skating every day. All the while, my uncle continued looking in that rear-view mirror, assuring me, "It's going to be a good vacation!"

When we arrived at my uncle's home, I saw that it was beautiful! Having only lived in an apartment building my entire life, I had never seen a large, private house with a yard. Oh, there were a few private homes in New York, but the yards were nothing the size of this one! It was great! We entered the house to be greeted by my aunt and my four cousins. The house was beautifully decorated for Christmas, with pine boughs cut and draped along the staircase banister, which was adorned with red ribbons and lights. Before I could take it all in, Uncle Butch put his arm around my shoulder and said, "Come over here, I want to show you something."

We walked through the living room to a huge curtain covering sliding glass doors. My mother was getting a tour of the entire house from my Aunt, who couldn't wait to show her every room and convenience they had—so it was just my uncle and I, standing at the window. He said, "I knew you didn't want to come, because I know you love skating. So I had this put in for you." As he drew the curtains back away from the glass and turned on the outdoor light, I could see what he had in store for me: He had installed an ice rink in his back yard! Maybe it was smaller than the one I was used to skating on—but it was all for me! My uncle pointed to his chair, which was placed very near the glass doors, and said, "I will sit here, and you will skate for me—every day, as much as you want!"

For the two weeks I was there, I had my own ice! My cousins actually asked me if they could skate on it with me! "Of course!" I said. Sometimes I would skate by myself and do what tricks I knew. Other times, I would teach my cousins. We also played a sort of hockey, slapping around a ball with brooms.

That vacation turned out to be terrific! Uncle Butch became my favorite adult in the world. And every day since that vacation, I have enjoyed the memory of being given the most wonderful gift. I think of that ice, and it warms my heart!

Stage II

10. There's a First Time for Everything

DURING HER TEENAGE years, my sister Genie was both rebellious and miserable. She slept for so much of the time, I actually thought at one point that she had a disease. She would come home from school and go directly to bed. By 3:30 in the afternoon, she would be sound asleep. Around 9:00, she would wake up, get something to eat, perhaps try to get out of the house for a little while to see some friends—but she would be back and in bed very soon after that.

My mother questioned her about this behavior—as if my sister could just give her an answer as to why she was doing this. At one point, Mom consulted a psychologist, who consoled her by saying, "She's home in bed. You know where she is. Stop worrying!"

My mother always told me that although they were trained professionals, doctors and lawyers were what they were only because they graduated from schools that taught that course of study. "That is not to say they were in the top portion of their class." Looking back, I always think she came to that conclusion because of the advice this doctor gave her about my sister.

Genie was absolutely lifeless during this time in her life! Consequently, she was dragged from one counselor to another, although I doubt she said much to them. She just withdrew from us.

After over a year of behavior like this, Genie began to get some spark back in her step and remained awake more often than not. She was gone and out with friends—but at least she was conscious! She was also very popular. I don't remember a time when my sister did not have a boyfriend. She always had someone in her life.

At one point, Genie was dating a boy who lived in the building. Like so many others in the neighborhood, he had been drafted and sent off to Vietnam. Genie was miserable that he was gone. Tours in Vietnam exceeded 12 months, so he was gone for quite a while. They would write back and forth, but even those communications were spaced far apart. With only the U.S. Postal Service to connect you, communication with someone in a war zone was limited, to say the least.

I remember Genie getting a phone call from this boyfriend while he was off in Vietnam. He had called collect. Up until then, it was totally unimaginable what a collect call from Vietnam would cost. Unfortunately, my mother was about to obtain this knowledge first-hand when the phone bill arrived! Heedless of this, Genie sat curled up in the red recliner next to the phone, talking up a storm with her soldier boyfriend. They talked for over an hour.

Coming home just long enough to change clothes and go to her second job, my mother saw that Genie was engaged in this conversation and asked, "Who is she talking to?"

Only a young girl at the time, I was very excited and blurted out, "It's Genie's boyfriend! He called her from Vietnam!"

"Oh my goodness, that must be costing him a fortune!" she exclaimed.

"He called collect."

"WHAT!!" My mother grabbed the phone receiver from Genie's hand, yelled into it, "Take care of yourself," and hung up.

"How could you?" Genie cried.

My mother just looked at her and said, "How could I?"

A few weeks later, a package arrived for Genie filled with souvenir-type items. Genie was very excited to receive this package, including a long letter from him. As she opened the box, I stood there being the nosey little sister. I couldn't wait to see what was inside! I had never known of anyone sending us anything from the other side of the world.

What I noticed, however, was something much different than I expected. The items, while very different, were not as startling as the smell coming from the box. It was an unusual smell, and I didn't know what it was from. It wasn't a bad smell—but it was distinctly different. It impressed me how alone her friend must have been feeling to be somewhere where even the air smells so different! I felt sad for him.

Inside the box were several different items: Christmas lights like small Chinese lanterns, a silk robe, photos and cards—and a circular, paint on velvet type picture supposed to be of an American GI, with his last name inscribed on the pocket and the words, "Missing You" around the border. Genie covered it in Saran Wrap and kept that picture on her wall forever.

Genie's boyfriend managed to come home from Vietnam as intact as could be expected. Others in the neighborhood weren't as lucky. Genie and he dated for some time after his return, but eventually they broke up and went their own separate ways.

Genie then dated one boy after another. I didn't think much of it at the time; I just assumed that this was what is done when you get to be a teenager. Boy after boy, Genie dated. It was almost a toss-up as to whether she was actually that popular, or whether she just couldn't make up her mind what it was she wanted in a boyfriend. Suffice to say, she was dating someone different all the time.

At the end of this one summer, my mother, Genie and I were all invited to California to visit my mother's older brother, his wife and their children. Again our tickets were paid for. This time it was easier for me to want to go, as the skating season had not yet begun. We were taken everywhere: Santa Barbara, Angels Flight, the Rose Bowl, and Disney Land. Every day it was some new adventure. After almost two weeks out there, we flew back home.

We weren't back 24 hours before Genie had a date lined up. She and my mother were talking beforehand. My mother seemed displeased that she was going—but that was nothing unusual. Genie and my mother were always at odds. Regardless, out Genie went.

She did not return home until the middle of the night. I awoke when she climbed into bed. I tried to go back to sleep right away, but I couldn't. Lying there with my eyes closed, I began to hear moaning. I didn't know what it was. I sat up and looked around the room, but saw nothing. It was pitch dark. "Genie, is that you?"

"Huh?"

"I heard moaning."

"Go back to sleep, you must be dreaming."

I was sure I hadn't imagined it—but she said nothing more. As I closed my eyes and tried to fall asleep again, I heard a loud cry. "Oh God . . . Help!"

"Genie? What's wrong?"

I sat up and crawled across my bed onto hers, which was soaked. I ran from our room towards the bathroom following Genie, but she passed the bathroom and went to my mother's bedroom door. I could see her collapse as she put her hand up to bang on the door. "Help me!" Down she went like a rock.

My mother came out startled and saw my sister lying in the hallway on the floor. "Help me get her to the bathroom," she said. She grabbed one arm and I grabbed the other, and we dragged her into the bathroom. Genie lay on the floor, blood pouring out of her.

"She's hemorrhaging!" my mother cried. "We have to call an ambulance!"

While Mom called for help, I stayed in the bathroom with Genie, trying to hold her and keep her calm, but I was scared to death myself. Both she and I were covered in blood, and Genie was getting weaker by the minute.

"They're coming," Mom told us referring to the ambulance. She tried to find out what had happened, but there was little talking and none while I was present.

After what seemed like an eternity of waiting for help to arrive, my mother was frantic. "Call Rachel's father. He's a policeman—he'll help us. He has a squad car."

Rachel's dad had been involved in an incident with work and thought our call was related to that when he first answered the phone. It was very confusing. However, he was quick to dress and come over. My mother had actually given my sister a cigarette to calm her nerves. Before that time, I had never seen my mother willing to allow Genie to smoke. When the officer arrived, there she lay on the floor, cigarette in hand, bleeding. "Who gave her a cigarette?" he asked.

"I did," my mother owned up.

Rachel's dad snatched the cigarette out of Genie's hand, shaking his head from side-to-side.

In one minute, he lifted Genie into his arms, carrying her out of the apartment and down the stairs whisking her away to a hospital where she was treated and her life was saved.

Not much was discussed with me at that age. I knew only that Genie had gone out and returned home bleeding badly. Most of all—I knew my mother was scared to death.

Mom sat me down and instructed me to talk to *no one* about this. Fortunately, I could talk to my friend, Rachel, because her father had taken Genie to the hospital. Rachel was my only outlet, my confidante. "Don't say anything to anyone!" I told her.

"All right—Jeez!"

The next day, as always, I walked home from school with my friends. I wasn't in the apartment five minutes before the phone rang. "Hello?"

"Hi, I'm a friend of your sister's. Is she home?"

"No, she's not in at the moment."

"Where is she?"

"I don't know—out."

"I saw you walking home from school this afternoon, you and your friends. You go to that Catholic school, right? I saw you in your uniform. You remember me, don't you?"

"No."

"I live just one house over. I'm a friend of your sister's, and I can be your friend, too!"

"I have to go."

"No, don't hang up. Talk to me."

"No, Mom will kill me if I sit on the phone. She gets mad." Click – I put the phone down.

By the time my mother arrived home, I was anxious to hear about Genie and how she was doing. She was to remain in the hospital for several more days, but she was expected to be OK and would return home by the weekend.

I advised my mother about the phone call. "You spoke to him? *What did I tell you?*"

"You told me not to say anything. I didn't."

"No—don't talk on the phone to *anyone*. Don't say anything. It's not safe."

"So I have to sit in the apartment alone? And I'm not safe?"

11. One Nightmare after Another

MY SISTER MOVED out promptly when she turned 18. I was 10 years old at the time. My mother worked five days a week, plus she continued selling Avon, both to the people she worked with and within her assigned territory. So she was busy most of the time. I was quite used to entertaining myself; even when my brother or sister had been home, I had still felt alone—isolated by the distance in our ages. This was to be no different; it was just that the illusion of having someone around had been removed.

My mother had taken over the room that was formerly occupied by my sister and me. My room became the smaller bedroom. I had gone to great lengths to create my own little oasis in that room. The single bed was up against the wall opposite the door. There were two closet doors with insets surrounded by molding, both of which I had covered in aluminum foil (for decorative purposes). The room décor was predominantly red, white and blue. I liked having my own room! I could go in there and shut the rest of the world out—leaving me alone to look out the window and ponder what life could be like.

Quite soon after this internal move had taken place, my mother was contacted by a relative who was returning to New York and had nowhere to stay. She agreed to allow him to stay with us until he found a place of his own.

At first our guest kept a reasonable distance, coming and going at will. We often ate our meals without him, as he had other things going on—looking for a job, an apartment, etc. It was no particular bother to have him there, aside from the knowledge that he *was* there. I had enjoyed having the entire apartment to myself, becoming quite accustomed to it. Anything deviating from that was a disruption, even though it didn't impact my plans in any way. Just knowing it wasn't all *mine* anymore was enough!

This stay of our houseguest became somewhat extended. I had originally thought when my mother said that this person would be staying with us, that it would last only a few nights. But the nights quickly became weeks. The longer he was there, the more used to it I got, I suppose. But I was still uncomfortable with it. Just the notion that someone else was there left me uneasy.

I began noticing that I was having trouble sleeping through the night. I would fall asleep easily enough, but by 2:00 a.m., I would wake up thinking I was hearing noises—footsteps. I would see shadows on the wall and check the window to see if someone was climbing in. It was a strange uneasiness that was coming over me.

After repeatedly being startled, I noticed one night that there *was*, in fact, someone walking into my room. It was our guest! He sat down on the bed, saying he wanted to talk to me. I was disturbed, but I remained still, telling myself that nothing was wrong. As he was speaking (and I was waking up), his hands were touching me. All the while, he was asking me, "Does this feel good? Have you done this before?" Before too long, he was touching me as if given free rein to do whatever suited him, and I—for the first time in my life—was stunned completely into silence.

"Do you want me to do this?" he asked.

"NO!" I replied.

"But you haven't done it before, you said so. Let me just show you what I mean. I think you will like it!"

The entire episode was so surreal, I couldn't move. I just remained there – frozen - allowing it to happen.

The next morning I awoke shaken. I looked around the room trying to find some piece of evidence that this episode had occurred (as opposed to my having dreamt it). My room was completely unchanged. Physically, there was nothing. But I felt different. I felt very uneasy. I was different—permanently.

I tried my best to return to the person I had been before, but there was no part of me that was the same. I couldn't think straight. I couldn't relax. I didn't want to be in the house—particularly in that room—ever again. Yet I had nowhere else to go. I wanted to tell my mother, someone. But what would I say? I was certain if I told some-one, anyone, I would be thought less of. With no ability to rationalize any of this, I kept the entire incident to myself. My behavior changed, however. From that day forward, I felt inferior.

In time our houseguest finally left with no words between us. I was glad to see him go and didn't care if I ever saw him again. *Out of sight, out of mind! Whew!*

But try as I did, I could not bring myself to a point where I trust-ed anyone, even friends I knew and had known for my entire life. Everyone was kept at a distance now. It was as if a cocoon were formed around my body. I could see out, but no one could get in. At least, I hoped they couldn't. *If they can't get in, they can't do anything to me.*

12. You Can't Pick Your Relatives

MY MOTHER'S PARENTS were Catherine ("Kitty" to her friends) and Lewis. Those who met them together could not believe they were a couple. They were nothing alike! Kitty worked for a dry cleaner in Manhattan. Her customers were quite often stars of the stage and screen. Lewis worked for Prudential Insurance. Together they had three children: Martin, Frances (my mother), and Raymond, nicknamed Butch (my favorite Uncle). Lewis wanted a life very different from the one he had made for himself, and it was not long before he made that known loud and clear. He left the family when his children were young.

My grandmother single-handedly raised all three children by working at the dry cleaner's six days a week, riding a bus back and forth (which actually meant several busses), and then walking up five flights of stairs to get to her apartment. After Lewis left, she did not date. Nana focused on working and taking care of her family.

In contrast, Lewis remarried multiple times, each time marrying up. His life was never that of the rich, but it certainly was that of the comfortable. He paid no child support what-so-ever.

I didn't meet Grandpa Lew until later in my childhood. In fact, my only real memory of him from when I was a young child was seeing him off at the airport when he departed from New York to move to Buenos Aires, Argentina. His last wife, Rosa, was from Argentina and owned a condominium there. Rosa was a registered nurse. She was also my mother's age. Her sole purpose from the time of their move to Argentina was to take care of Lewis. She did this quite well. It was a match made in heaven. They both thought Lewis was the most important person in the world!

Argentina has weather in contrast to the United States. Our winter months are their summer months, and vice versa. So when winter came to Argentina, Lewis and Rosa began coming to the United States to vacation with my mother at her home in Florida—for the entire season. I found this not only surprising, but on another level, unnerving. Why my mother went out of her way to accommodate this man after he had abandoned her as a child, I could not understand. When I asked, she would just shrug her shoulders and say, "He's still my father." While I never came to terms with this, more than once I found myself doing what Mom asked for Grandpa Lew, simply because she asked me to. She was my mother!

Rosa was in the habit of going to market each and every day to purchase fresh fruit, vegetables, and whatever meat she intended to prepare for dinner. Rosa's preparation of such good foods, we all believe, was the very reason Grandpa Lew lived to the ripe old age of 99. She really did take excellent care of him. We could appreciate that Rosa was a great cook, but this custom of daily shopping ran my mother ragged, as she was the designated driver to get Rosa to and from the market.

Here are a few typical snapshots of Grandpa Lew and Rosa—being Grandpa Lew and Rosa:

During one of my mid-afternoon visits to the family at my mother's home, Grandpa Lew announced their intention to sit and watch Rosa's favorite show, *Kojak*. In his own narcissistic way, Grandpa Lew grabbed the most comfortable seat in the room, a rocker recliner facing the TV. For Rosa to sit by his side, she had to open a lawn chair and place it next to the chair he was in. My mother was left to the couch on the other side of the room. I chose to sit on the floor.

There we were, watching a re-run of *Kojak*. Rosa sat intently watching, interjecting commentary all the while. Grandpa Lew, taking full advantage of the opportunity to demonstrate his superiority, commented on her comments. "Will you be quiet so the rest of us can watch this? We haven't seen these 300 times like you have!" He continued with his very heavy New York Jewish accent, "She always does this. She doesn't think!"

In the episode we were watching, the character Stavros was

shot while in pursuit of a perpetrator. Wanting so much to make conversation with Grandpa Lew, Rosa blurted out, "Oh, Lewis! Oh goodness—he's been shot! I am a nurse. I know how serious a gunshot wound is. You see, this is why actors get paid so much money! I know for a fact he will be out of work for 5-6 weeks recuperating from this."

Grandpa Lew rolled his eyes and in his very condescending way said to the rest of us, "You see what I have to put up with? This is why I don't think she should speak. She doesn't know what she is talking about."

Rosa then argued, "Of course I know! I am a nurse! I may be retired to take care of you, but I am certain of what I say." Sadly, Rosa had the early stages of both Alzheimer's and dementia. Her thought process was a bit disconnected. Though she realized that the man was an actor, she couldn't put together in her head that the gunshot was just a part of the act. To Mom and me, Rosa was funny. But Grandpa Lew didn't see it that way. He was growing tired of her confusion.

Another time, while flipping channels, Rosa stumbled onto a cable channel showing two people active in love making. She blurted out quite loudly, "Look Lew, they're fucking! It's mid-afternoon and they are fucking!" This had very little to do with Rosa's dementia and more to do with her limited understanding of English language usage and local customs. Often people from other cultures tend not to make such a big deal out of what we consider to be curse words. They just use them!

My mother, on the other hand, has never used that word in her entire life! She was vacuuming at the time this happened. The vacuum literally left her hand and flew across the floor into the furniture. I laughed so hard I thought I would cry! Grandpa Lew, however, was not amused.

My mother, the classic middle child, always wanted to make peace in the family. She would invite whoever was around to come for dinner when Grandpa Lew and Rosa were there, just to entertain the illusion of family.

My brother and his family lived in the same city as my mother, as did my daughter and I at that time. With several generations of the family at her disposal, Mom decided to immortalize this vision of family by having us pose all together for a photo. She announced this during dinner one evening—and she was not going to let the idea alone until she got what she wanted! She instructed each of us to "Get ready!"

My daughter, only three at the time, was in a party dress and ready. However, Grandpa Lew was *not* dressed. Much like Hugh Heffner, he spent the day in silk pajamas. Grandpa loved fine clothing, but he wanted the comfort that pajamas would provide. After grumbling a bit, he acquiesced and went to the guest room to change into more suitable clothing.

We waited for quite a while for Grandpa Lew to return to the living room for this family portrait. When he finally emerged, he was dressed in a very beautiful white silk dress shirt with cufflinks, an ice blue necktie, and dress socks with garters holding them securely in place—and his boxers! He walked very stiffly, much in the same manner that Tim Conway used to walk across the stage in character as the old watch maker, one little step after the other. All the while, Grandpa had his hand pointing at his waistline, saying, "Francey, just shoot me from the waist up."

Now it was bad enough that I was going to have to pose for this family portrait. But I would have nothing to do with sitting next to old Grandpa Lew and his knobby knees, simply because he was too lazy to put on a pair of trousers! I looked at my mother as if to say, "Please don't make us do this!" But Mom was insistent. We all crowded onto the couch and smiled as sincerely as we could for that photo.

This was to be the last photo of us all together. Grandpa Lew lived many more years, but he never visited the United States again. His health deteriorated, and the trip was just too much for him to endure. Oddly, our health was fine—but Grandpa Lew's visit was more than *we* could endure! So in the end, we had something in common with Grandpa Lew after all: our inability to endure another visit.

13. Do Nice Guys Finish Last?

MY MOTHER'S MOTHER, my Nana, had a sister and a brother: Harriet and John. They were actually Nana's step-siblings, but they were close and never thought of themselves as being distanced in any way. Now the sisters had facial similarities, but Nana (Kitty) was a very stout woman. She was also extremely down to earth. What you saw was what you got with Nana!

Harriet, on the other hand, was very refined—both in appearance and in speech and mannerisms. These two sisters were the real-life equivalent of Patty and Kathy Duke (from *The Patty Duke Show*). Harriet (Hattie, as we called her) was married to Sidney (Sid). Uncle Sid, a Texan and one of ten children, was also very refined in his manner. He was a manager of Standard Oil. Hattie and Sid had a very comfortable life. They lived in a very nice apartment just outside the New York City limits.

Once a month or thereabouts, Hattie and Sid would plan a day to visit with my mother and me. These visits always took place on a Sunday, beginning at about 1:00 pm. They would drive down, pick us up in front of our apartment building, and take us to a fancy restaurant. Then they would take us either for a drive in the country, or back to their apartment to visit and look at pictures. The trip was always very well planned out and nice, but nothing a child would get excited about. The conversation consisted of adult topics—and I felt as though I was just *there*.

Every visit took us to a different restaurant and a different part of New York on our drive. One restaurant that we went to was a place called Patricia Murphy's. I remember it well, because Patricia Murphy's had a floral garden that contained a working analog clock made exclusively of flowers. It was huge! The diameter of the face was at least 15 feet, and it was filled with all sorts of beautiful flowers. I used to get up from the table and watch that clock trying to figure out how they had made it. The food was also delicious! I was always given permission to order absolutely anything I wanted ". . . just as long as you eat what you order." No problem there! I would typically order a Delmonico steak, medium rare, with a baked potato, some vegetable my mother had selected for me, and as many dinner rolls as I could consume! Dessert was always a parfait. Then, lulled into submission with a full belly, I would sit back and try to make the best of the drive, groggy though I might feel.

Uncle Sid enjoyed driving us around. He would take us on these little tours of the country, where we would admire different houses, landscaping, and countryside. We would drive for a few hours looking at things.

After my Nana passed away (which happened when I was eight years old), part of our Sunday visits would include a trip to Nana's grave to place flowers on it before we went to the restaurant. We did that at least four times per year. While these trips didn't seem like anything particularly special to me at the time, I will always remember from those trips my impression of how much Hattie loved her sister—my Nana. We would stand at the headstone with Nana's name on it, talking about her and listening to stories they would tell about her.

Next to Nana's headstone was the headstone of a Chinese ma n we did not know. Oddly, though we had never met this man, the proximity of his headstone to Nana's made him sort of him a neighbor. Invariably, on these visits to Nana's grave, someone would always comment, "There's Mr. XXX," (as if we would find his having moved somewhere else!) On his headstone, there was always an arrangement of fruit (not flowers), much like what you would see in a fruit bowl on a table in your house. Every time I went there (which was always before we went anywhere else), I would stare at that fruit and wish I could just reach down and take an apple or a pear—something to hold my hunger at bay until we made it to the restaurant. Some days, the conversation about Nana would last longer than others. My stomach would be growling the entire time!

Sadly, as a child, I really took those trips for granted. Had I not been forced, I wouldn't have chosen to go. Yet now I have very fond memories of those outings. I remember each and every restaurant. I remember the roads we drove on looking at things afterwards.

Uncle Sid was a really nice, good man. He treated us very well. As he aged, he developed Parkinson's disease. I remember this, because Uncle Sid always ordered soup before his main course, and as the disease progressed, he had much difficulty getting the spoon with soup on it to his lips. The shaking made it almost impossible. Then one time we went for our usual dining excursion, and he didn't shake at all. It was a noticeable improvement—almost as if the problem were gone completely. My mother explained to me later that his physician had prescribed a new medication for him, and that it was working quite well. I believe that medicine was called L-DOPA. It worked for a while, but later became ineffective. Our visits with Aunt Hattie and Uncle Sid became less frequent, until they were completely non-existent.

By the time I was in high school, Aunt Hattie and Uncle Sid had retired to San Antonio, where Sid was from. They remained there the rest of their lives. Now our only outings with Aunt Hattie and Uncle Sid are the memories we have of those drives. Mom and I have talked about them over the years—how good Hattie and Sid were to us, how nice they were.

During one of our reminiscences, the conversation took us outside the parameters of just remembering.

"How did they ever meet?" I asked my mother.

"Well," she said, "Sid met Nana first. They went out a time or two. Then Nana said to him, 'You're very nice, but I think you would really like my sister.'"

After all those years, I had finally found out . . . *the rest of the story*. Every time I think of it, I find my head shaking from side to side in disbelief. This great guy comes along, and my Nana passes on him, introducing him to her sister instead. Then she marries Grandpa Lew. Oh, Hattie and Sid belonged together, there was never a doubt. But I can't help but think how sad it was that my Nana didn't find a man who was kind to her. Truth was—she *did* find one. I guess she just didn't want one.

14. Missing the Window

THE LEAP ONE takes from grade school to high school is a big one. In the Catholic School system in which I was a participant, there were choices to be made and a test to be taken first, known as the Co-Op. This is an examination testing the knowledge of the student in basic subject matter such as English, Math, Science, etc. for the purpose of screening them for acceptance into a high school. Fortunately, if we had been taught anything in Our Lady of Angels, it was how to take tests successfully.

The next big step is applying to the schools of choice. A student is allowed four choices, to which applications are submitted, along with the results of the Co-Op scores. At that point, a decision is made to accept or reject the student at each school, based solely upon those scores. This process is very similar to what is done in preparation for college or university acceptance.

Before I took the Co-Op test, my mother and I sat down at the kitchen table and studied the choices of schools. We then listed the four schools in which I was interested (the maximum number allowable). Despite the time and amount of serious thought put into this effort, my personal goal was to be accepted into and attend the Bronx High School of Science. Science, as it was affectionately called, was a public school, yet very well-known both for its high standards and its curriculum. Besides offering a very demanding science academic program, it also offered Russian as a foreign language course. This was of great interest to me, as I very much wanted to be a translator for the United Nations.

Now to get accepted into the Bronx High School of Science, simply listing this school on your sheet of choices was not sufficient. In fact, they did not even subscribe to the Co-Op program. The only way one could be accepted into the Science program of study was to take the Bronx High School of Science test. So in addition to enduring the six-hour testing required for the Co-Op, I also registered for and took the Science test.

The waiting period after this testing is, from what I remember, six weeks or so. I waited anxiously for the results of both tests. Finally the day came when the letters from the schools were expected to be coming in the mail. This was 1970. There were no cell phones. Your communication about such things was limited to word of mouth or visual observation. By that I mean you could see 8th graders chasing mail trucks or mailmen on foot to get their letters before they even hit the mailboxes!

Our mailman had a huge bag that he carried on his shoulder as he walked into the building. I managed to intercept him in the courtyard and begged him for any mail addressed to me. There were four envelopes: St. Nicholas of Tolentine, St. Barnabas, Cardinal Spellman, and St. Thomas Aquinas—applied to in that order. I was accepted to three of the four. The school that held my real interest, however, had not responded at all.

It would be days later before the envelope bearing Bronx High School of Science would arrive. I waited anxiously for that mail delivery. On the day it arrived, the mailman walked down my street with the letter held up in the air, waving it as if to attract me from the window. But I was further up the street playing. When I realized he was coming, I ran the length of the block, my neighborhood friends following behind. Upon ripping the envelope open, I read only the first line: "We are pleased to inform you…"

I could not believe it! I was in. I had made it! All those years of studying and doing work that I didn't want to do—and this is what it was all for. The teachers always told you it would pay off. They were right! They were telling the truth!

"*Mom!*" I shouted up to the window. Before she even had a chance to poke her head out the kitchen window four stories above me overlooking the courtyard, I ran up the four flights of stairs, letter crumpled in hand. "I'm in! I'm in!" I told her.

"That's terrific, dear. Congratulations."

"What? You don't look excited. I can't believe this! I wanted this so bad, and now I have it. I'm going to Science!"

"No, you're not," she said in quick reply.

"WHAT?"

I said, "You're not going."

"Mom?" My stomach began to knot up and I felt anxiety everywhere. For a quick moment, I thought surely she was kidding. But she wasn't.

"I'm proud of you for taking the test and getting accepted. That is quite an achievement. But I never said you could attend the school."

"Are you crazy?"

We literally fought about this for days on end. Every chance I had, I would question my mother (or more accurately, beg). "Please, please let me go to Science!"

She wouldn't budge. "You're going to Tolentine. We discussed this, remember?"

I remembered us discussing it, but I had thought that when we listed those four schools on the other application, the purpose was to have a Plan B—something to fall back on if Science rejected my application.

"You were always going to attend Tolentine. And that is where you are going. Period."

"NO!" I shouted back at her. "I worked my butt off studying; taking tests, doing everything I was supposed to do—and now I'm going where I want to go. This is an honor! Don't you get it?"

The arguing escalated both in volume and in frequency. Finally I found myself screaming at my mother, tears streaming down my face, "Why can't I go? Why did you sign the paper for me to take the damn test if you never intended me to take them up on their offer?"

"Because I never thought you would get in."

"What? What did you say?"

After all the badgering, arguing, and begging, the truth finally came out. The fact was, if the school had rejected me, there would have been no argument to be had. And that was what my mother had counted on. Now that I was accepted, the plan had backfired.

Too bad for me about being invited to attend the best school in the area! I wasn't going.

15. The Brothers Grimm

BY THE TIME I had entered seventh grade, there were some new additions to our group of friends. Two brothers, Kyle and Kinnon, had begun to hang out in the park with us. Although they did not attend the same school, they became a prominent part of our social group rather quickly. These two were as diverse as two brothers could be. Kyle was tall and had a rough exterior, almost like that of a longshoreman. He was young, but his face was seasoned, as if he had been out in the world. Kinnon, the younger brother, was the more handsome of the two. In fact, handsome would not be the appropriate definition. He had a pretty face. Kyle and Kinnon were fixtures in the park where we played. They were well known and, for the most part, well liked.

Kyle and Kinnon had their pick of girls with crushes on them. It was rare to have either of them without someone of interest. Now, since we are talking about seventh and eighth graders, this was not overly involved. To be defined as going out with someone constituted their walking the girl home, kissing, dancing with her at parties, and exchanging gifts on special occasions.

The two brothers lived just up the hill from my house. Quite often, we found ourselves walking home at the same time. We would talk about everything from sports to parties to sharing information about girls or boys of interest. We would talk for hours on end.

The closer I got to age 13, the more interested in the opposite sex everyone got. The group of friends I associated with was made up of real social butterflies. There were parties being held every weekend. The girls would dress up in whatever that week's fashion attire was, and the boys would wear slacks and a nice shirt. We would go to whomever's house was designated as the party site, and the records would play! Dancing was a part of this ritual, as were treats. We would eat snacks, dance, listen to music, and socialize.

My friends were all predominantly nice kids. Each of us was lost in one way or another, but all OK to be around. I was not considered one of the most popular girls, but I had friends. Boys, however, did not take a particular interest in me. In fact, what I remember most about this period in my childhood was that the few boys who *were* attracted to me were not any of the boys I was attracted to! Bottom line: I was quite intimidated by boys. If there was one in particular that I liked, I couldn't speak around him. Not the most conducive means of getting someone to notice you!

The one boy that I really did like was Kinnon. He was handsome, charming, funny, and athletic. He was no star—but I thought he was terrific. If he was around, I noticed him and in fact, had difficulty looking away. I enjoyed just watching him. Thinking about Kinnon took up a great deal of my time.

The truth is that thinking about Kinnon was an occupation for several of the girls I knew. I was not the only one who was impressed by him. There were several. The reality was that these other few girls had much more likelihood of getting noticed and asked out by Kinnon than I did. I was just *there*. For all intents and purposes, I was just one of the guys.

Every now and again, something happens that takes you completely by surprise. It was just another afternoon at the park. As the sun went down and dinnertime approached, it was time to head to the house. I said my good-byes and went for the hole in the fence to leave the park and walk home. Kinnon shouted after me, "Wait up!"

Kinnon lived just up the hill from me, so for him to be walking home with me was not completely out of the ordinary. However, we were usually in a group. Now it was just the two of us. We talked about all sorts of things—basketball, other friends. We talked all the way. When we got to his house (which was before mine), I said, "OK, I'll see you tomorrow."

Then Kinnon said, "What, you don't want me to walk you home?"

I was shocked! *Hell yes, I want you to walk me home!* I thought. But dare I say that? "Oh," is all that came out of my mouth.

We continued down the hill and around the corner to my apartment building. Kinnon began telling me about the party that was coming up the next weekend, and how he was wondering, "Would you like to go out with me?"

I was thinking to myself, *I have talked to other girls about this. Don't seem too eager!*

"OK." I said. "So . . . we're going out?"

He smiled. "Yes. Is that OK?"

I kept thinking, *Oh, God—keep my feet on the ground!*

Kinnon leaned towards me and kissed me. I thought my heart would stop! It was over before I realized what had happened. WOW!

The next day, I tried my best to keep myself contained. Outside, I was cool, calm and collected. Inside, I was screaming at the top of my voice, *Kinnon asked me out!!!* It was brutal waiting for someone to bring it up in conversation.

Fortunately, my friend Rachel was well informed, and she mentioned it—right in the middle of math class. "Hey El, is it true?" The smile on my face was huge. I could feel it. "Holy cow—it *is* true!" Pretty soon everyone was talking about it. I couldn't believe it! I just wasn't one of those girls who got the guy; I was the one that got passed over. But the more I heard people talking about it, the more I knew it was real.

The party now became even more important. For the first time, I had someone waiting for me when I got there. I had to get just the right outfit, do my hair just the right way. I must have spent hours getting ready. I couldn't decide if I should eat before I left or not. My stomach was in knots.

I arrived at the party, which happened to be at my good friend Lizzy's house. Lizzy and I had gone to school together since before 1st grade. I had been in her house before, many times. So the environment was not exactly unfamiliar.

There were lots of people there. The house—or should I say apartment?—was crowded, but it was fun! The music was loud, and the conversation louder. I walked around trying to be discrete. I looked everywhere for Kinnon, but he was nowhere to be found. I began asking people, "Have you seen Kinnon?"

"Nope, he's not here."

I reassured myself that he had said he was coming; therefore, he would be there. But as the evening went on, I realized I had reason to be nervous. He should have been there by now, but he wasn't.

When Kinnon finally did appear, he was quite under the influence. There was commotion outside the apartment upon his arrival. I remained inside the apartment, thinking it would be best if I stayed put until he came to me.

As Kinnon made his way in, I could tell instantly that this was not going to be good. He took my hand, walked me into a corner of the room, and told me, "This isn't going to work out." That was all he had to say.

Inside my head, my thoughts were racing. *Not going to work out? Wouldn't we have had to try it before we decided it was not going to work out?*

Then, like a gunshot, the thought went through my head, *I've been set up!!*

I began to cry and could not stop. I literally cried all night, through the party and after I got home. I cried for what was probably 12 hours, fell asleep, and then cried some more when I woke up.

It had been so hard for me to trust anybody! Kinnon, I had *wanted* to trust.

I was a fool!

After a while, it became clear that Kyle was the brother I would be spending the better part of my time with. We had become close friends. Even though he dated other girls, I was his confidante. He walked me to school every morning. We talked on the phone every evening and thought about what we would talk about in between times. We were sewn together at the hip.

It was odd that Kinnon was the object of my affection, yet I spent most of my time with Kyle. In retrospect, I think perhaps I enjoyed the safety of thinking about what might have been rather than the reality.

And perhaps Kyle took me under his wing after witnessing my sadness from Kinnon's rejection. Nonetheless, this is how it was: Kinnon was simply out of my reach, while Kyle was always there.

Kyle and Kinnon came from a fairly large family—six children in all. Their parents were odd. That is not to say that they weren't the nicest people in the world. But just to look at them, one could easily see that they had their eccentricities.

Kyle and Kinnon's father had some sort of connection to the New York Coliseum. I am unclear what his role was. But suffice it to say, this connection afforded him access to tickets to virtually every show in New York. He would get tickets to car and boat shows, concerts, and the like.

One afternoon, Kyle very excitedly told me that his dad had gotten us all tickets to the Armory for a concert that was going to be held over the weekend. "It's going to be like a mini Woodstock," he said. Now to make that claim was quite a statement. It was, of course, incorrect. But the list of performers was impressive. In no particular order, the performers were The Byrds, The Ike and Tina Turner Review, The Beach Boys, Lighthouse—and the list went on. This was to be a three-day event, and we had complete and total access—thanks to Kyle's dad. Kyle's cousin Regina joined us for the event also. She was a riot! A year or two older than we were, this girl was every inch a kleptomaniac. But she had a good heart!

My mother, none too happy about my taking off with these boys, gave in to my begging. Whenever I wanted to do anything, I would beg and whine and not let up until she would just give out and give in. The trick was to wear her down—and the effort involved in accomplishing that was a small price to pay!

So we all ventured to the Armory to partake of the party atmosphere. We entered this huge facility on a Friday afternoon. At this point, music was playing, but it was more preliminary background music. It was not a performance. We investigated the tables of trinkets being offered by vendors who had set up their wares for sale. There were also many choices of snack foods such as pizza, hot dogs, cotton candy, and popcorn. It was an indoor festival—an amusement park with no rides.

We had brought blankets to place atop the floor of the Armory so that we could sit and listen to the music. But once the first band appeared on stage, we were up dancing. It was great! One act was better than the next. The excitement was freeing—and the fact that my mother was nowhere to be found was the cherry on top! Kyle's mom was there, but she had a very loose grip on us. We were allowed to run free and explore to our hearts' content—just so long as we did not leave the premises.

By 11:00 p.m., the show for that first day had concluded. We all walked home. The Armory was only a few blocks away from our houses, and it seemed that the walk was just long enough for us to unwind from the music and dancing. Kyle was told to walk me to my building so that I would not have to walk the additional block alone—and he did. We talked and laughed all the way home.

Early the next morning, the telephone rang. It was Kyle: "Are you ready? We're leaving!"

I jumped up and dressed quickly, running for the door almost before hanging up the phone.

"Where do you think you're going?" my mother yelled.

"To the Armory, Mom. The show starts again in 30 minutes."

"You don't expect me to let you just stay gone the entire weekend, do you?"

Well, yeah, I thought to myself, but I didn't say it. Instead I began to beg and plead again, urgently. "Mom, come on—you know they got this ticket for me, and I want to go! I'm not leaving the area. I'll be right at the Armory, and Kyle's mom is going to be with us. We'll be OK!"

I don't remember my mother actually saying yes, but I was out the door of the apartment in a shot. I ran to the corner and saw the group at the top of the hill, waving to me, "Come on, let's go!"

The second day of the show was even better than the first. By this time, we had learned the lay of the land inside the Armory. We knew all the neat places to go and how to maneuver through the crowd to get a good place to stand. This day seemed to go more quickly than the first, but it was great fun anyway. There were encore performances, and the show ran later than expected. Kyle's mom suggested that I just stay over at their house, since it was so very late.

I called my mother from a pay phone. She was furious! "Have them walk you home—NOW!

"Mom, come on. Kyle's like my best friend! His cousin Regina is with us. His mom is home. It's all good." I basically hung up before she could argue with me anymore. I was going to stay there, and that was that!

We arrived at the apartment at about 1:00 a.m. It just so happened that it was July 4th weekend. Kinnon had stashed some fireworks in his room, which he conveniently brought out for us to celebrate with. Since we were in an apartment, the only option was to shoot the fireworks out the window. Kyle and Kinnon had firecrackers, bottle rockets and roman candles. I was unfamiliar with fireworks and how they were to be handled. In short, I was afraid of them. I enjoyed watching them go off, however, and was perfectly willing to observe from behind them.

The two brothers were out of control, lighting one firecracker after another—as if they were trained military. We had a Coke bottle to launch the bottle rockets from the window sill, which conveniently shot them across the street at the building opposite ours. One actually hit someone's window! We all ducked down so that we wouldn't be seen. (How stupid we were! Where else would it have come from? Our window was directly opposite theirs—and wide open!) These antics went on for a few hours. We laughed so hard our sides were splitting. It was a great time!

As much fun as we were having, it had to end at some point. We were all getting tired, and we were out of any fireworks, having lit all that they had in the brown paper bag. I was told to sleep on the floor in the living room in a sleeping bag that was brought out to me. Kyle and Kinnon went into their room to go to sleep. Regina passed out in another room.

I had just about fallen asleep when I felt someone behind me. Before I could realize exactly what was going on, I felt hands around me from behind. It was Kyle. He was kissing my neck and pulling me around towards him. I was half asleep and completely caught off guard.

"What are you doing?" I asked him.

"What do you think?"

I was absolutely terrified at the prospect of his advances. "But we're friends!"

"Yeah, we are," he agreed with me all the while continuing with his advances. "But I like your brother, remember?"

As quickly as I realized what was going on, it was over. Kyle stormed out of the room and slammed his bedroom door.

The next day I awoke and went home after a short conversation with Kyle's mom. I felt strange, but I hoped that things would blow over and all would be forgotten.

Hell may have no fury like a woman scorned, but hell was about to freeze over with the likes of how angry Kyle was! From that day on, every time he saw me, as long as I was within ear shot, he screamed at me. He called me names, he told me off. He was hateful! I would go to the park where all our friends played. Kyle would be there. Before I was even able to enter the park, I would hear him screaming at me. To say that Kyle hated me was an understatement! He was determined to hurt me—and he was going to succeed.

I soon realized that I could no longer go to the park without suffering through the yelling and screaming that Kyle was prepared to inflict. He was relentless. Not only did I retreat; I felt myself cowering. I withdrew, emotionally and physically. After eight years of being friends with everyone at that park, I banished myself. Some of them told themselves that I had moved on, making friends at the high school I was about to enter, and that I had dumped them. In reality, I was run off by the closest male friend I had.

16. Girls Just Want to have Fun!

ATTENDING A SMALL parochial elementary school in the Bronx was very much like being segregated. We were in New York City, but we were separated from much of it at the same time. Our school, small as it was, had only one class of each year—first through eighth grades. At the time we were in third grade, the school/parish announced that the school would be expanding and adding an additional class to each year. The following school year, there would be two first, second and third Grade classes. While exciting for some, that announcement thrilled our class—simply because it meant we would miss the cut. The 40 or so of us in that class would remain together for all time, or at least until we graduated from eighth grade.

There were, if memory serves, about 25 girls and 18 boys in the class. In fact, there were a handful of us who were second generation classmates, meaning that our mothers or fathers (or both) had grown up and gone to school together. Regardless, it seemed that everyone knew everyone else, and this was true of our parents as well.

At varying times, some of us became closer friends than others. Such was the case with Lizzy, Marie and I. Both Lizzy and Marie had attended Park School with me—a pre-school activity of sorts that took place in the park house of the local park. We also all attended PS 86 Kindergarten. Although not all in the same classroom at that time, from first through eighth grades, we were practically inseparable. With the one exception of figure skating (which I did on my own), there was not a single childhood activity that one of us did apart from the other two.

During the summers, Lizzy, Marie and I all attended Visitation Day Camp. We traveled to a different recreational site each weekday by bus. For being so young and in the midst of New York City, we were actually afforded quite a lot of freedom.

So there we were, in the same classroom every day; the same sports practice every afternoon; the same social activities in our spare time. There were distinct differences between us all, but the common threads were so basic and ingrained that looking back on it now, I feel we were surely destined to be together forever!

Lizzy and Marie had only brothers. Lizzy had four, Marie, two. Unlike them, I had one brother and one sister. Marie was a middle child. Lizzy and I were the youngest of our families. The one common denominator we all shared, however, was that we all had alcoholic fathers. While behaviors varied from steady maintenance drinking to falling down (as in my own father's case) all three were absolutely committed to their drinking.

Marie lived across the street from the park we all played in. Lizzy and I lived four blocks away from the park, quite close to each other. Oftentimes, we would walk to and from the park together. When my mother remarried, we moved down the street—right into Lizzy's building. It was the one silver lining in that cloud! This building was HUGE: Seven stories high, with apartments labeled from A-Z, 26 on each floor. It was built into the side of a hill known as Kingsbridge Terrace, overlooking the Hudson River. The main floor of the building faced the Terrace side. If entering from the Sedgwick Avenue side, you would find yourself immediately on the second floor.

A very old lady lived on the second floor of that building. She would walk in and out all day long, mumbling to herself in a foreign language. At times, I would see her stopped at the building entrance speaking as if to the door, with no one else around her. It was only after quite some time of living there that someone told me they thought she was telling the door not to let anyone into the building who didn't belong there. We thought she was crazy!

On the main floor on the terrace side were a maintenance room, the superintendent's and porter's apartments, a very large laundry room, and two sitting rooms. These sitting rooms were identical mirror images of each other, flanked on either side of the elevator doors. Their only distinguishing features were the wall murals in each. One had a view of daytime, the other, night. Lizzy and I told ourselves that these "living rooms" were ours, and we often talked about which one we preferred—Day or Night. On weekend evenings when boys would walk us home for dates, Lizzy and I would meet in that lobby. Whoever made it there first got her pick of the rooms Day or Night. The other got what was left. Not that we felt unsafe, but there was a certain comfort that came from knowing your girlfriend was just on the other side of the elevators!

In those days, it was quite uncommon for anyone to have a washer/dryer in their individual apartment. Most often, the tenant would use the laundry room. Rather than spend any length of time in that area alone, Lizzy and I would do our laundry together. It wasn't so much of a chore then—just another opportunity to hang out together.

At the tender age of 13, we were beginning to get into mischief! Together we concluded that if we combined Lizzy's laundry with mine, we would have half the loads, one dark and one light—which would mean we would save half the money our mothers had given us. So we crammed our laundry into the machines together and then ran to the cigarette machine in the lobby to purchase a pack of cigarettes with the money saved. We would then sit and smoke while the laundry was being done. It was, we thought, an ingenious plan! So at least once each week, Lizzy and I would spend an hour and a half in the laundry room smoking and talking.

The laundry room was massive. There were many washers and dryers, and several extractors. In case you've never seen one, an extractor is a stainless steel machine that spins so rapidly it literally extracts more water than the average washer. This is useful for things like blankets or quilts, which hold an excessive amount of water and take an excessive length of time to dry otherwise. These extractors were positioned on a riser on the center wall of the room.

Oddly, on the wall over the extractors was a moose head! This was an actual moose head that someone had shot and then mounted up there. Lizzy and I would sit smoking, talking, and wondering why this moose head was there. *Who shot this thing?* After hours of pondering, we concluded that it really didn't matter who shot it, but we were convinced that they had needed to hang it on *this* wall—and no other. Where else would they have hung this thing? It was tremendous!

Lizzy could not seem to resist the moose head. Admittedly, I was fascinated with it myself. But Lizzy felt the need to touch it. She would climb up on top of the extractors and pet this moose on its nose, talking to it as if she had stopped to pet a dog in the street. "Nice moose," she would say. Lizzy wasn't crazy; she was just adventurous! What she was not, however, was knowledgeable of taxidermy. The moose head had been on that wall for long enough that it had dry-rotted. As Lizzy stroked the nose of the moose one day, a piece of its skin fell off. "Ellen, oh God, grab that!"

"Grab what?" I looked back up at her. "Are you nuts? I'm not picking that up!"

"Come on, we need to put it back on."

"On its nose? Are you serious? Climb down here and let's get out of here. We'll just leave it!"

Many a Saturday afternoon we would sit in that laundry room and talk, our conversation consisting of boys and sports.

Of all the sports we three participated in, cheerleading was the most equal, in that we were all equal participants. Lizzy and Marie were very good at basketball; they were starters, while I was not. But cheerleading was something we had all done together since third grade. By eighth grade, we were in the top of the heap at our school.

Mrs. Noonan, our coach (as she was in basketball, volleyball and everything else we did), was very proactive. I don't know how it came about, but she had arranged for us to cheer for an all boys' high school (All Hallows) during a city championship game. Being an all boys' school, it made perfect sense that they did not have cheerleaders of their own. But how ingenious this was of Mrs. Noonan, we thought! All Hallows was *the* school for boys (as far as young girls were concerned). It was chock full of the best looking, athletic, high-school boys around. Now we were their cheerleaders—even if only for one night.

There was nothing about cheerleading that seemed to require our focused concentration. We had, after all, been cheering since we were eight. This was merely a matter of our showing up and doing what we did while watching the best looking boys in the city play basketball. What was not to like?

There was a large crowd at the championship game. This was a very big game and, as expected, an exciting and active one. Geraldine, our captain, stood at the end of the line and motioned to us what cheer we would perform next, as we led the crowd in cheers as if focusing the energy of the room towards our team to assist them in achieving victory. The cheers were to be done on the sideline of the court, while the game was in play. We were paired in twos by size order, and two at a time would each do this very deliberate clap and then a jump—together. The first two would do their jumps and then proceed to walk apart towards the end of the line. Lizzy and I were the tallest and subsequently, the last to perform. Ours was not a jump, but rather cartwheels at the end.

"Let's go!" Clapping, *One, two – three, four, five – six, seven, eight, nine* – "Let's go!" Then another two would jump, the crowd roaring with excitement during this two-point game all the while. Lizzy's and my turn came up: Clapping, *One, two – three, four, five – six, seven, eight, nine* – and we ran and cart-wheeled.

As my hands hit the floor, I heard a thunderous roar from the crowd! I jumped to my feet and looked around. *Did Lizzy forget her bloomers?* I wondered. The game was stopped, the ref visibly shaken, and Lizzy was crying on the side.

"What the hell happened?" I ran over yelling.

Marie held Lizzy, trying to console her. "She cart-wheeled into the ref as he was running down court!" she told me. I could tell by the expression on Marie's face that she was trying everything she knew not to laugh! Lizzy was beyond distraught, crying her eyes out.

Mrs. Noonan spoke to us after the game ended, telling us how wonderfully we had performed. At least a few of us rolled our eyes in disgust thinking, *Oh, yeah! I'll never be able to show my face at an All*

Hallows Dance! Not in this town!

Mrs. Noonan, however, saw a different view of this event. "Girls—are you kidding? They loved you guys. What's more: They will NEVER forget you!"

The upside of this was that All Hallows did, in fact, ask for us to cheer for them again. We cheered in the city finals—which were held at Madison Square Garden.

17. Rock – Away

DESPITE THE NEGATIVITY of my early childhood, I always felt very fortunate to be born in New York City. I loved being a New Yorker! I loved everything about it. There was an entire world out there, and yet the only part of it that interested me in any way was New York. There was no other spot in the world in which I wanted to be more—and I was already in it! In my mind, those not born in New York were somehow at a disadvantage. We had the Yankees; we had the Knicks. We had everything! No matter how bad life got, as a New Yorker, I was still a winner.

Between the end of the eighth grade and the beginning of the ninth, Lizzy and I began to explore what we considered to be our right of freedom as teenagers. We wanted to explore! We wanted to go places! We were about to enter our new high school, St Nicholas of Tolentine, and we were quite keen to meet as many people as we could from that school. On the invitation (and scheming) of a cheerleader from Tolentine (Midget) whose family had a summer place in Rockaway, Lizzy and I plotted to sneak away and spend the night at Rockaway Beach.

It took every bit of two and a half hours by train to get to Rockaway, which is located in Queens. The "D" train took us to 59th street in Manhattan; the A train then took us to Brooklyn; and finally the E train into Queens. We were 13 years old. There was no way that either Lizzy's or my own mother would allow us to make such a journey—particularly on our own. Midget had the perfect solution: Lizzy would tell her mother that she had been invited to stay the night at Midget's house (in the Bronx); Midget would tell her mother that she had been invited to stay the night at my house; and I would then tell my mother that I was staying with Lizzy. The success of this plan was contingent upon our mothers failing to call one another to verify this. It worked!

We rolled up towels, packed a snack, and put on our bathing suits underneath our shorts and shirts. We had no extra clothes with us and very little money. But we were off!

Now Lizzy and I had been to Rockaway before. Not only had we gone for the day with Visitation Day Camp, but some families of classmates had rented bungalows every summer. Of course, when travelling with Camp, we did not have the time or the freedom to go from one block to another searching out people we knew. This was going to be different!

With Midget's directions, we found her summer house easily. She and her friend, Tina, were expecting us. It was exciting to travel unescorted. We all got along well and were determined to have a good time. Midget's house was a one-block walk to the beach. We set up by laying our towels side by side and embraced both the sun and the surf. Midget was very, very tanned already. She was blonde haired and blue eyed and very pretty. And she was twice as popular as she was pretty. Midget knew everyone!

The sun was hot, the water cool, and the day perfect. We all had a great time. There were many kids our age in different groups at the beach. It was as if we had hit the mother lode of places to hang out on a summer's day. One by one, Midget introduced us to yet another friend of hers, most of whom were from Tolentine. Lizzy and I were meeting everyone in the school we were about to attend ahead of time. It was a perfect beach day.

As nighttime fell, we all went to Tina's house to shower. Evening was party time! Midget was more of an experienced party-goer and began to advise us: "You should drink about a quart of Colt 45. Lizzy, you might want to have two—just 'cause you're a bit bigger than she is." How we would purchase beer at the tender age of 13 was no hill for a climber like Midget, who quickly assured us both that she had connections. The beer was purchased at a nearby deli by someone older. Then, with beer in hand, we all proceeded back to the beach where we planned to spend the night.

This would have been frightening, if not so exciting. Here we were at the largest party ever, with all sorts of high school students to meet and greet. Life just doesn't get any better than this! We met one new person after another, Lizzy and I. Midget seemed to know everyone!

There were quite a few boys from Tolentine. Our conversation centered on our going to the school in the fall and what class we would be in. Before long, Lizzy had settled into one spot on the beach, talking with one particular boy, Peter. He was very good-looking. One year older, Peter seemed very interested in Lizzy. Most of my time was spent conversing with Peter's friend, Kenny, who was very nice and very polite. Coincidentally, Kenny had a friend named Steven who, with his younger brother, Peter, had attended Visitation Day Camp. So theirs were familiar faces to me.

As the evening progressed, the moon rose, the alcohol kicked in, and everyone was getting friendlier. There was a lot of kissing going on among the paired-off couples. Lizzy was with Peter, and I was with Kenny. We would kiss for a while, then stop and talk. He would tell me all about what to expect at the school, as well as asking questions about things I liked to do when I wasn't at the beach.

In the midst of the conversation, Lizzy emerged from underneath the boardwalk, seeking us out. "Hey, Midget!" Lizzy called, giggling all the while.

Midget smiled at Lizzy and asked, "You like him?"

"Hell, yeah!" Lizzy said. "What's not to like? He's a doll!" Lizzy whispered into Midget's ear. I tried, but could not hear what she was saying. I could, however, hear Midget.

"A hickey? Are you serious?"

Lizzy needed instruction on how to give a hickey. My thought was, *why?* But Lizzy wanted to know, and Midget knew—and told her. Lizzy always has been a bit of an over-achiever. She was the best basketball player the school had. She was a straight A student. Why would this be any different? Lizzy ran back to Peter, where she remained for the better part of the evening. They kissed and talked all night.

By sunrise we were all looking around for each other to regroup. Lizzy, Midget and I each had a wonderful time!

As the sun grew stronger and the light brighter, evidence of Lizzy's evening became more and more apparent. Peter had a string of hickeys around his neck like a necklace. "Oh my God!" his friends exclaimed. "Geez, Peter—what are you gonna do?"

What did they mean, what was he gonna do? I wondered. It was funny, I thought. But nothing that required action of any kind.

Little did any of us know—Peter's girlfriend, Melanie, and her best friend (nicknamed Animal) were both on their way out to Rockaway. And Melanie would be none too happy to see a string of hickeys around her boyfriend's neck when she arrived! Lizzy became concerned, as did I, but for different reasons. Lizzy worried that Melanie and her friend would want to beat her up. I was worried that Lizzy would expect me to help her if that happened!

When they finally showed up, Peter and his friends had concocted a tale of how he had gone to an amusement park and gotten mugged. I don't think his girlfriend believed the story. There was talk that she "wanted to" beat Lizzy up—but I don't know that Melanie ever laid a hand on her. Nor did anything more come of the relationship that began between Kenny and me that night on the beach. He did visit my house once or twice, but I kept him at arm's length. Nice or not, I had no interest in getting any closer.

Stage III

18. The Religion of Basketball

FOR THE KENNEDY family, it was known as Camelot. For those of us who grew up in the Bronx, it was Angels' basketball. Basketball is as Irish Catholic as baseball is American. The name of the parish was Our Lady of Angels. It was located near the reservoir on Claflin Avenue. Students there learned that basketball, like Catholicism, was a religion. Playing was fun and introduced both boys and girls to the advantages of athleticism at a very young age. Winning was everything. "Angels" were winners!

I was on my own from a very young age. Consequently, my friends were my family in many respects. It was with my friends that I learned about life in the city, passing the time, entertaining myself, and having fun. Without them, I would have been nothing more than a spectator. And together we played basketball and other sports.

We began playing organized basketball on a team in the third grade. Our coach, Mrs. Noonan, was an icon in the parish community, heading up all athletic activities for girls on a volunteer basis. She was a very smart, very powerful woman who stood with her head held proudly, her chest out, and her hand pointed out as if leading a charge to victory! Mrs. Noonan taught us the fundamentals of basketball when we were merely 8 years old. Her intention was simply to nurture players from a very young age to groom them into becoming an unbeatable team. And for many years, her plan worked. We practiced in the gymnasium several times a week after school and played in the park when there was no practice. We played basketball all the time!

Despite my Catholic upbringing, I was not what you would call "born with it" when it came to basketball. I enjoyed the game and the camaraderie that came with being on a team, but I did not have the natural ability coaches like Mrs. Noonan saw from afar and then said to herself, "This kid is terrific!" My belonging to the Angels' basketball team was more like what causes some people to take in a lost puppy. As for me, I did not need the training to become an athlete as badly as I needed to belong—particularly since my number one sport of choice, figure skating, was largely a sport of isolation. With the exception of my coach, I did not spend a great deal of time "speaking" to other people. To be more precise, I spoke to anyone who would listen—but I only shared personal information with a select few.

Mrs. Noonan was a great person with a big heart. But she was no fool! To have a winning team, you play the best players. Our Lady of Angels parish had many very talented players to pick from without having to avail themselves of my services. So I was on the team, but I rarely set foot on the court. My role was more in a support capacity. I would "dress out" for each game, wearing my uniform as if ready to play. But during the second quarter, I would leave the bench to go cut oranges for the players. Then as soon as the buzzer sounded, I would appear at the bench with a tray of oranges to replenish all the tired, sweaty, stars of the team. It wasn't a glamorous job, but it did have its perks! I was in an Angels' uniform—and Angels ruled the courts!

Being a member of this elitist group afforded me much in the way of good times. There was practice two times a week, games two or more times per week, and social occasions sprinkled in between. Angels were on the go—constantly! When you were on the team, everyone knew your name, and you met everyone *they* knew. This provided players with a very wide range of acquaintances all around the city.

On the up-side: Another perk to being a member of the Angels' basketball team was being invited to participate in many activities outside of basketball. This stemmed from the rationale that if you were a member of the Number One basketball team in the city, you must be athletically inclined and good at everything! Therefore, you were now welcome to participate in cheerleading, softball, volleyball, swimming, track—or anything else your heart desired. In fact, it was considered "out of character" to refuse to participate in any of these sports. Before you knew it, ". . . your cup runneth over." Not a day would go by that there wasn't some practice, game or event that beckoned. I attended every single event. In fact, someone would have had to kill me to keep me from going. Socializing was more than my life's blood; it was a fix to which I became addicted. From the moment of my 3rd grade introduction to the wonderful world of sports until 7th grade, I focused my attention on watching, cheering, and cutting oranges. Conversely, my mother was in favor of figure skating, but NOT BASKETBALL—or anything else. She took me to every single skating session I ever attended, paid for every lesson, and hand-sewed every single performance costume (excluding the competition dress). Basketball, on the other hand, was something that did not interest her in any way. Therefore, she did not participate. She never attended one game.

Securing the last berth on the third string of a winning team affords a person the luxury of never having to pay much attention to what is going on—as she stands very little chance of ever being asked to take an active role on the court! However, on one occasion, the Angels were up 20+ points, and Mrs. Noonan was feeling more benevolent than usual.

"Ellen," she yelled down the bench over the backs of the others who were seated on the bench. "You're going in!"

A time out was called, and instantly I was in a huddle receiving instructions from the coach. My excitement was overwhelming and caused me to suffer from detached hearing. I saw Mrs. Noonan's mouth moving, but I didn't hear one word she was saying to us. All I knew was *I was going in.*

Seconds later I was on the court. The crowd's yelling was almost deafening. The excitement was unbelievable. In an instant, the point guard threw me the ball. I was wide open. I shot without hesitating . . . . *Score!* I was so happy, I thought I would cry. My first basket! Regrettably, I had just racked up two points for the other team, as I had tossed the ball into the wrong basket! Team members on the court looked in disbelief at what I had done.

"What are you doing? Are you nuts?" The crowd appeared hostile. Angels never gave points away! And there was my biggest dilemma–I was thrilled that I had scored, even if it was for the competition. Not until the fall of my freshman year in high school did I set foot on the court again.

Although St. Nicholas of Tolentine was not my first choice among the high schools I could attend, it was, in fact, my mother's first choice. Therefore, I was Tolentine-bound in freshman year. Several other friends from my grammar school team also headed for Tolentine: Lizzy, the point guard and captain of the team; Marie, starting guard; Nancy, starting forward; Geraldine, cheerleading captain; and Janet, co-bench warmer! Six Angels in total headed to join the rival Tolentine family.

If I had learned one thing in grammar school, it was that the key to a social life was participation in sports. Knowing that I was not exactly a "hot property" coming to a rival school, I decided to take the "net" approach to fishing and try out for *everything*, including cheerleading, hoping to secure a position on *some* team.

Cheerleading was something that I truly enjoyed, and combined with a fair amount of acrobatic ability, this gave me the hopes of securing a position on the team. Cheerleading try-outs were as much based upon learning ability and talent as they were popularity and looks. So day after day for one full week, I learned cheers to demonstrate for members of the entire existing team.

Better safe than sorry, however, I also chose to attend basketball tryouts. As I had not been a starting member of the elementary school team, tryouts for me were limited to Junior Varsity. The first day was limited to drills, lay-ups, foul shots, dribbling, and passing. By the second day, we were assigned to scrimmage teams. I was put on the same team as Nancy who, despite being a starting member of our grammar school team, had not made the Tolentine varsity. Whenever I am in an unfamiliar environment, I find great comfort in having someone around me that I know. So, being on the team with Nancy gave me a sense of security.

That first day I didn't get much play time. I wasn't in the game two minutes at tryouts. I remember thinking that the word was out on me being more of a mascot than a player. *How can I be trying out if I'm not playing?* I wondered. I knew that I would have to do something to be remembered in a group this size.

The third day of try-outs came, and I was as nervous as ever. I could see my chances quickly slipping away. I needed luck! My sister had what her friends used to refer to as a "Captain America" shirt. It was a long-sleeved navy blue jersey with a white star across the chest, outlined in red. *This will make me a star,* I thought. *This will make me lucky.*

We kept the same teams we had had before. This time my name was called early, and I was to have my chance. I had it in my mind, *Make this count!* My knees were buckling as I watched the jump for the ball begin play. *Don't screw this up,* became my mantra. Several trips up and down the court, watching nervously as the ball was in play. My hands were up in the air waving to signal that I was open and ready. Suddenly the ball came at me mistakenly from a member of the other team! I intercepted the pass and ran with it, dribbling the length of the court into a lay-up—and scored two! *Oh my God,* I thought to myself, *and it was in the right basket!*

Now I am a viable member of the team. My counterparts are looking to see if I am open; they pass me the ball. I take it around the top of the key and pass it back, thinking all the while, *don't get too full of yourself—luck runs out.*

Then the sophomore on the team calls to me, "Hey you, star girl!" and passes me the ball. Again I take a lay-up and score!

Twice—that's twice I've scored, I'm thinking to myself. *I can't believe it!*

For the full length of the quarter that I played that day, I scored six points and intercepted the ball three times. People at the try-out are high-fiving me as we walk out of the gym.

Then Nancy gave me the strangest look and said, "What—d'you play a lot this summer?"

I know she meant it as a compliment, but all I kept thinking was *don't let people hear how surprised you are—at least until they make up their minds.*

The fact is that there was magic for me that day. I had always imagined there was such a thing as magic. At times I had had glimpses of it—brief glimpses that were so swift to come and go that I almost questioned the feeling. This time was different! It was as if somebody really good at basketball used my body for the day and let me enjoy watching her play. It wasn't me! But it sure was fun.

19. Freshman/Senior Day

ENTERING HIGH SCHOOL is a rite of passage from youth to the teenage years. Basically you go from being the elder of an elementary school to being the new kid in a high school. Freshmen are often the targets of much humor and practical joking as a way of being indoctrinated into the mainstream of the program. In St. Nicholas of Tolentine, this rite of passage was marked with a formal celebration known as Freshman/Senior Day.

Each freshman girl was paired with a senior sister. This coupling was to serve as a sort of mentoring program for the freshman new to the school and its routine. For the senior, however, it was often license to torture, if only for the one day!

The seniors collectively sat down and decided upon the "festivities" for the day. No detail was left to chance. For attire: Freshmen were to wear the standard summer uniform, which was a pink cotton A-line dress. That was the only norm. Additionally, opaque stockings were to be worn, but cut at the ankles so that the stockings would roll up and down. The hair of the freshman was to be loosely rolled in curlers. There was also to be a braid of hair stemming from the crown of the head. Attached to that braid was a balloon, causing the braid to move about. It should be mentioned that the boys in the school, fully aware of this ritual and its requirements, came to school that day armed with straight pins with which to pop the balloons of the girls. Should your balloon be popped, a replacement would have to be obtained immediately. On the front and back of each freshman girl was an oak tag (poster board) heart, stating the name of the freshman girl and the senior to whom she belonged.

As if this were not enough, each freshman girl was to carry with her a 6 x 6 inch velvet cloth. At any point in the day when she would encounter a senior girl, she must immediately kneel, recite the official pledge, and with the cloth, shine the school ring of the senior. Directed to the seniors, the pledge began, "We plebian freshmen, diminished by your dazzling presence, existing solely for your benefit, hereby pledge to you . . ." and went on to commit ourselves to being of service to the seniors for the duration of their tenure at the school. Should a freshman either forget the pledge (word for word) or not please the senior in some way, a punishment was assigned. The punishment could be anything from dancing a jig in the lunchroom during the boys' lunchtime to cleaning the bathroom.

This tradition had gone on since the beginning of time. No one had ever been hurt physically; it was entirely about humiliation. The good news was that all the freshman girls were enduring this together. Oddly, the more popular you were, the more of a target for abuse you were. It was the one time in my life I welcomed obscurity!

Our high school had programs for both boys and girls. However, as the saying goes, "Never the twain shall meet." The boys occupied one side of the building and the girls the other. There were swinging doors in the center of each floor's hallway separating the two sides and two populations. Of course, we managed to mingle at class changes, slipping notes under and through the doorway to friends on the other side. But for all intents and purposes, we were banned from association during the day, so we did not share lunchtimes.

But Freshman/Senior Day allowed a change of plan. During lunchtime, while the senior boys were in the lunchroom, the freshman girls were led in parade-like fashion to the cafeteria. Upon entering, music was put on and the girls were instructed to perform the senior hop; a dance created by the seniors for their amusement. If not for it being rather degrading, it would have been comical. Photos were taken to preserve the memory for all time. Those photos appeared in the yearbook!

Until the day before the event, I had no assigned senior sister. With the help of some well-wishing friends who put their networking skills into action, I was introduced to a senior who had not been assigned a sister. Her name was Angelina. I had never met her before.

Despite our relationship as "sisters" being created as the result of last minute necessity, she was perfect! Angelina was both very nice and extremely pretty, not to mention smart. She was not at all what one would expect to find at the last minute.

At the close of the day's activities, Angelina handed me a gift box which, when opened, revealed a beautiful silver necklace with a pearl pendant. It was one of the nicest gifts given that day. Although the entire Freshman/Senior Day experience was geared towards humiliation of the freshmen, this was done in group. On a personal level, Angelina was kind, quiet, and very classy. I felt very lucky!

Throughout the remainder of my freshman year, Angelina made herself available to me for any of my questions or concerns, or just to serve as a sounding board when I had a run-in with a teacher—which was more often than not! She was never intrusive. Rather, she was simply there if I needed her—very much like the behavior one would expect from a guardian angel!

Once my freshman year was over (and Angelina graduated), I lost contact with her. Over the years I have thought of Angelina, wondering how she is, hoping she is happy. That experience was the first conclusive evidence I had in proving to myself that you do not have to be popular to end up perfectly happy!

20. Egg Cetera

HALLOWEEN, CELEBRATED EACH year on October 31st, has been a time of celebration for centuries. The term "Halloween" comes from Hallows Eve, or holy evening, the day before All Saints Day, a holy day in the Catholic Church. Halloween inspires playful traditions, such as dressing up in costume, trick-or-treating, carving pumpkins into jack-o-lanterns, touring haunted houses and watching horror films. Perhaps not part of official tradition—but certainly engrained in Halloween practices in New York—is egg throwing!

Although not part of the normal Halloween occasion when I was younger, egg throwing was something I noticed more and more as I grew older. By the time I was 13, I was quite aware of the tendency for eggs to be thrown on Halloween. There were always the occasional neighborhood boys who would throw eggs from the rooftops towards the sidewalks below. They would not deliberately hit pedestrians, but rather just frighten them as they were walking.

After a few months of attending my new high school, I had made many new friends. Some were members of the cheerleading squad of which I was a part; others were in the same classes as I. Many of this group had grown up in the area of the Bronx where this school was located. They had known each other for many years already. I, on the other hand, was very new to the group, having come from a different parish and associated with them for only a few months.

The girls were all fun to be around. Most of them had very out-going personalities and quite a sense of humor. It was often that we found ourselves laughing and talking about the most current news of the neighborhood.

As Halloween grew nearer, conversation focused more around what would be happening in the neighborhood pertaining to that event: candy, parties, etc. There was no having this conversation without exploring the possibility of eggs being thrown. With only days away, Halloween was sure to bring at least a few eggs our way. It was just something boys did for fun!

One afternoon as the girls gathering in the park grew in numbers, we all found ourselves very pre-occupied with the potential threat of egg throwing. One of the girls, Melissa had seen the boys carrying grocery bags heading towards an alley up the street.

"What, what are you talking about?"

"I saw them! I'm sure they had eggs. They must be stashing them up Andrews Avenue."

"Are you sure?"

"Yeah! What do you think—they ALL went shopping for their moms?"

All the girls laughed out loud. Melissa clearly had a point. If several of the boys were carrying grocery bags, it was no coincidence. They must have bought eggs!

"Come on—let's go see," she encouraged us all.

"Oh, sure; like they won't be mad as hell if we find them!"

"*Find* them—I think we should break them all!" she told us. Melissa was obviously fearless and void of any rationale. If we did that, the boys were going to be more than just mad.

One by one, we bolstered one another up. Before we could stop ourselves, we were all walking up the street in a mob in search of the eggs! Melissa was out in front leading the search party. We went up the street and into the alley as she instructed us, climbing over the fence, up one side of the alley and down another, until we came to a sort of cove in the yard surrounded by trees. Just as she had suggested, there they were. Eggs! Dozens upon dozens of eggs. They were everywhere! Holy Cow! The boys were planning to get us! We all laughed.

The excitement filled us with power, and we each began grabbing the boxes of eggs and smashing them. We didn't throw them at each other, but rather smashed them so that they could not be used against us. We enjoyed the idea that we had beaten the boys to the punch. Our giddiness, however, was interrupted by the thought of one clear-headed girl who uttered, "They're going to be pissed when they realize we broke all their eggs!"

"What?"

"Yeah—can you image how much this cost them? They're not going to like this!"

"Oh, well," Melissa exclaimed, letting out a guttural laugh. "Too bad!"

We all laughed big, hearty, belly laughs as we broke every last egg.

Two days later was Halloween. We had enjoyed ourselves immensely finding the hidden egg stash and breaking them all. We especially enjoyed the knowledge that we had somehow defeated the boys. But our joy was about to come to a screeching halt.

As darkness fell upon the day, we realized the time of reckoning was drawing near. "Hey, John and Malcolm are down the street, and they are pissed! We'd better get out of here!"

It only had to be said once. We all headed in different directions. Some lived only a short distance from the park. I lived the farthest away, having to walk 6 blocks to even get into my own neighborhood. I headed towards the largest street, thinking that with more people around, less would be likely to occur. Not so!

Malcolm was furious! As I saw him within a half block from me, I began to run. I was a pretty good runner, but Malcolm was angry, and that was fueling his speed. I found myself standing face to face with him in the street. He smiled at me. It was an evil smile. He looked me right in the eye and said, "You're dead!"

I knew instantly that he wasn't kidding. Before I could get going, Malcolm reached back and threw an egg right at me. It hit me in the face so hard that it literally cut my cheek open. Blood and egg yolk ran down my face as I took off into the wind. But once was not enough. Malcolm ran after me calling to the others. I was now being chased by a gang of angry egg throwers!

I managed to get to University Avenue where the #38 bus ran. I had just missed the bus. Knowing that it was my only hope, I ran alongside the bus as it went down the street, banging on the door. "Please stop! Let me on!" I cried. "They're chasing me!" The bus driver slowed down and opened the door. I hopped on, and the doors closed behind me.

As I walked into the bus, the other passengers looked at me very strangely, seeing the blood running down my face. I was quite relieved to be separated from the mob at this point. Still, I wondered if there was some way they would get to my street before the bus did. Fortunately, my mind was just playing tricks on me. The mob was far behind by the time I made it to Sedgwick Avenue. But just to be safe, I ran down the block and up the four flights of stairs into my apartment!

It was days before I returned to the neighborhood where we had smashed the eggs. I decided that "laying low" was the best solution. I heard that the other girls had gotten "egged" as well. Some had been drenched with eggs; others, just one or two.

Time filled the space following Halloween. As the fear subsided, all the girls agreed that it was far better to have fought back and broken all those eggs than it would have been to just "take it" another year! In retrospect, perhaps our standing up to the boys was all it took; I don't recall them really launching a major egg-throwing campaign against us ever again.

21. "Playing" with the Band

THE PARTICULAR HIGH school I attended was divided up into three academic sections: "A," "B" and "C." These groupings were arrived at rather predictably by test scores and grade point averages. For the purposes of education, "A" and "B" were given strictly academic programs of study, while Section C was given a commercial program, consisting of typing, bookkeeping, etc. In addition, Sections A & B were assigned French as the second language to learn; "C" was assigned Spanish.

Now, good grades or not—it is not difficult to arrive at the conclusion that one's use of French in New York City (the assigned language for Sections A and B) would be limited at best! On the other hand, Spanish (Section C) was widely used and would be considered quite an asset.

I was in Section A.

It was no secret that my goal had been to attend Bronx High School of Science. There I could have taken Russian as a language, which would have enabled me to work as a translator at the United Nations—my first noted ambition. Not only was I not permitted to attend the school of my choice, I was not going to be permitted to take a language that would be of any use to me in New York City either.

To say that I was unhappy would be a colossal understatement. I did try to make the best of my situation (or so I thought). In reality, I was miserable in my own skin and couldn't find a way to make myself happy. I couldn't attend the school I wanted, couldn't take the classes I chose, and I no longer cared about the things that I *could* do. I was floundering!

In a feeble attempt to switch gears, I began looking at the potential to study architecture. Skyscrapers were something that had always fascinated me. During a "counseling" session with my guidance advisor, Mrs. "P" *as we referred to her*, she asked (going through the motions of her job), "Isn't there *anything* you are interested in, Ellen?"

I replied, "Yes, I would like to build skyscrapers."

"Don't be silly. That's not something a woman does. That's a man's career! What would YOU like to do?"

I sat with a look of disgust on my face, mouth hanging open, my eyes glazed over, thinking to myself, *You dumb cow—I just told you what I wanted to do. In fact, I told my mother what I wanted to do, and she sent me here to you geniuses. Maybe I should have taken ENGLISH, since no one here seems to understand me!*

I left Mrs. P's office certain that I would grow up to be of as little value to society as she had been to me. This was the environment I was in, and therefore the best I could hope for. I was screwed!

For an unnatural length of time, I became preoccupied with the dilemma of what to do. I felt trapped in an institution that was neither there to serve me nor capable of doing so. The best I could hope for was to have fun while I was there.

Then at a high school dance, I met a boy, one year older than I, who was a musician. I had never met a musician before! He was the bass player for a local band. We met right before Christmas and became instantly inseparable. My life revolved around the band's jobs. It was great! One weekend, we would be going to a high school dance, another time, a local pub. Although I had no musical ability greater than selecting a radio station to listen to, I was glad to be tagging along every weekend.

Band life is exciting. You are there with the center of the action. You get the best seats in the house for the show. And, you aren't "thinking" you are interacting with the band—you actually are! They will look at you while they are playing, make comments to you about the show. You are part of the action! As if this were not enough, you are now able to walk into local pubs and places that normally require scads of identification proving you are of age to be there, which I was not. Arriving with the band causes details like that to be glossed over! There was music, dancing, laughing, and drinking—every weekend.

Life was getting better!

During the week, I would continue to attend cheerleading practice and scheduled games. All other free time was spent with my new friend and his band. I was hardly ever home—which also suited me. My mother and I were literally arguing about EVERYTHING every time we were in the same space. I hated going home! True to life, the more I resisted going home, the more my mother would try to put her foot down and make me come home. "You are too young to be out in the street till all hours of the night!" she would yell at me.

"I'm not in the street—I'm in a bar with the band!" I'd yell back at her. "Is it safer for me to walk home alone than it is to be driven to the door and walked up? Think, Mom!"

She *was* thinking, but we were using two completely different frames of reference. My mother was big on remaining calm, but making her point. She decided that the best way to enforce her rules and get me to come home at what she considered to be "a reasonable hour" was to stipulate, "OK, you are to be home at 11:00 p.m. If you are not here by 11:05, the top lock will be put on, and you will not get in." I did not have a key to the top lock. Her rationale was that I would certainly come home if I was faced with the threat of not being allowed in afterwards.

Not so! Hell, I didn't want to come home anyway! So when Mom said, "You won't get in," I thought, *OK, we agree!* From that point on, I planned to stay over at a friend's house any night the band was playing. Implementing my own plan B, I was gone all the time, going home only long enough to change clothes.

In the meantime, my grades were taking a nosedive. I was doing no homework or studying of any kind. Why would I? I wasn't taking the courses I wanted; I wasn't in the school I wanted to be in; and—by the guidance counselor's own admission—I would NEVER be what I wanted to be in life. What was the point?

My mother was called in for parent/teacher conferences, one after another to brainstorm about what to do with me. If those conversations were as successful as the earlier ones trying to inspire me, I completely understand why nothing was accomplished! I was rapidly becoming my mother's worst nightmare—a "street urchin."

The weekends had become my reason to live through the week. Music and dancing formed the backdrop for the introduction to life I was getting. Traveling around with a band, you meet all sorts of people from all walks of life.

One was the manager of the band, Jack. Jack was a middle-aged man, who managed the band's bookings and pay. I never paid much attention to the details of that. Suffice to say, everyone who was in the band was paid every time they played. But how much each one received or how much Jack got was irrelevant to me. Jack was a fixture—even more so than I was. He drove the van that carried all the equipment and, at times, the band members themselves. I don't even remember if Jack had a regular job during the week. All I knew was that he managed the band—and that was enough. Jack was a bit of a character, but there was never any impropriety. He never made advances towards any of the girlfriends of the band members. In fact, I don't remember seeing him hit on any females, ever. He behaved like a middle child—trying very much to keep the peace among the group. He spent week after week traveling with the band, going to the jobs—which were usually in bars. Jack just remained in the background, watching.

Night after night, I would have to make plans to stay over at someone's house. This usually wasn't a problem. Most of my friends had large families, and one more body in the morning wasn't even noticed. I would just walk in like I belonged, sleep there, and leave in the morning.

For whatever reason, on this one particular night, no overnight arrangements had been made, and I had nowhere to go. It was time to test the water on this threat my mother had issued. I was driven home by the band and dropped off in front of my building. I hurried. As I reached the apartment, I thought to myself, *Think positive—she didn't lock the door.*

I put the key in the lock and turned. "Click," I heard the tumbler of the lock disengage. But as I pushed on the door, it didn't budge. *Damn! She actually locked the door! Where do I go now?*

I had to think. I could try to go to my friend's house, but she lived six blocks away. That's a long walk at 3 o'clock in the morning! Not too safe in New York City.

With few options, I decided to just find someplace to stay in the hallway. I went to the landing between the top floor and the roof and sat on the stairs. It was darker up there, as there were no overhead lights illuminating the area. Perhaps I wouldn't be seen. I leaned over onto my arm against the stairs and went to sleep.

22. Holiday Hills Forever

THE CONCLUSION OF Freshman Year brought many things: The prospect of summer—FREEDOM; the awareness that we were all one year closer to completing our high school education; the knowledge that we were no longer the new kids on the block and were "indoctrinated" into the mainstream of the student body.

It was also the time of year that brought acknowledgments of achievements during the year. For the purpose of this writing, the achievement I refer to is the completion of a successful athletic season—which was of great significance in my Catholic school. All members of the girls' athletic program were invited to attend an end-of-season trip. Our destination, Holiday Hills, was a place that would become infamous in Tolentine history—for it was there that all but 3 members of the athletic program were suspended!

Holiday Hills, located in upstate New York, was a resort filled with log cabins, buildings to board groups, and a main facility meeting area. The amenities at this establishment included horseback riding, as well as swimming. We were out of the city for a long holiday weekend.

There were approximately 50 girls in attendance, ranging in age from 14-18, as well as several chaperones, nuns and teachers. Of those in attendance, six of us were former classmates from our grade school, Our Lady of Angels. In one way, shape, or form, we had all managed to secure a berth on a team at Tolentine. While we each intermingled with the entire group, we remained a sort of sub-group core.

We considered any entertainment that presented itself to us while in high school to be a backdrop to drinking some type of alcohol, be it beer, wine or liquor. This trip was no exception. Each girl purchased her substance of choice beforehand and packed it carefully, concealing it within her clothing. (Alcohol was not, of course, sanctioned by the school.) This was going to be one heck of a party! We all boarded the buses and departed from the school on a Friday afternoon. There was some singing of songs—as there always was as standard practice for riding on the bus—along with laughing, excitement and banter.

The ride itself took several hours. We arrived at our destination Friday evening and were instructed by our chaperones to get ourselves settled in. We had a large cabin, where all the girls could stay somewhat together. The nuns were staying close by, but not right with us. We decided to explore the grounds and get ourselves familiar with the area as quickly as possible.

Everyone had brought something different to drink, depending upon their preference. I had brought two bottles of wine. Others had brought vodka or rum, with the intention of mixing it with Coke, orange juice or the like. There were some who were assigned the task of taking plastic cups from the kitchen area to be used outside. We found a suitable place for our outdoor party part-way into the woods. It was pitch dark—which was actually perfect, despite its drawbacks, because we couldn't be seen by the teachers. The plans and the party itself rapidly grew in size.

As expected with sundown, it was getting a bit chilly outside. We were excited to be outside—having fun and partying—but we were feeling the chill. One of our "core group" members, Nancy, decided to look for a place for us to get in out of the cold. We wandered around for a bit until we came upon a small cabin. It had a few furnished rooms inside that we could see through the window. "This is perfect. Let's go in here." Unable to get the door open, we decided to climb in through the window. Nancy removed the screen, slid up the bottom window, and one by one, in we went! We partied in the living room of this little cabin for hours, laughing, telling stories, and drinking. I am unclear as to why we did this, but we exited the exact way we had come in—through the window.

Back to the woods we went to join the rest of the main group.

There was so much going on in such a small area—seniors, juniors, sophomores and freshmen all drinking together in the woods. It was great fun!

The two seniors present were actually captain and co-captain of the basketball team. Trying their level best to act responsibly, they were encouraging us to keep a lid on our wildness so as not to get caught. Clearly we were having fun and had developed serious cases of the giggles. At 11:30 p.m., we began heading back to the main cabin where we were to sleep that night. We were having too much fun to simmer down! The laughing and carrying on went on throughout the night.

With very little sleep, we awoke the next morning to venture out for a horseback riding excursion. There were all of us city girls climbing up on these very large animals and taking off in a line. The horses were quite tame, for the most part. They did, however, have some difficulty accepting direction from a bunch of New York City girls—who knew nothing about steering a horse! Occasionally one of us would get off the beaten path, but soon enough, the horse would rejoin the group, seemingly on his own.

After dinner, it was again our intention to go into the woods to partake of round two of the drinking. It was as if someone had rung a bell, declaring *Round 2*. Out we scurried into the woods, substances in hand. We were more relaxed this second night—thus, much more confident of our ability to do whatever we pleased without being caught.

This time, several of the girls had had more than a reasonable share of the alcohol. They got plastered! A few made an effort to contain those who were laughing and falling down out of control, but to no avail. While they were being brought back to be put to bed (which is where they belonged), the nuns heard the commotion and went to investigate. There was no hiding this—they were caught!

Before too long, we were all being rounded up, both by chaperones and by local authorities. Nothing will kill a good party faster than to have local police shining lights in your face! We were escorted back to the main cabin, where we were lectured. Nuns thrive on lecture. It is amazing we are not still being talked to about this, what with all the material we had provided them!

As we returned to our sleeping quarters, we speculated on how this was going to turn out for us. We knew it was going to be bad; for some, it would be worse than for others. My mother was no stranger to my antics, so I assumed she was going to take this in stride—much in the same manner with which she dealt with everything else I threw at her. Others, having never given any trouble to their parents, sat wondering just how bad this was going to be when their parents found out.

Morning came soon enough. We were informed, in group, that each of us would be telephoning home to advise our parents of our behavior. What this entailed exactly was a line of everyone waiting to use the one payphone that was at the facility. Picture this: Fifty or so teenage girls standing in line, flanked by teachers, coaches and nuns, in anticipation of calling home to confess to drinking in the woods. It wasn't a pretty sight!

One by one, girls would complete their phone call and be escorted back to the main building, some crying, some sneering in disgust—all in trouble. My mother made a remark when I told her—something along the lines of, "You couldn't just go and have a good time?"

I did! I thought to myself. *I was having a great time until these idiots broke it up!*

The bus ride home was somewhat more subdued than the ride there. There was no singing. There were lots of mini-conversations about strategy: How were we going to handle our parents when we arrived home?

Some girls found out all too soon just how their parents were going to react; they were standing at the corner of the school property when the buses pulled up. Mine was at home, *thank God!* I walked home, gear on my back, ready for yet another good time to be completely ruined when I got home.

The news was fairly basic: "You're grounded." That was to be expected. The question was for how long? But I was in no mood to start up another argument at this point. I was tired; I hadn't slept much in the time I had been gone and just wanted to crawl into bed and forget about it. Sleep was a welcome relief to the episode.

Tuesday morning brought a new stress with it: An assembly for the entire student body was called at 8:30 a.m. Each of us knew it had to be something to do with Holiday Hills! "What now?"

The principal, Sister Rose Patricia, had made the announcement over the loud speaker that we were all to gather for the assembly. Typically, any announcement from Sister Rose Patricia would elicit some one of the many class clowns to utter under their breath, "Rosie, Rosie, Rosie on the PA!" Not this time! There was no joking this time. We just stood and allowed the home room teacher to usher us to the gymnasium downstairs.

As the crowd entering the gym grew in size, members of the athletic programs sought each other out and herded up together in the center. A few of us were holding hands. Even a sweaty palm is support when you are about to be publicly chastised! This was going to be bad—and we all knew it.

As Sister began speaking, she described very matter-of-factly and without detail or embellishment the incident that had occurred at Holiday Hills. It was an accurate portrayal of the weekend—but with the fun taken out. Her account took only a few minutes. At the end, she declared, "Because of this incident, the following girls (and then named each and every one of us), are no longer, members of . . ."

I grabbed my friend's hand thinking. *Oh, God—she's going to expel us!*

". . . the St. Nicholas of Tolentine Athletic Program."

"What?"

"What did she say?"

All the athletes looked around to find each other in the crowd.

"Is she kidding? *That's it?* Oh, my God! We're safe!"

23. Sophomore Year

MY LIFE WAS changing drastically. In an effort to find a distraction from arguing every time we were at home together, my mother volunteered at the local Veteran's Hospital as a sort of candy striper, bringing magazines around to patients. As a result, she became involved with and married a man who was a patient at that time. Admittedly, I didn't care much for him— nor him for me. But fate had brought us together. My mother would no longer be working every day (and many evenings), which meant I no longer had the apartment to myself. I also had to accept the fact that we would have to move. Mom's new husband was confined to a wheelchair and therefore would be unable to ascend four flights of stairs. We moved down the street to a building with an elevator to accommodate his condition.

The wedding was planned for February 3rd, right before Valentine's Day. My mother wore a red velvet dress. I always laughed about that. It was a beautiful dress, and she looked wonderful in it. But I always regarded the color choice as symbolic of how many times she had been married. Each time the wedding dress got a little darker!

My grades had deteriorated substantially during my freshman year, causing my reassignment within the grade system. I had originally perceived this to be a good thing, as dropping my grades would push me towards Section C—which would place me in a business curriculum and Spanish for a language. However, the school placed me in "B" which gave me neither. Now not only was I separated from my elementary school friends in "A"—I still did not have what I wanted, a curriculum that I thought would be useful!

Cheerleading was also a thing of the past. With my suspension from any athletics for the remainder of my stay at this school, I had an abundance of free time on my hands—as did everyone else I knew. In addition, my days of trotting around the city with the band had subsided abruptly, since I was no longer dating the bass player.

So there I was, left to my own devices. I made the acquaintance of some new friends that year: Harry, a member of the swim team, who lived on Andrews Avenue, and his best friend, Kevin, who lived closer to where I lived. As I became better acquainted with Harry and his family, I realized that I had attended dancing school with his sister, Maxine. In fact, she and I had danced in the same routine more than once.

From the time we met, Harry and I saw a great deal of each other. Our time was not spent in the same manner of excitement as I had previously spent with the band. It was more day-to-day activities. At one point, we painted a hallway for his mom. This required a base coat of one color and then taking a feather duster and applying gold paint on top of the base color by twisting the feather duster around as we applied it. The family had obviously done this routinely, as they were all quite good at it. I, however, had never seen it done and made quite a mess of my portion! Fortunately it could be fixed, and the job was completed as desired.

In autumn of that year, a trip was planned for any students wanting to go. The destination was Washington, D.C. One of the parish priests (and a teacher in the boys' school), was taking those who wished to go on this weekend trip to meet the author of *The Exorcist*. A panel van was rented for the journey. It was completely empty inside, with just two seats in the front. There were about 8 of us travelling. We all piled in with our knapsacks and sleeping bags—and away we went!

The drive took several hours. By the time we were told we had arrived at our destination, we had nowhere to go! No hotel reservations had been made, and no real plans solidified. Father, being resourceful, pulled into the parking lot of a school parish at which he had formerly taught, Carroll High School in Maryland. As we approached the rectory of this parish, music could be heard. Upon entering, we soon discovered that we were in the midst of a party in progress! The former graduating class from this high school was there visiting, and a party had ensued.

"Where have you been?" someone walked up to me asking.

"What do you mean? I've been on the road for 6 hours."

"Really? Where were you?"

I looked at this person in disbelief, stating, "New York isn't exactly just up the road."

"*New York?* You've been to New York?"

"No, I'm *from* New York. What is it with you? Are you drunk?"

"No, I'm not drunk! You're late."

"Late? I thought we made excellent time getting here. By the way, where is it that I am right now? Is this Washington DC?"

"Will you knock it off?"

Clearly, this individual had mistaken me for someone else—but I really thought it was just a prank. As time went on, it was apparent that he had been waiting for someone that I strongly resembled, and she had not shown as promised. As he realized that I was not that person (and therefore, he was not angry with me), I relaxed and we became acquainted.

Murray, a native of Baltimore, Maryland, was an absolute doll! Not tall or dark—but definitely handsome. We talked and talked! We discussed New York, Maryland, Washington, sports, schools—you name it! We talked all night long. At the end of the evening (which in our case was morning), we exchanged phone numbers and promised to keep in touch. Living six hours apart was hardly the best of scenarios. But the connection was strong enough that it seemed the only logical thing to do.

That introduction turned out to be the most significant part of the weekend for me. Our group did continue on and meet the author, as intended, but my focus was on meeting Murray! Upon returning home, I called him. This was prohibitively expensive, particularly when speaking for longer than five minutes. Back in the day, phone calls were placed from land lines and were charged based upon long distance rates per minute. Speaking for 30 minutes could result in a $20 cost! A few of those phone calls, and the bill was mounting up considerably. So Murray and I decided to write letters to correspond. Letters were not continual, but went back and forth several times over the next few months. Never having been to New York, Murray proposed a trip north for himself and a few friends to tour the Big Apple. I agreed that this was a wonderful idea, and that I would serve as tour guide.

Murray and two of his closest friends arrived in the Bronx that spring for a weekend in the city. My friend (and older sister of the bass player I dated in freshman year), Mo, and I had made all the plans for showing them around. No tour of New York is complete without at least one subway ride! So we took the visitors into Manhattan by way of the subway. We rode all the way down to Wall Street. While unable to go inside the Stock Exchange building on the weekend, we did look around outside and decided to proceed uptown from there. On foot, we walked from Wall Street to Greenwich Village, then uptown to the Empire State Building, the Pan Am Building, and further still to the Museum of Natural History. We walked for over 10 hours touring the city. The boys were exhausted!

The next day, Murray and I had the day to ourselves. We decided to stay around where I lived and just talk for the day. Seeking privacy, I decided to take him to my favorite spot—the roof. Now the building I lived in at that time was seven stories tall. Any building over five stories must have an elevator. (I never knew where that rule came from, but it made perfect sense.) We took the elevator to the seventh floor (which was the floor I lived on) and then proceeded up the stairs to the roof.

Once on the roof, we walked around until we found the top of the elevator shaft. This section of roof extends up even higher, almost an additional story in the air, and must be accessed by ladder. We climbed the ladder to reach the top of the elevator shaft, where we remained for the afternoon. From that spot, we had a 360 degree view of the city—and all the privacy we wanted!

Murray and I talked and talked for hours on end about everything under the sun. I remember him thanking me for taking him and his friends all over New York, which was great fun. He then said, "I can see now why you love it here so much. I didn't think I would love it—but I do!"

All I could say was, "Of course you love it! I never doubted that you would. It's New York!"

24. When the Cat's Away

SEVERAL MONTHS INTO their marriage, my mother and new step-father planned a trip to Florida as both a vacation and a honeymoon. The trip was to last 10 days. My mother, not wanting me to be alone for that length of time, suggested that I stay with a friend. However, I persuaded her to allow a friend to stay with me in their absence. The friend I called was Mo—my partner in crime!

Mo, the older sister of the base player, and I had been friends for over a year and had a great time together. She was two years older than I, but it made no difference. The bottom line was that we both enjoyed the same things—partying being at the top of the list. We bid my parents a quick farewell and instantly put on our thinking caps to determine what mischief we were going to get into!

First things first: We examined the money that had been left us for food and planned just how far we could get on that amount. Our destination: The Pic-n-Shovel—a bar on Webster Avenue. In the early seventies, the Pic-n-Shovel was host to several local bands, one of which was Kiss. Since Kiss was playing that weekend, we made it a point to attend.

Mo and I dressed and left for the bar at about 8:30 p.m., with all intentions of closing the place! We were on our own, we had cash—and we had NO chaperones! Life was looking up.

We went straight to the bar, where we proceeded to drink and dance for the best part of the evening. While there, we met two college students from Fordham: Dougie and Killer! Don't let the name fool you; this guy was no Killer. How he got that name, I will never know! He was a clean-cut, ironed-shirt-wearing, college student who, accompanied by his friend Dougie, was just looking to get out on a Friday night. We all became acquainted, had drinks, and ended up making plans to go out the following night.

In the meantime, whenever I was at the apartment, more than not, I was on the phone to Murray, my friend in Maryland. These calls were 30 minutes in length if they were a minute! I would talk for a while, and then Mo would get on and talk. The slogan "Reach out, reach out and touch someone . . ." was created around Mo and me! For the duration of that vacation, Mo and I were on the phone constantly.

In addition to the phone abuse, there were the visitors to the apartment. Friends in the neighborhood began learning of our situation—the two of us being alone in an apartment for 10 days! News like this travels very fast in teenage circles! Whether invited or not, people would show up at all hours.

One night, the older brother of a friend came with a friend of his, ringing the doorbell at 2:00 a.m. Naturally, we looked through the peek hole to see who it was before opening the door, but it was "only" Paul (Lizzy's older brother) and Dennis (his best friend) —so we felt totally safe. These two had been drinking. Paul, bottle in hand, looked at Mo when she opened the door and stated, "Six bells and all is well!" That was Dennis's cue to begin to gong like a cathedral bell. Mo and I laughed so hard we couldn't breathe. We told them to go home, as we knew things were going to get way out of control with them in the apartment. We thought they had already partied enough for one day. Occurrences of this type were non-stop.

The big evening with Killer and Dougie was coming up. Mo and I took what was left of the money my mother had given us for food and bought outfits to wear that night. I was quite anxiously anticipating this date. These were college guys. This was the big time!

Oddly, the memory of Killer was much more exciting than actually being in his presence. This entire hubbub about meeting him and going out fell flat. Once we were out on the date, all I wanted to do was go home! Mo, conversely, was really enjoying Dougie's company and invited the two back to the apartment. Now they were both there, and I wasn't interested! Instead, I reverted back to the trusty telephone to call Murray. Yes, this was quite rude. But then, I was quite selfish in those days.

All this partying in the middle of winter had run me down to the point where I caught the flu. I was burning with fever. To make matters worse, we now had no money! We had spent every last cent my mother had left for us and had no food in the house. Mo decided to take matters into her own hands and search through the cupboards to find whatever she could find to whip something up. Meanwhile, I slept on the couch for the better part of the day, only rising to get more medicine and liquids.

At one point, I noticed something sizable and pink on the dining room table. I still had a fever, so my vision was strange and uncertain. I got up to see what it was I was looking at. Mo—in her boredom (and creativity)—had managed to bake three dozen cupcakes, frosted with pink butter cream icing! With wooden matches from the kitchen, she had spelled out "Eat at Mo's." I laughed so hard I almost fell down. She had gone to work at the movie theatre, so I went to the phone and called her. "What the hell did you do?"

"Hey, we needed something to eat, and we both like cupcakes. It's the basics of the food groups: milk, butter, eggs, sugar. We're good to go now!"

For the next few days, we "ate at Mo's"—cupcakes and milk—to our hearts' content.

Mom called to check on us, see how things were going, and see if we were both still alive. She also mentioned that she and her new husband, Wally, would like to extend their trip another week. I was instructed to go downstairs to a neighbor's house and get money from them. My mother had made arrangements with them to give me a certain amount, "So don't ask for more than they give you."

I ran down to the neighbor's house and got the money. I then ran back upstairs to the apartment to call Mo. We were now back in the game and had cash to spend!

By the time Mom and Wally returned from Florida, Mo and I were literally exhausted. We had been out every night, partied every weekend, and had eaten nothing but junk food. It had been heaven—but now it was over. Mo returned back to her own parents' house, while

I returned to my routine of staying out as much as humanly possible!

That plan lasted until the phone bill arrived.

Upon entering the apartment from a long day, I found both my mother and Wally seated at the dining room table, bill in hand. "Would you like to explain this?" my mother asked sternly.

I remember rolling my eyes and thinking, *No. Do you think I want to?*

I think it was supposed to be a rhetorical question, because Mom never stopped talking long enough for me to actually answer. The yelling went on for a good 20 minutes, with Wally interjecting his comments when she slipped and took a breath. "You did this for spite!" she yelled.

"No I didn't; I did it because I like Murray and I was bored silly!" For someone twice my age, she sure didn't understand much about my life!

When the yelling stopped and rational thinking returned, I was informed that I would be responsible for paying every cent of that phone bill back to them. Now I was also not allowed to use the phone in the house without express permission beforehand.

"Whatever. . . ."

25. Down and Out

BY THE END of my sophomore school year, my grades had deteriorated even more than they had in freshman year. My logic was that allowing this would most assuredly secure me placement in the commercial class—where I could finally take Spanish, typing and the like!

Fate was not on my side, however. Neither was logic! With two failing grades to my credit, I was informed that my summer would consist of summer school for both failed classes. *Hell, no!* I thought. *There is no way I am going to endure one more day of this—particularly when it will only keep me where I do not want to be!* It seemed to me that instead, my one and only option was to enroll in the business school, The Assissium, located on 63rd Street between Fifth and Madison Avenues.

The Assissium offered a business curriculum of strictly commercial courses. It began at 7:30 in the morning and went straight through until 12:30 p.m., at which time each student would go directly to a job to work for the rest of the afternoon. This was a requirement of the program. If it was the working world you were after, this was the road to get there! With little argument left, my mother agreed and I was enrolled for Fall Semester.

Attending The Assissium meant that I would be riding the subway to and from school each day. This did not suit my mother at all. The only other option was to put me on an express bus, which was far more costly. So - the train it was! The IRT was an above-ground train until about 125th Street, at which point it entered a tunnel and became an underground train. The #4 train went right past Yankee Stadium. It was an exciting journey. I felt very grown up taking the train every day, despite my appearance in a plaid Catholic school uniform.

The school building itself was a brownstone. It appeared no different than any other brownstone on the street. In fact, if you did not see girls going in and out, you would not recognize it as a school.

7:30 came awfully early in the morning, and I was not known for my punctuality. In fact, I was late almost every day. As I was now taking classes that I actually wanted, my grades were good. Still, lateness is cause for discipline, and I was rapidly becoming a target of the principal of this school.

After only a short period, the school arranged a job for me after school. I was to work as the secretary for the owner of a very upscale beauty and facial salon in Mid-Town. The salon itself was a very beautiful place filled with foreign workers. They spoke very little English, while I spoke nothing else. Everyone on staff was to be addressed as "Ms." and their first name. I became Ms. Ellen.

I was cautioned from the first, "If you feel the need to request an autograph from any of the clients entering the salon, make it one that really thrills you—because it will be your last! Our customers do not come here to be bothered by fans. They come here to relax. And relax they shall!"

"OK—got it!" Little did I know that I was to be surrounded with celebrities. It was very exciting, even if not relaxing for me.

My duties were easy. I was to answer the phone, do moderate typing, and send out Christmas cards to all the clients and friends. This was not to be a permanent assignment. Rather, I was filling in for the permanent secretary, who was on a three-month maternity leave. I tried to do my best, mailing the cards out every day, answering the phone politely, and staying out of the customers' way.

At the end of my first week, the owner sat me down and asked, "How do you like it here so far, Ms. Ellen?"

"Oh, I love it! It's very exciting to see all the movie stars coming and going. And I enjoy the work."

"That's wonderful. May I say something to you?"

"Why, of course. Have I done something wrong?"

"No, you are fine. But—when you answer my telephone - well, we all know that you are from the Bronx, but we certainly do not want the people calling to think they have reached Yankee Stadium!

Try to lose the accent."

Sadly, the first thought I had was, *Huh?*

I left that day and spent the better part of my weekend speaking to myself in the bathroom mirror. I practiced until I developed some sort of Midwestern accent—a twist between Pennsylvania and Illinois. I returned to work the following Monday, the new and improved "Ms. Ellen"!

By the time I received my first paycheck, I had two full weeks of salary coming. Granted this was no fortune, but it was my first check, and I wanted to do something special with it. I walked the streets of Manhattan looking in one store window after another, trying to find just the right something to reward myself. Before I knew it, there it was! A purple velvet angel blouse embroidered at the collar and cuffs with small mirrors inside the embroidery. (This was the 70's, after all!) I ran into the store and insisted the blouse be taken from the window for me to try on. It fit like a glove—or rather, a beautiful blouse. My very first purchase with my own money, and it cost just under $25!

Oddly, work was a much more positive experience for me than school. The class I was placed in was filled with misfits from other schools all around the New York City area. It was obvious from the beginning that everyone was there because they did not fit elsewhere. That is not to say that the girls there were not bright. On the contrary, they were high functioning to the point of being bored. And they were mischievous! Not long after getting to know them, I realized that the gatherings in the girls' restroom on the first floor were in fact drug deals being enacted before class. It became so common-place, so casual, that several of the girls would take hits of acid and then begin their day. I never could figure out how they could do it. How could they sit in class straight-faced and higher than kites all the while? But they did.

The school building itself resembled the set from the movie, *The Trouble with Angels*, starring Haley Mills. There was a spiral staircase going right up the middle of the building, enabling the girls to access three floors of classrooms. At the base of this staircase was a HUGE statue of the Virgin Mary, haunting me from my encounter in the 2nd grade. The fourth floor was reserved for the nuns' quarters, which is where they slept. It was strange to me that they would be confined to this building all day and night. Didn't they get cabin fever having to stay there all the time, I wondered?

I remember one girl in particular who was brilliant! She was so skilled in shorthand that she would take her class period in the principal's office taking dictation from her directly. This girl was much faster than everyone else, and as a result, it was felt that she should not be slowed down or held back. Italian by birth, she was a beautiful girl with long, dark, wavy hair. She prided herself on her appearance. Each day, she would come to school with her make-up and hair fixed just so.

It was not until overhearing a conversation between she and another girl that I realized how she managed to fix herself so elaborately every day. (After all, we had to be in at 7:30 in the morning). I found out that, smart as she was, she actually put her make-up the night before and then sprayed her face with a substance called Fixative; an aerosol spray used by artists to hold fast charcoal or pastel drawings to keep them from smudging. Clever girl! But was that safe? I didn't want to ask.

I managed to complete a year at The Assissium unscathed. There were many discussions about my lateness every day—but it was concluded that with my grades being what they were, it made no sense to discipline me any more severely than the talking to I was receiving weekly.

While my school life was settling down, my home life was coming apart at the seams. Arguments with my mother turned to bickering, and the bickering intensified two on one, as my mother and Wally gave me their opinions every time I turned around. I tried to stay clear of the home front, but it was wearing thin.

I decided to respond definitively. When I could take no more, I announced In the middle of a heated argument that I was going to live with my sister in Brooklyn! There, I had said it, *"I'm leaving!"*

What I failed to do, however, was to discuss this with my sister—who was, coincidentally, having dinner with my mother that evening. *Who knew?*

Over dinner, my mother blind-sided my sister angrily, asking, "Are you crazy—letting her stay with you?"

"Who," Genie asked.

"What do you mean, *who*? Ellen—that's who!"

At this news, Bill, my sister's live-in boyfriend, raised not one—but both eyebrows. By the time dinner was finished, Genie was caught between my mother and Bill, not knowing what to say or to whom.

With no knowledge of the dinner or the conversation, I phoned Genie. Honestly, I don't know what I could have been thinking; I just needed some place to go, and Genie's was the first thing that popped into my head.

My sister first and foremost, Genie said, "Get on the train and get out here. We'll figure this out."

26. Bouncing Between Boroughs

TO AN OUT-OF-TOWNER, Brooklyn, the Bronx, Queens, Staten Island, and Manhattan may all seem like different parts of the same big old New York City. But to those of us who live there, they are vastly different. Brooklyn was 90 minutes or more away from anywhere I wanted to be—socially.

The apartment that Genie and Bill had was the top floor of a duplex with roof access, which was like having a patio. The space was large for New York, but not for all that was in it! Bill was an artist. To say that doesn't really capture the true feeling of it. Bill was head to toe an artist—and a great one! He could paint anything, and he did. There was one painting he did of the inside of a diner. The counter top, stools, glasses, and the mirror behind the counter were perfect. The only deviation was the area in between the back mirror and the counter top; it was filled completely with soapy dishwater! I loved that painting. I could stare at it for hours, just admiring how realistic every detail was.

Bill and Genie had a very controlled life—by their standards. They got up for work at a certain time every day, worked from 9-5 in Manhattan, and then rode the train home at the same time every evening. It was routine to the point of mundane. The controls were as stringent on the weekend time as they were during the week, just filled with different activities. The weekend was "their" time to do with as they wanted. If there was to be any getting high, it was done on the weekend. All substances were kept in a locked tool box in the house and Bill had the only key. As soon as everyone was home on Friday, the box got unlocked.

Bill would sometimes stay awake painting all weekend, round the clock. I didn't ask—and he didn't discuss it with me—but I was sure that he had "help" staying awake for that long a period of time. Bill would focus all weekend on painting. Then on Sunday evening late, the painting would be put aside, the toolbox would be locked, and Bill would go to bed, resting for the beginning of the work week.

At this point, I was a junior in high school. My schedule had to be maintained. I went to school, then to work, then home. During the summer, I had a full-time job provided me by the school, at a printing company near Chinatown. The name of the business was Hudson Printing. One of their big accounts was the Muscular Dystrophy Telethon. We were often doing printing of advertisements with Jerry Lewis (the spokesman), who would then come in to review the work. This wasn't something I had set out to do, but it was interesting.

At the same time, I was 16 and wanted to have fun during the summer! I started to notice that fun was an hour by train away from work. I wanted to go to the Bronx to see friends, but I worked in Manhattan and I lived in Brooklyn. I was riding the train more than I was doing anything else, it seemed.

I had made friends with some people in a local bar in the Bronx called Chickie's Pub. Chickie's was out of the neighborhood I was familiar with, but not terribly far away from where I grew up. The people in there were a bit older than I was used to; still, I enjoyed meeting people and found them interesting. An entire afternoon could be spent hanging out in Chickie's playing pool, just waiting to see who showed up. It was mostly the same people—the regulars coming and going.

I have noticed that in meeting people, one tends to assume that all people are as they appear. Until something happens that tells you *this person is different,* you don't know or expect that they are different. This was true of the people I met at Chickie's. They appeared gruff, but underneath, they seemed nice enough; just regular people wanting to have a good time.

It was not long before I became a regular at Chickie's myself. As I spent more time there, I became more aware of the behaviors of the people. It wasn't my imagination! They *were* different. Some of them were involved with more serious "substances" than I had been around before. No matter! I was determined that they weren't going to make me do anything I didn't want to do. So I didn't mind so much.

I had become friends with one girl/woman named Kimberly. Kimberly was a single parent of three smaller children, ages 8, 5 and 3. She lived in New Jersey, just over the George Washington Bridge. Kimberly was originally from this neighborhood (the Bronx) and, like me, she would return to visit rather than trying to make new friends in New Jersey. Having three small children does not permit one to spend much time socializing!

Kimberly got it into her head that the perfect arrangement would be for us to share her house–which had more than enough room for one more—and I could stay for free if I watched her children, in lieu of paying rent. I considered this. Granted, I had a place to stay with Genie and Bill, but they wanted their privacy on the weekends. I wanted to be closer to the city anyway. With Kimberly having a car, she could drive me into the city on those days I wanted to come in. That would get me off the subway by myself—which was no fun. So I thought, *Let's give this a try.*

Kimberly may have had it tough, but her kids were sweet. They watched cartoons, asked for cereal, wanted me to help them pick out clothes to wear, and color with them—regular stuff. It was not hard to watch them at all! They did what they were told and were easy to deal with. Kimberly was nice to be around, too. She was one of those people you would classify as low maintenance.

However, Kimberly had one drawback: her boyfriend. Don was an iron worker—and a bad ass! He appeared older than Kimberly by several years. That could have been due to his living hard. Or, he could have *been* that much older. I didn't ask. He would say hello to me and make small talk, but the majority of the time that he was there was spent visiting with Kimberly.

It always seemed to me that there was more to Don than met the eye. He was one of those people who you just *knew* had something "bad" about him. I wouldn't ask, and no one offered to tell me. Because of his relationship with Kimberly, I ran into Don more and more. The danger in getting used to anything is that you tend to let your guard down around familiarities. My acquaintanceship with Don began to extend beyond running into him in New Jersey. He would come into Chickie's pub every now and again when I was there. We would not socialize particularly, but Don would always send a drink down to me via the bartender, and I would give him a wave thanking him.

One afternoon while I was playing pool, Don came into the bar. Although he had just arrived, it appeared he had been at a pub for quite a while. He staggered around saying "Hi" to different people, working his way towards the pool table. On this occasion, he was more touchy-feely than usual. Don was not normally the kind of a guy who would go up to anyone and put his arm around them. But today he was. He was hugging and hanging all over people.

Sure enough, my turn was coming up. Don slithered his way over to the pool table, calling, "Next game," and became a fixture by those of us at the table. As I moved around to take a shot, I bent over the table. Don, then, bent over me.

"What the hell are you doing, Don? Let me take the shot!" I thought if I put it that way, he wouldn't take offense at it. (Listen to me, though; I was worried that Don would be offended. UGH!) He went ballistic!

"What! You don't want me putting my hands on you? I'll put my hands on you whenever I want! Don does what Don wants to do!"

Don was screaming throughout the bar and becoming so agitated that I knew I was going to get hit. I could see it coming. Apparently so could several others, because in an instant, guys sitting at the bar and elsewhere jumped over and grabbed him before he could do anything. One guy (a bartender) pulled me by the arm and said, "Get out of here while you can." So I did.

Later that night, I returned to Chickie's. I was cautious, checking as I walked in to make sure that Don was not still there. Kimberly was, though. I walked over to where she was sitting. Kimberly was not happy! In fact, she would hardly look at me. I asked her what was wrong.

"What do you think is wrong?" she said in a huff.

"I don't know."

"Don tried to rape you?"

"What? No. Don was drunk and got pissed. A couple of the guys thought he was going to hit me, and so they told me to leave."

"Then why are you here?"

Wow! Kimberly was mad at me! I hadn't seen that one coming at all. I suppose that was the easiest thing to do. Kimberly loved Don— or at least, she thought she did. If she acknowledged that he was the type of man that he was, she would have to leave him. And she didn't want to do that. So she turned on me, which was easier. After all, I was just the babysitter.

I found myself on the A train going back to Brooklyn at 11:00 that night. Not exactly where you want to be at that hour, alone. But it beat going back to Chickie's.

So I returned to Brooklyn and decided to try to entertain myself as best I could there. My life was in Brooklyn now. I should make the most of it.

I wasn't interested in making new friends. But I did need something to pass the time. Every now and again, Genie and I would make our way to the rooftop and lie out in the sun to get a tan. We called it "Tar Beach." Everyone in New York was familiar with Tar Beach (the rooftops). It was the next best thing to a real beach. We would go up there and lie out and talk, smoke cigarettes, listen to the radio, and just hang out—relaxing. That summer I planned to get a tan, if nothing else.

Genie had also shown me her most recent purchase, a sun lamp. This lamp looked very much like an ordinary extension lamp for a desk, but the bulb was special for tanning. I asked her if I could use it.

"Sure, just be careful."

I remember thinking to myself, *Who is she telling to be careful? I used to be out in the sun every day. I get black dark tan all the time. My skin doesn't burn!*

I set the lamp up on the floor, so that it would hang over the middle of my body—right above my stomach. Then, so as not to be bored during the process, I brought in a portable television so that I could watch TV while lying there.

There is so much wrong with this plan I cannot even list everything! There I was, lying on a make-shift beach towel on the floor, with a sun lamp over my stomach and the television down by my feet. "This is heaven," I thought to myself. "I'm going to get really tan!" I was so comfortable, I fell asleep.

I awoke two hours later—burnt! This was no ordinary sunburn. This was serious! The entire front of my body, except the areas covered by a bathing suit (thank God for that!), was burned to the point of being blistered. It was visibly bright red.

My sister was furious and scared all at the same time. "What did you do? I told you to be careful! Oh crap. I'm going to get in trouble now—because you're hurt." Genie carried on so, she actually started to sound like my mother!

I ended up going to the emergency room, where I was declared to have second-degree burns.

As bad as this was, Bill thought I should still go to work. I had done this to myself, was the reasoning. That was no excuse to miss work—and lose a day's pay!

My problem was that I couldn't get dressed. I literally could not stand clothing touching my body. Genie and I had to wrap me in Vaseline and then tissue paper to cushion the clothing against my skin. It was ridiculous! I went to work that way for a week.

It wasn't until I got up one night to get a drink that I realized how bad it was for Genie. She was in her room crying, saying over and over again, "It's my fault she's burned! I should have watched her."

Bill kept telling her it was going to be OK. "She's 16! She's not going to listen to you. She doesn't listen to anybody!"

Bill was correct.

27. The Last Hurrah

THE SUMMER WAS long and hot in 1974. My job, although bringing in money, did not particularly interest me. I missed my friends. I missed *life*. More times than not, I found myself sneaking back into the Bronx. Doing "the responsible thing" did not appeal to me at all. I was miserable. I made a conscious decision to spend more time doing what I wanted to do, rather than what I should be doing.

While in the Bronx one evening, I visited with friends associated with the band with which I had spent so much time in freshman year. It was just as much fun as it had been then!

One evening, we went out to a club. Knowing it was going to be late when our evening ended, I made arrangements to stay at a friend's house in the area, because the train ride back to Brooklyn would have taken hours and wasn't exactly safe late at night. My original plan was to stay there, then get up in the morning and borrow some clothes to wear to work.

But just having a plan is not enough! Morning came quickly. I awoke to realize that it was already 8:15. Even if I jumped up right then and ran to the train, I would not make it to work on time. My friend woke up at the same time and said, "Just call in sick." When ideas such as this go through your head, they don't sound as though they will work. Yet, because you *want* them to work, you talk yourself into it.

"OK, where's the phone?" I called the office and told them that I was not feeling well and would be unable to come in today. I offered no details. The fact is that I really didn't want to go and didn't much care. That must have been obvious, because the voice at the other end said, "Please give me an address where you can be reached."

"Excuse me?"

"I'd like to know where to mail your final check."

Oops!

In the end, this was what I wanted. I hated going to work every day. It was summer. I wanted to continue being a kid and spending time with my friends. That's what I wanted. That, however, is not how my life was set up. I was now living with my sister and her boyfriend and responsible for my portion of the bills. I was also responsible for my own spending money. This "being an adult" was for the birds! I tried to enjoy the rest of the day with my friends, but became preoccupied with the knowledge that I now had no work and had to find another job. It was very conflicting to have lost a job, need another one—and not want either!

Upon returning to Brooklyn, I broke the news to Genie and Bill that I had been let go. Rather than admit the real reason, I told them that that the person I had been hired to fill in for had returned.

Genie looked suspicious. But Bill just wasn't going to believe this at all. He spoke very calmly and said, "Go get your house key." I brought it and gave it to him. "OK, I'm going to call your employer tomorrow and ask them for a reference. I'll tell them that I am an employer and am considering hiring you. If they back up your story, you get the key back. If not, you're out!"

I remember being stunned! It had never occurred to me that my bluff would be called. The shock must have been evident all over my face, because I looked at my sister and she looked worse than I felt. She was beginning to cry, as she often did when things were not going well. It was bad enough having things fall down around my head, but making Genie cry was much worse.

"OK, that's not what happened."

"No kidding," Bill said sarcastically.

I told him the simple facts of what had transpired; thinking that telling the truth now would get me off the hook. It didn't. Now I was finished.

Genie must have telephoned my mother, because within 24 hours, my mother was pursuing me, wanting me to come back home. I hated it there and didn't want to return, but this time, there was no crowd around me trying to advise me differently.

We met in mid-town Manhattan, which I determined to be half-way between my mother's house and my former one. We had lunch and talked about what we each needed from the other. It felt like a treaty meeting. At the conclusion, I agreed to come home.

Murray—who had happened to be in New York at the time I moved out—was conveniently there again. He could help me move home! Murray's timing was impeccable for me, but lousy for him. "I wish you'd stop doing this every time I come to town," he said. But he was a great friend, and he took it all in stride. Murray loaded up his car with my things and drove me back to the Bronx.

Just when I had placed the last item back into my old room, my mother came to the bedroom door and told me that she and Wally wanted to speak with me. This was one of the things I really hated—these "meetings" with the two of them! I reluctantly went to the table and sat down. They both had that "cat that ate the canary" look on their faces, trying to suppress a sort of smile underneath a scowl. My mother then announced that she and Wally had found a place they really liked in Tampa and that they would be moving by Halloween.

Stupidly, I asked, "If you're moving, why did you have me come back here?" Talk about missing the point. I had been duped! "So, what—now I'm moving? Are you serious? I can't move!!"

My mother then assured me that everything was going to be great. She had consulted a psychologist, who advised her that it would be better for us to move while I was still in school, so that I would make friends more quickly.

Who was this genius? "Did you mention to them that I was a SENIOR?" Now I was really screwed! I was not only leaving New York and my friends, but going somewhere where I knew no one, somewhere where I would have to drive to get anywhere. Somewhere that was not New York!!!

The good part came when Mom and Wally told me that I had no curfew until such time as we moved. "Just be here on this date—and we will leave for the airport together."

"OK. I have 60 days to party!"

From that instant, I could feel myself getting physically ill. I was no longer myself. Looking back on it, I am convinced that this was the onset of severe stress. But at the time, I didn't know what it was. We had been fighting, or at least at odds, for years. Now I was about to relocate with the only two people with whom I was sure to fight on a daily basis. This was no "plan"—this was a disaster!

One by one, I informed my friends of this travesty. I began bouncing like a pinball from one group to the other, trying to take in all that I could before "D-Day" (departure day). I knew a lot of people in New York. Until then, I hadn't thought about how many. Now I had to spend as much time as I could with each of them—just to be able to savor the friendships.

When waiting for a bus, Genie and I used to joke. She would always tell me, "Light a cigarette! As soon as you do, the bus will appear—like magic!" Genie had a dark side to her—but about this she was right. Whenever standing at a bus stop waiting for what felt like an eternity for a bus, I'd light a cigarette—and there the bus would appear!

It seemed to me that this same principle was holding true for guys, as well. Now that I was about to move, I met the most terrific guy! I was supposed to be saying good-bye to all the friends I already had, and out of the blue, this guy appears, like magic.

Cameron was as adorable as he was charming. He was also a great deal of fun! We met quite unexpectedly at Chickie's pub. (I know - I can't believe I went back there either!) I walked in one afternoon, and a bartender I knew was there. He introduced us (sort of). Anyway, the conversation between me and Cameron took off as if no effort were required at all. We talked all afternoon—about everything. He then invited me to get something to eat. We went to a diner up the street and ate and talked some more. Next we walked all over the neighborhood. We must have walked around for hours, just looking at the city. As we walked, we looked in the windows of businesses and imagined what was going on between the people we could see inside.

Cameron was older than I. At that time, I was 17. Cameron was 24. I had never dated anyone that much older than myself. As I thought about it, I realized I wasn't going to be dating anyone that much older now either. I WAS LEAVING!!! *Damn!* I remember finally telling him that I was about to move out of state.

Cameron just looked at me and said, "You're not gone yet!"

That pretty much sums up the approach Cameron and I took. *Live today. Enjoy today! Don't think about tomorrow.* So we didn't. We spent every possible minute together.

Cameron had a job working in Manhattan at a delicatessen. I remember thinking; *you go all the way to Manhattan to work in a deli?* That never made sense to me. But that's what he did! I would sit in Cameron's apartment while he was at work, listening to his records, entertaining myself. Either I would call him or he would call me on breaks. There was a pay phone in the store, and that is the number I would call to reach him. He would come back to the apartment and tell me stories of all the characters that would come in during the day, how unique they were. We would then devise some plan as to what we were going to do in the evening to entertain ourselves. Sometimes we checked the local pubs around the neighborhood to see if there were any parties going on—and then crashed them!

We talked about plans for the future. Cameron wanted to work in Alaska on the pipeline. At that time, many people were being enticed to work there. The money was advertised to be fabulous! On the other hand, the expense of living in Alaska was also fabulously high. But if you could go in with others, share a place, and then work there for a year or two, you could save a bunch of money and make it worth the effort.

Cameron also talked about wanting to be a fireman. I didn't think he could get any more attractive to me than he already was, but it happened then. *A Fireman! Firemen rescue people from burning buildings. How great is that!*

The more "perfect" Cameron got, the closer my date of departure came. Without being overly dramatic, it felt very much like waiting to be executed. I knew the day my life was "going to end" and was just watching as it got closer and closer. I tried to enjoy every minute with Cameron, being in New York. But the reality was that this time had already begun to end. In my heart I knew it was over, and I was sickened at the thought.

Although spending what seemed to be every waking moment with or around Cameron, as the departure date grew nearer, I did go see other people to try to get in as much visiting as possible. I found myself one evening visiting with two of the members of the band. They were very much a part of my core. We had been friends for several years, and despite any separation, we were solidly friends. I was unable to talk about anything besides leaving New York. I was consumed by the thought of it. After listening to me pine over what I was sure would be impending doom, the one friend finally looked at the other and said, "Oh, just tell her."

"Tell me what?" *What could possibly be wrong now?* I thought, dreading hearing anything else bad.

My friends looked at me and smiled. "We know you don't want to leave. Believe us—we know. We don't want to leave either. But we're going to!"

"What do you mean? You're leaving?" I instantly went from miserable to miserably confused. "Where are you going?"

"We're going to Florida! We have wanted to get out of here for a while now. So we're going to go too. We'll be right behind you! We are leaving in a week or two. We'll be right down near you. Don't worry! You're not going to be alone. We just didn't want to say anything yet. Nobody else knows. But you're so unhappy, we figured, *just tell her.*"

"You're not lying to me? You're actually going to be in Florida?"

"Yes."

Life was throwing me a lifeline—a HUGE one. I loved these guys and knew that life would be tolerable if they were there. I still hated the idea of leaving New York. But now, at least, I wasn't leaving *everyone.*

Not everything was going well, though. The Assissium, my school, had scheduled the ring ceremony when school rings were given out to the seniors. I attended the program, received my ring, and then was pulled aside in the back of the church by the principal, who informed me, "Since you won't be graduating from this school, we'll have to take the ring back."

"WHAT? You must be joking!"

"No, anyone who wears a ring from our school must graduate from it. I'm sorry."

"You're not sorry—you're crazy! My mother paid for this ring. I'm not giving it up!"

I went back to the school with my classmates, complaining the entire way. "They can't do this to me. Can they?"

One girl in the school, with whom I was fairly close, told me, "They can't do something to you if the majority of people are against it. Start a petition to make them let you keep the ring. You have to stand up to them!"

I later thought that it was ironic that the girl who did so much acid during school had the clarity of thought to tell me exactly what to do to beat this thing!

"OK—I'll do it!"

Every day I was at school, I was sneaking around getting signatures from students, teachers—and yes, even nuns. Apparently everyone thought depriving me of my ring was a crazy idea—everyone but the principal, that is. But when I presented her with pages of signatures, she caved in and agreed to allow me to keep the ring. It was my first victory in defying authority.

My glee would be short-lived, however, as the day of departure arrived. One last time, Cameron and I walked up the street where I lived. It was a beautiful, sunny, autumn day. The leaves had all turned different colors, and the sounds of traffic and people bustling around were like music. I tried everything I knew to do to keep myself from crying all the way up that street . . . and I succeeded. I didn't cry.

In fact, I don't think I cried during my teenage years at all. In many respects, I functioned as someone striving for numbness. Every time something happened to me, another layer of cocoon was added on. Crying would have amounted to cracking open. I was completely and totally frightened of the idea of opening up, despite the fact that I desperately wanted to feel love.

Of all the times I had tried in the past, Cameron was about as close as I had come to allowing myself to be open. In a very short period, I had become as fond of him as I had ever been of anyone in my life. I remember him kissing me goodbye and telling me, "Keep smiling, kid."

All I could think was, *What for?*

Stage IV

28. Dan & Dave vs. the Major Deegan

FLYING TO DAYTONA Beach for any other reason would have been exciting. I loved to travel, primarily because I loved the sense of adventure a trip brought with it. But the fact that this was a one-way flight and I was never coming back to New York put a dark cloud over it.

Travelling with Wally was no small endeavor either. Before his joining the family, I had had no experience with anyone in a wheelchair. All sorts of special arrangements had to be made ahead of time. My mother seemed to like taking care of those details. She was a literal paragon of efficiency when it came to his care. Staff from the airlines had to lift him from his chair, place him on a special airline chair that would fit down the aisle of the plane, and then place him in his assigned seat (which, thank God, was in the front of the Coach section). He and my mother smiled at each other as if this were so great—all of us moving to Florida. I just kept to myself, looking out the window at the tarmac of the city trying to rationalize saying goodbye to the city I loved.

Our flight landed in another city first before arriving at our destination, but it was not necessary for us to change planes. There was a pause of about 30 minutes or so. For those passengers who were continuing on, permission was given to deplane, so long as they returned quickly. My mother and I got off to look in gift shops in the airport. Mom was always looking for postcards to send people. She wrote all the time—letters mostly. She would never type any letters, but insisted on using her own special fountain pen and putting down on stationery whatever she wanted to say. "My letters are too important to be jotted down on loose-leaf," she would tell me. I didn't much care about that, but I liked letters, too, both writing them and receiving them. I liked the idea that you had something to hold at the end of reading a letter. Conversations were great, but you couldn't hold on to them!

We returned to the plane, which departed immediately. The flight continuing on to Daytona was short. Upon arrival, we were greeted by Wally's brother, Rob, and his wife, Gabriel. I had met them before at the wedding. Rob and Gabriel had three sons, the oldest of whom was my age. When I got to the house, the middle son, Teddy, showed me to my room—which had been his until I got there. He was nice about it, showing me around and making conversation. Josh was the oldest. He, too, was nice, though they were polar opposites.

At this point, the circumstances made Teddy and Josh my only social outlet. When they went out in the evenings, they would offer to take me with them. It was usually no place special, just out. But they had friends, and this was, after all, better than sitting around with my mom, Wally and his relatives. Kids trump adults any day of the week!

Often we walked down to the strip (as they called it), where there was hotel after hotel. I had confiscated a fist full of quarters for the pay phone and was on a mission! I could barely wait to call Cameron, who was at work at the deli. I would call him just to hear a familiar voice. We would talk for a few minutes, and then the operator would come on, asking for more money. Sometimes Cameron would call me back so that I wouldn't have to put any more money in. Other times, he couldn't call back, so we were limited to only three minutes.

It was very much like hanging from a rope, making those calls. That phone line was my only lifeline to what I knew as reality. I became more and more lonesome as the days went on. Josh and Teddy's friends were nice enough, but I was homesick, and there was nothing I could do to stop it. The feeling overpowered me.

So my daily goal was to snag enough quarters for the phone calls in the evening. Surely my mother must have realized that all these quarters were disappearing right out from under her! At times, I felt as though she put them in the same place night after night so that I could make those calls. I don't know. We have never really talked about it, before or since. That was my social life, in a nutshell—stealing quarters and going to the pay phone at night.

We were to stay at Rob and Gabriel's house for several weeks until the apartment we were moving into was ready. The apartment complex Mom and Wally had picked out was being renovated (or something), and we had nowhere to go until such time as they were notified of the completion. I never understood why we left New York so early, if we had nowhere to go when we got there! Perhaps Wally wanted to visit with his brother and sister-in-law. Perhaps they left New York just to avoid paying another month's rent in the apartment—or even worse, signing a new lease. I wasn't told. Daytona Beach was like limbo for me. I felt that I had sinned somehow, yet what I was experiencing was not terribly bad, so I surmised that I hadn't been sent to hell—not yet anyway. I was in a holding pattern until I could earn my way out of "limbo"!

The "way out" seemed to be forthcoming in the not-too-distant future, as my two friends from the band, Dan and Dave, were heading down to Florida soon. I was unsure of exactly when they planned to depart. I assumed it would be as soon as they both got their money and belongings together. I was treading water, and the lifeboat was out there. I just didn't know where!

My only contact with anyone in New York was with Cameron, and even that was becoming increasingly more difficult. We would talk every night. But despite my desperation, I knew this was a dead end. What were we going to talk about? He was certain to find or meet someone up there sooner or later, and a warm body beats a warm phone!

The schedule of phone calls to Cameron went from daily to every other day. Standing in the street on the strip in Daytona glued to a pay phone grew weary – contributing more towards my dwelling on what I no longer had, and I decided to limit this. Instead, I sat around just outside the living room, eavesdropping on conversations between the adults. They would sit around every evening and watch television and make small talk. It was dull. I think it was even getting old for Mom and Wally. There is only so much *Hee Haw* anyone can stomach!

One evening while we were sitting around the house, the phone rang. My Aunt Gabriel answered it. "Yes, she is. One moment, please. Ellen—it's for you!"

Huh? I thought it was a joke or a solicitor—something other than an actual call. After all, who knew I was here? People in New York knew I was in Florida generally, but that was about it.

"Hello?"

"Hey—it's the snow queen!"

"Mo! Oh, my God! I'm so glad to talk to you! Where are you? What are you doing? What's been going on? Tell me everything!"

"Hey, slow down. You sound crazy!"

"I am. *You* try sitting around with a bunch of adults and no friends. I'm dying down here! Hey, how did you find me?"

"I knew Wally's last name, I called information looking for a family with that name. Looks like I found you."

"Oh, no—what's wrong? You must be calling for a reason."

"Yeah, I am. Dan and Dave left for Florida last night."

"Really? That's great! Wait—how do *you* know? I thought they weren't going to tell anybody?"

"They weren't, Ellen. They're not going to make it. There's been an accident. They no sooner got on the Deegan [the Major Deegan Expressway], than a car sideswiped them and caused a terrible accident. Ellen, Dave is dead."

"NO-O-O!! Oh God, no! Please tell me you're making this up. You're not—this really happened. Where is Dan?"

"Dan is alive, but he's a mess."

I don't remember hanging up the phone. I do remember looking around the room, as my mother looked right at me as if she knew something was up. I told her, "I need to go back. I need to go back to New York! Dave is dead. There's going to be a funeral, and I need to go."

"No, honey. Now, I'm sorry about your friend—but he's gone. There is nothing you can do. You going to the funeral isn't going to make anything better. You need to just say a prayer for him and let him go."

The only prayer I could think of was one praying to bring him back. But I knew the answer to that one. *No.*

29. Inconsolable

WHENEVER YOU THINK it can't get any worse, look out! I was disappointed and depressed upon my arrival in Daytona Beach. Later, upon hearing the news of Dave's death, I became literally inconsolable. I couldn't eat, couldn't sleep, and wanted nothing to do with anyone or anything.

In addition, now I was having another problem. My period, due ten days earlier, was a no-show. I needed a doctor—fast! Yet there I was, in a city where I knew only three male cousins and a few of their male friends, my mother, and my aunt. The pickings were slim! Bottom line: With my back to the wall, I approached my mother and my Aunt Gabriel in the kitchen, blurting out in mid-conversation, "I missed my period."

Cool as a cucumber, my mother turned to me and asked, "Do you have any reason to think this might be a problem?"

You really had to hand it to her. My mother was willing to look in the face of disaster and ask the question, "Is this an issue?"

"Yeah, it's an issue! We haven't spoken three words since I've been here, and now I mention this. Yeah; I think I have a reason."

My Aunt Gabriel was even taken aback by the way my mother wanted to brush this off. "Gee, Fran, I think she needs to go to a doctor, eh?"

Plans were made via telephone for me to go to a local OB/GYN for an exam.

It was bound to come up on the ride there: "Who is this lucky fellow? Do I know him?"

"No, Mom—you don't."

It was clear my mother was not happy to be dealing with this.

The doctor was very matter of fact. "Well, we'll give you a test and do an exam. Then we'll see."

The exam was pretty basic. And then there was the peeing in a cup! At the end of the day, I was given some pills to take. They were not "morning after" pills. However, I was assured that if I was not pregnant, my period would be brought on and my cycle restored to normal. I went back to the house and took the pills. My mother, though dabbling with the urge to lecture me, decided to leave well enough alone.

By the next morning, my cycle was in full swing. I felt like crap, but that was par for the course.

The doctor telephoned to discuss the results of the test. My mother and I were both present. Making a long story short, he was concerned about why my period had not started on time and wanted me to be seen by a regular physician. This was taken on advisement and tabled until we arrived in Tampa.

Moving to Tampa was just another step towards numbness for me. My mother and Wally both discussed fixing up the new apartment as if they had selected this grand manor. It was an apartment! It was OK, but it was nothing fancy. In fact, it was on the first floor. Apartments, as I knew them, were in buildings several stories high. That was something I had always loved about New York apartment living: that sense of comfort knowing that in order for someone to break in—say on the seventh floor—they would really have to want to get in, as they would have to be willing to hang from the roof to do it! This was a duplex with all apartments on the first floor. Thieves could be virtual idiots and still manage to climb right in through your window, with little or no skill involved. *Who lives on the first floor?* I thought to myself. *It isn't safe!*

Our plans around arriving in Tampa went beyond what we needed to do in the apartment. The movers pretty much took care of unpacking and placing furniture. Our tasks involved running around to banks, schools—and yes, a doctor.

The visit to the doctor was something different entirely. I was discussed as if I weren't in the room. My weight (or perhaps I should say lack of it) was of concern to the doctor, as was my attitude—which was one of utter disgust. It was recommended that I be "monitored," that is, watched to ensure that I made progress in adjusting to my new surroundings. "I wouldn't wait too long for that to happen," the doctor added.

Beginning in November of the school year, my first day at school was with an entire student body that I had never met. To make matters worse, the school was not a small Parochial school, but instead, a huge public school. It was a massive campus that had all the appearances of being an indoor/outdoor facility. I had no interest in it, despite the school's size and all that it offered. I was only going there because it was the law and because I needed a high school diploma. *Let's just get this over with and get me out of here,* I thought. People in the halls were coming up to me asking me to say things like "hot dog" or "water" to hear my New York accent. I was pretty fed up. As if this were not bad enough, I had to ride a school bus. Yes, a native New Yorker with no driver's license had no means of transportation to get to and from school, so I was riding the bus! I spent the better part of my entire Senior Year unable to get around, with nowhere to go if I could. It was a nightmare of culture shock.

My school day began with catching the school bus at the entrance to the development where we lived. Clearly, I was the only student in senior year riding the bus. This was inconsequential to me. I was officially in hell; so be it if hell included a bus! The students were conscious of "the new kid" being in their class, but they didn't much care. There were a lot of cliques, and I'm not much of a clique person! *Easy enough to overlook,* I thought.

I also discovered that there were physical education teachers who doubled as coaches for the basketball team. They were not so easy for me to overlook.

There were two coaches for the girls' team. Word had been conveyed to these women that I had played basketball in New York. This gave them reason to pursue recruiting me for the team. Now, for a team to be pursuing *me*—the prognosis was not good for the team, in my opinion! Clearly, they were desperate for talent. Girls' basketball was not as big an item in the South as it was in the Northeast—at least not in those days. Also, it had probably been suggested that because I was resisting fitting in, being on a team might help me. Be that as it may, I was talked to repeatedly about it until I agreed to participate in this team sport.

The girls on the team were OK. They weren't overly friendly, but they weren't stand-offish, either. There was just one girl with any real talent on the team—Julie. She was all but carried around the school like a queen.

We began with drills and layups and then went on to learning plays. It was pretty basic stuff, but it did give me something to do. Because I was staying after school to practice, I needed transportation. The school bus does not accommodate students who deviate from the regular daily schedule. Mom would usually pick me up after practice. But it was obvious that she didn't want to. "Can't you get a ride from someone on the team?" she would ask.

"No, Mom, I can't. I'm not friends with them. We're just on the same team."

"Well, try. I have dinner to fix and things to take care of for Wally."

Our first game was on a Friday night at another school. I barely knew where I was, let alone having a way to get there and back. Fortunately, the school bus would take the team to and from games. We went, we played, we lost—and we came back to the school. It was now after 10:00 p.m., and I had no ride home. Everyone went in their own separate directions. "Hey, I need a ride!"

Both coaches looked at me dumbfounded. "We don't provide rides from the school. You will have to call someone to pick you up."

"Are you kidding?" There I was—stuck. I called my mother, but she winced about leaving the apartment so late in the evening. I was angry and frustrated at this point.

"Look, I have no way home, and I'm not walking. Come and get me!" She eventually did, but it was obvious that this was not going to be something I could do more than once.

Monday morning I returned to school with my uniform and all my gear in the bag they had given me. When I met up with the coaches during the day, I threw the bag down at the gym door and said, "Here you go. I'm out!"

"What are you doing? I don't understand."

"No, I don't guess that you do. You follow me around the school for days on end, asking me to play—and then strand me at the school with no ride. I'm not going through this twice. Keep your damn team!"

As one might imagine, this caused a great deal of ruckus among the student body, particularly those who heard me tell the coaches what I thought. But I had no interest in leading a rebellion. I just wanted to be left alone.

A few more encounters along these lines and the parent/teacher conferences went into full swing. In addition, the doctors I was seeing were so many and the visits so frequent, that it was as if I had a terminal illness. After much conferring amongst themselves, the doctors decided that I was clinically depressed and making myself sick to the point of shutting off my own bodily functions—causing my period to stop, my weight loss, etc.

A psychologist selected by my mother to "fix this" advised her, "Send her back."

"WHAT?"

"Send her back. She is miserable here. Send her back."

At first, my mother must have thought this would be construed as taking a loss in her battle with me. But the psychologist explained it to her this way, "Do you want to win the battle or the war? Ellen is making herself sick. Send her back."

It was Christmas break. My mother and Wally reluctantly purchased an airline ticket for me to return to New York. Finally—I was going home! I called Cameron and informed him of my impending arrival. He extended an invitation for me to stay at his apartment. It took me all of six seconds to pack my bags, and I was ready to go.

The plane departed from Tampa International Airport mid-morning, non-stop to JFK. When we touched down, it was snowing. SNOW! It was perfect! It snowed for my homecoming! I quickly hailed a taxi to take me to the Bronx. I was back! The air smelled different. The crowds, the noises, and the skyline: It was good to be back! I could feel myself recovering as we drove closer to the city.

I was so excited! As we pulled onto Fordham Road, I began directing the driver exactly where I wanted him to take me—right to the corner of Andrews Avenue and Fordham. We pulled up just past the traffic light over to the side so that I could pay. I leaned forward and began getting my money out of my pocket, all the while looking around taking in the scenery. To my right was the OVAL—the name given to the park where I used to hang out (which was an oval shape). To my left, the pizza shop.

In front of the shop were several of my friends. They were standing in front of the pizza shop shivering, smoking cigarettes, and hanging out. It caught me so by surprise! It was the exact scene I had observed the day I left (minus the snow). There they were, standing there in the cold—doing nothing!

I don't know why, but this shocked me. I began to think, *damn, what would I be doing if I were still here? I'd be standing there in front of the pizza shop or standing in the park—doing nothing! How long would that last?*

I loved my friends. I missed New York. But we hadn't been *doing* anything. We had just hung out every day. For some reason, it had never occurred to me that as I got older, my usual lifestyle would be less and less acceptable to me (to say nothing of unproductive). It was as if someone had slapped me right across the face.

There was nothing for me here, and I knew that my relationship with Cameron was impossible in this situation. In the spirit of the holidays, I did what any red-blooded American girl would do: I stayed the two weeks, spending every dime my folks had given me, and then when Christmas break was over, I got back on the plane to return to Tampa.

Sending me back to New York turned out to be the smartest thing my mother and the doctors could have done. I was there just long enough to realize that I didn't fit any longer. I still hated Florida—but I knew I had to make it work somehow.

30. Mary Frances Noonan

AT THIS THE conclusion of my existence in New York, it seems most appropriate to insert the account of my last visit with the woman who was the head coach of every single sport I participated in (less figure skating), Mrs. Noonan. During my Christmas break exodus from Florida, I learned that during my absence, Mrs. Noonan had been diagnosed with cancer and was quite ill. At the time of my visit, she was enduring yet another episode and had been hospitalized. Fearing that her illness was going to continue to worsen, I wanted to see her.

While in the vicinity of Tolentine, I ran into Sister Mary Doris, a former math instructor from the high school. "Doc," as she was affectionately named by the girls in the school, planned to visit Mrs. Noonan that day and offered to give me a ride to the hospital. I gratefully took her up on the offer.

It always feels strange to meet with a former teacher—particularly a nun—once you are out from under their tutelage. Sr. Mary Doris was quite a math teacher; she definitely knew her stuff. It was *I* who didn't know her stuff, or rather care! Still, our conversation was cordial, even pleasant. I wondered if this was what it would be like to be an "adult"—talking to teachers and adults as if I were an equal!

We arrived at the hospital early in the afternoon, just as visiting hours were beginning. I had been cautioned by Sister that Mrs. Noonan had been very ill and that she did not look the same. So upon entering the room, I tried not to display my shock at her physical appearance. She was about half the size she had been the last time I had seen her. The Mrs. Noonan I had known was a large woman, both tall in stature and large in body weight. She had had a commanding presence everywhere she went. When she spoke, everyone heard— because you didn't dare *not* listen! The woman before me now was petite and frail. I was looking at what was left after the battle.

Mrs. Noonan recognized me immediately. "Well, look what the cat dragged in!" she exclaimed. Her voice was timid, but she was still the same woman behind those eyes. "How are you, dear? Come sit over here so that we can talk." Both she and Sister Mary Doris commented on my moving to Tampa and having to make new friends and work through the challenges of a new school, etc. All of that paled by comparison to what Mrs. Noonan was facing. It was quite humbling to see such a strong woman so challenged by illness—yet willing to battle for life. We talked about all sorts of things. Naturally, she gave me her opinion on various things that she thought I should do. She even commented on my making the basketball team in Tampa. "I always knew you had it in you!" she said. I didn't have the heart to tell her that I quit when they wouldn't drive me home.

As the afternoon turned to evening, Mrs. Noonan seemed to tire. Yet her main concern was the upcoming Fordham contest. Fordham University sponsored a cheerleading tournament every year. It was *the* tournament to enter. Every school entered its team in the hopes of capturing the title that year. Mrs. Noonan was a dominant force behind every athletic team at Our Lady of Angels and had single-handedly built the cheerleading program to what it was today. She was troubled that the Fordham contest was coming up and the cheerleading team did not have the cheer ready for the tournament. "I need to get this together for them. I don't think I'll be here for it, and I don't want them to be unprepared."

Here we were, sitting in Mrs. Noonan's hospital room because she was terminally ill, yet what she considered to be her biggest problem was that the cheerleaders would be unprepared for the Fordham contest! It was classic Mrs. Noonan. "You have to help me!" she said. "Can you help me?"

"Sure. What do you want me to do?"

"Let's put this cheer together and get it down on paper for them."

"OK, let's do it!"

For the next 3-½ hours, Mrs. Noonan and I worked on that cheer. She actually made me go through it in front of her so that she could see how it would work. The woman wore me out! She was amazing. She was really ill, spitting up blood, having to take treatments in between planning segments of the cheer. But she wasn't stopping until she was through.

We finished the cheer. Mrs. Noonan thanked me for helping her; for coming to visit and for staying as long as I did.

Honestly, I didn't want to leave. I knew I would never see her again. Mrs. Noonan had been in my life in some way, shape, or form since I was in third grade—and technically, she was probably involved in things I was doing even before I realized it. We had locked horns many times. I was quite a handful as a child, and she was not going to have her buttons pushed! Many times she had put me in my place—deservedly. But what I will always remember of her is that she *listened* to me. When I would come to Mrs. Noonan with a question or in need of some guidance, she listened and then advised me. She never once backed away because she was angry at me for something I had done—which she could very easily have done.

Sister Mary Doris came back to drive me back to the Neighborhood. I remember getting in the car and not being able to speak. Sister asked me, "Are you OK?"

"Yes."

I kept remembering something Father Tracy, one of the parish priests, had said when a sister in the Parish had passed away. When he announced that she had died, he commented, "She died as she lived—with grace, strength and dignity." I hoped that someone would say that of Mrs. Noonan. She was one of the best!

31. Baby, You Can Drive My Car

THOUGH FEELING ALONE in Tampa, I was fortunate to be taken in by a group of friends/neighbors and *their* friends who were students at the local University. Most of them were extremely high functioning mentally, although mischievous in their own way. Some were veterans of the Vietnam conflict, now students on the GI bill. There was a social worker; a drug dealer; and even a male prostitute working his way through medical school! These misfits of their generation were now my adoptive foster friends, and they were great fun to be around. Upon my high school graduation (for which I was virtually alone), my new friends arrived at my apartment door with two bottles of champagne in each hand—and there were seven of them! We partied into the night. All these years later, I often wonder if they realize how they saved one of the milestone events of my life from becoming a total disaster for me!

At any rate, these friends were very eager both to induct me into the Southern way of thinking and living and to promote my development in whatever way they could.

As mentioned, I was from New York. Previously, I had neither wanted nor needed to learn to drive. Driving was for people who lived in the suburbs and for those friends of mine who were in a band and needed transportation for their instruments and equipment. Not something necessary for the average New Yorker to function. Yet here I was now in Florida, with no means of transportation.

So I begged for a vehicle as much as ever I could beg for anything! Just when I felt I had finally succeeded in talking both my mother and step-father into accepting that they had foisted me into this land of "no transportation"—and that therefore my predicament was entirely their fault and responsibility—they arrived home, proudly announcing, "*We got you your own transportation!*" I flew out the door, thinking I would find a suitable used car parked in the space in front of the apartment. But NO! Instead, I was greeted by a neighbor who was helping my mother hoist a 10-speed bicycle out of her trunk, as my mother declared proudly, "It's peach! Have you ever seen a peach bicycle before?" I thought I would literally die! How could someone genetically so close to me so profoundly not get what I was saying to her day after day?

Disgusted and forlorn, I went to seek solace at the apartment across the way, the hub where my friends resided. After sharing several tokes with me to calm my nerves, they collectively convinced me that the way to get something to drive was to just get up and drive! I told them, "I have nothing to drive! I don't have a car—I only have a bicycle!" At this moment, Matt, one of the guys there, threw his keys at me and said, "Here, take my car and learn to drive!"

"Are you kidding?" I asked, hoping he would say no, he wasn't kidding.

"Go ahead!" he insisted. "But watch it on the turns; it's pretty fast." The keys fit the ignition of a 1976 Dodge Charger, which I fell in love with almost immediately. I had some trepidation about driving alone in Florida on roads with which I was not all that familiar. But what the hell, I was driving!

My driving outings became a daily routine. I would ride my bicycle over to Matt's house and then take his keys and be on my way to escape on another driving lesson/venture—ALONE! At one point, I took the car and headed down I-75. My logic was this: *If I'm going to learn to drive, I had better experience the highway.* Thinking that I-75 meant 75 mph, I had my justification to zoom on down the highway. Well, all I will say is that I experienced the highway and the highway experienced me!

All summer long and part of the fall, I drove that car all over town–with no driver's license. That I was never pulled over or caught is still a mystery. The fact that I was not in any kind of accident, an even bigger mystery.

The February after I graduated from high school, I obtained my

Driver's License. My mother and her husband allowed me to take the road test in their car, a 1973 Chevy Malibu. However, this was to be the only time I would ever drive that car. Since my stepfather was in a wheelchair, the car represented mobility to him, and he was not about to lend it out. So it was made clear to me from day one, *don't even ask; you will not be allowed to use it!*

After I took the road test, I convinced my mother to take me shopping at the local mall, which was about 5 miles from our apartment. I was to begin a new job the next day and needed some new, more suitable clothing to wear. After a few hours of shopping, we loaded the trunk with our purchases and were about to head home. My mother, feeling benevolent said, "Why don't you drive?" I quickly reminded her that the rule was that I never drive the car, period! I was not about to be used as a ping pong ball in an argument between my mother and my stepfather—not over driving home from the mall! So my mother climbed in behind the wheel, sighing as if to say, "Oh well, you had your chance."

We pulled out of the parking lot and headed for home, which was a straight stretch of four-lane road. We were no sooner halfway home, than a beautiful new, metallic blue Mustang—headed west, while we were traveling east—made a left turn in front of us. It was too quick for my mother to stop. There was no time.

In an instant, I had one thought, *damn, the seatbelt!* In 1973, the Chevy Malibu was equipped with a safety feature that caused an alarm to sound any time the ignition was turned on while the seatbelt was not in the locked position. I hated seatbelts! Habitually, I would get in the passenger seat and lock the belt behind me to keep the alarm from sounding as we traveled down the road. I had apparently done this once too often, and now was about to pay dearly for it, I thought.

When you are in a car accident, motion takes on a frame-by-frame sensation. You are no longer moving in a flowing fashion, but in clips or frames—like photographs of the impending doom you are about to experience. I put up my arms and crossed my head and face with them in a last ditch effort to protect myself, when all of a sudden, the regular motion of the momentum returned and we crashed with a loud crunch of the car and began to roll off the road and out of control. I felt a horrible sickness in my stomach instantly, as though I had been punched.

Smoke began pouring from the engine. I then realized that I was still in the seat—intact—and was about to die in an explosion (rather than going through the windshield). I tried and tried to get my door open, but the luxurious feature of both power locks and windows now had us trapped like mice. The car was up on its left side like a beached whale, which meant I was up in the air. In my dress, stockings and platform shoes I twisted around in the seat and attempted to kick through the window of the car. *Damned if I'm going to live through this wreck only to get blown up afterwards*, I thought. *I'm getting out of here!*

Almost immediately, passersby were stopping to help with crowbars, trying to pry us out. My door flew open, and several people put out their hands to help me climb out, but I was stuck! My seatbelt! It was on! People kept shouting at me, "Take your belt off!" I couldn't believe it. I never wear my belt—NEVER. They pulled me from the wreckage, then reached down and pulled my mother out. We were banged up something fierce, but we were alive, well, and able to walk away.

As I rode to the hospital in the ambulance, my one thought was, "How did that belt get around me?"

33. The Magic of Mushrooms

I LIVED IN Florida for several years. During that time, the friendships I made with my neighbors and their friends fostered much in the way of socializing. Some of the members of this group were in a southern rock/country band. I believe most of them met while attending a college and discovered their mutual interest in music. The band consisted of two brothers, one a drummer and the other a lead guitar and banjo player; a rhythm guitar player; a mandolin player; and one official singer—a girl. In truth, they all sang. Further, several of the "friends" of the band would occasionally get up and play something with them, ranging from guitars to tambourines to maracas—and even a kazoo. It was a grand time whenever they were playing!

The band was not with us all the time, because they travelled to play. When they did come around, their presence would create an "occasion" of sorts, and everyone would gather accordingly. Between the music and their personalities, they drew people to them.

I remember one time in particular when the band played in a local bar and everyone, it seemed, was in attendance. It was not just an evening in a bar, but more of a reunion. As the evening progressed, the word got around that the band had been invited to a big party in the northern part of the state—and by osmosis we were all invited to go with them! I couldn't imagine a party that could accommodate so many people. Others assured me that this was no ordinary party! We would be going to a house on a great deal of acreage, and there would be plenty of room for everyone.

The group broke into smaller groups to carpool to this location in North Florida. Naturally the party began before we left. Everyone packed light except for whatever they wanted to consume. The party house was very nicely prepared for the expected (and unexpected) guests. But I was totally unprepared for what I was about to experience. The party was entirely about *Mushrooms*. Not cooking mushrooms—Magic Mushrooms! No matter where you looked, there were Mushrooms for the taking: Mushrooms on fresh garden salad, dried Mushrooms like potato chips, cooked Mushrooms in spaghetti, Mushroom tea, Mushrooms a-plenty!

Now, besides smoking marijuana, I had very limited experience with any "substances," and no experience with Mushrooms. This was not about peer pressure for me, but more that I trusted these people, having known them a good while. They were all doing this. In fact, they were looking forward to it. So - I decided to partake. *When in Rome . . . .*

My first taste was of Mushroom Tea. It did taste somewhat different—not a "bad" different, just an *unfamiliar* different. Within a few minutes—and in mid conversation—I noticed that I was beginning to feel the effects. The picture above the mantle in the room where I had been sitting and talking began to change in appearance. I spent quite a bit of time laughing—happily.

Because there was nothing negative about the experience, I grew more confident about trying the other servings of Mushrooms. I nibbled on the Mushroom Chips, and then just sat down to the salad and spaghetti with full commitment. By the end of the meal, I was FLYING!

Everyone was having a marvelous time. There really was nothing I didn't love about this. I drifted from room to room, meeting new and interesting people—all of whom were really nice. The music was excellent, with several musicians in every room playing all sorts of music, people singing along. The house was very comfortable and inviting, and the property was vast.

Now, I had only lived in Florida about a year. Before this, I had spent my entire life in New York City. I was very unaccustomed to seeing large parcels of land with nothing as far as the eye could see. Without exaggeration, looking out from the front porch, all you could see was a four-way stop on two intersecting dirt roads. That was it! Nothing else. No other house, no fence, no lights. Nothing, that is, except a cow.

Before I knew what hit me, I was walking out into the field with the cow. I had seen one in a petting zoo when I was very young, but I had never seen a cow just walking around as if it belonged there—free! I walked and walked until I got pretty close to the cow. As it turned around, I couldn't help but be impressed at the size of this animal. It was HUGE. It had a particularly large head with very big eyes, and it looked right at me! There I was in this field, staring at a cow that was staring back at me.

We stared at each other just long enough. The cow began to approach me. I began to back up. As I continued to back away, the cow continued to come after me. I began to walk a bit faster. So did the cow.

The Mushrooms had noticeably altered my judgment. I could not discern if this was, in fact, a cow! Or was it a bull? How would I know? I was from New York!

Fear was beginning to set in. I knew I needed some assistance, but wasn't sure how to go about getting it. I didn't want to yell, because that might incite the cow/bull to charge at me. *Oh, goodness!* In the faintest of voices, I said "H e l p. Somebody, HELP!"

All I could hear was laughter coming from the porch, which was a good distance away. As I got a bit closer, I realized they were, indeed, laughing at me. Not *with* me, but *at* me. A smile came over my face, as I admitted to myself how foolish I must appear.

Then the cow MOOed at me! That did it! Scared witless, I ran back to the house.

Some might consider this an early form of diversity training—saturating a native New Yorker with Magic Mushrooms, then leaving her out on her own to meet with a cow. For me, it was in part nerve-racking and in part hilarious! Suffice it to say, I spent the rest of the weekend party venturing out no farther than the porch. Good music, good food, good friends—no bull!

33. DWI – Driving Wally Insane

OUR APARTMENT IN Tampa was a two-bedroom, two-bath, with a living room, dining room and very small kitchen. My room was small, but big enough for the amount of time I spent in it.

Because of his condition, Wally slept in a hospital bed equipped with a trapeze lift for him to be able to pull himself upright and a Hoya lift which assisted my mother in getting him into and out of the wheelchair. There was also a lift secured to the roof of the car, which assisted her in getting him in and out of the passenger seat. Being paralyzed is a complicated existence. Being a quadriplegic is even more complex. Wally and I were hardly buddies, but I wouldn't have wished this on him or anyone else.

The Veterans Administration was very supportive with regard to Wally's care and treatment. Any supplies that he needed pertaining to his physical condition, they provided for him. His paralysis was the result of a skiing incident while he was in the army, in uniform. Wally qualified as a disabled vet, so his chair—which was electric—was provided by the Veterans Administration.

Wally's chair ran off a battery, much in the same manner as a car, with one exception—the chair had no alternator. Therefore, after so many hours of use, the chair battery had to be recharged. This was similar to how we charge our cell phones at the end of the day, or when we see that the battery is low. My mother would put Wally to bed and then before she went to sleep, she would plug in the chair to recharge it. It didn't happen very often, but occasionally the amount of power left on the battery would be misjudged, and a problem would arise.

One afternoon as I tried to come into the apartment after school, I put my key in the door and pushed—only to find I could only open the door about 5 inches. I could not budge it another inch! As I pushed, Wally yelled to me, "I'm here."

"OK, I'm here too. Can you let me in?"

"No, the battery on my chair is dead, and I'm stuck."

"What?"

"Wait till your mother gets home."

I thought to myself, *is he kidding? My mother's not going to be able to push the door, Wally and the chair out of the way. I'll just go get my friends.*

I immediately went to my friends' apartment across the complex and rounded up a few large college guys to come and help me. "Hey, Wally got himself stuck in the doorway of the apartment and can't move the chair. Can you guys come over and give me a hand?"

"Sure."

I had interrupted them in the midst of passing around a joint or two, so while they were quite willing to help, they were also quite stoned. But they were coming!

On the other hand, Wally HATED anyone coming to help. He felt helpless enough being a grown man stuck in a chair and didn't want the likes of my friends coming over to "move him" out of the way! Nevertheless, they were on their way. Oh, well . . .

My friends picked the lock on the sliding glass doors, gaining access to the inside of the house, and proceeded to walk to the hallway to pull Wally out of the way. Now this electric wheelchair was nothing to sneeze at. It weighed considerably more than the regular unpowered wheelchair—and also had the weight of Wally in it. The guys surrounded him and in seconds, picked Wally up off the floor and lifted him into the living room. Then, thinking quickly, they plugged in the charger so that by the time my mother arrived, his chair would have enough power to move on its own throughout the house.

I thought my friends had done us a big favor. But Wally was furious. "They just waltzed in here and shoved me out of their way!"

"No, they didn't; they came over here to help because I asked them to. Stop complaining! They got you out of the doorway, didn't they?"

"Why were they laughing at me?"

"They weren't laughing at you, they were stoned." As it came out of my mouth, I realized what I was saying and wanted desperately to make it stop—but it was too late.

Another afternoon, we were all sitting over at my friends' apartment getting ready to go see a movie, as we would do together from time to time. There must have been 15 of us. It was great fun having so many people go together. Beforehand, in the apartment, the atmosphere was like a pre-movie party; everyone was smoking a little pot to set the mood.

So we were all having a good time, but growing anxious as we were about to be late. As usual, Richie had not shown up yet. No matter what the plan or what time it was, Richie was late. He was always late—for everything. Everyone really liked him, but it was a pain to have to wait for Richie all the time. Today was no exception.

We were getting higher and higher, and Richie was later and later. Finally he showed up. Everyone jumped him the moment he showed up, complaining, "Where the hell have you been?" What kept you?"

Richie looked sheepish as he reported, "I was *here*. As I drove in on my bike (his motorcycle), I saw a man lying on the ground. His wheelchair had gone over a speed bump and thrown him out onto the pavement. I stopped to help him, but he was pissed and told me to leave him there! I couldn't do that."

"Oh, God—it's Wally!"

I looked over at a few of the others and we burst into laughter. This was so like Wally! He had been riding around the complex and gotten himself thrown out of the chair. In the midst of the laughter, we asked Richie, "Did you get him back in the chair?"

"Yeah—but I had to stop three cars to get help first."

After several years of feeling really helpless, Wally was able to obtain a van with wheelchair accessibility and hand controls, which had by then become more common and affordable. This enabled Wally to drive. It was a huge step towards his independence. He had not driven since he was 18—his age when he had sustained the injury.

Now, at 40 something, he was about to be able to drive again.

The van obtained, with the help of the Veterans' Administration, was a beautiful blue Ford Econoline van, with tons of room inside. There was a lift on the side of the van that would act somewhat like an elevator to slowly raise Wally's chair to the level of the van, so that he could then maneuver himself into the driver's area, which had a removable seat. On the rare occasion that my mother wanted to drive, the regular van seat could be reinserted.

Mom had only just learned to drive a few years prior—and then only in a car. A van was much larger, and she was unsteady driving it. Wally would encourage her to take it for a spin, but she would limit her driving to just around the complex.

There was a laundry room building on the other side of the complex, just beyond where my friends' apartment was. Wally would drive Mom over to do the laundry and then drive her back. This one day, he was more insistent than usual on her learning to drive. Mom gave in and decided to give it a try. The seat was in, and Wally was in his wheelchair behind her. Apparently, they had made several trips back and forth, and Mom was becoming more comfortable with operating the van. Unfortunately, although she was gaining confidence driving the van, she was still quite unfamiliar with the hand controls. Now, she didn't *have to* use the hand controls; the van had the regular gas pedal and brake on the floorboard. But Mom was giddy with confidence and felt that she knew what she was doing.

She didn't. Grabbing the hand controls, Mom accelerated, rather than braking to stop. The van jumped down the hill and crashed into the laundry room building, taking out three washing machines and two dryers!

Naturally, I heard about this from my friends talking about it over dinner. The van had crashed so hard into the building that it required a crane to hold the roof up while other heavy equipment pulled the van out! All this was happening when my friends got home from work. It was quite a spectacle!

Hearing all of this from my friends—and knowing full well it was my mother they were talking about—I returned to the apartment. "Hey, Mom, did you hear about what happened at the laundry room this morning?"

"No. What happened?"

I just looked at her. She had that same expression on her face that Lucille Ball used to get on hers when Ricky would ask her about some stunt she had pulled. Inside my head, I could hear that same sound that "Lucy"—and my mother—used to make, "Euhhhh . . . ."

All Mom said was, "I thought I was applying the brake."

I thought to myself, *was she stoned?*

34. Where There's Smoke . . .

TAMPA WAS A strange place to me. As beautiful a city as it was and is; I never could make myself fit there as if I belonged. I was always the square peg in the round hole.

Conversely, my mother was turning into Suzie Homemaker right before my eyes. No longer having to work outside the home, she devoted her day to taking care of Wally, cooking, cleaning, and planning to entertain. There was always something going on. She had neighbors who were friends, Women's Circle at the church, civic associations. She was into everything—and loving it.

Wally came from a fairly large family. His brother, Rob, and wife Gabriel (that we stayed with before moving to Tampa) lived on the East Coast of Florida and visited often. His other siblings that lived out of state would also visit yearly, at different times. In Florida, we were either preparing for a visitor, entertaining one, or just seeing one off. It was a completely different existence than we had had in New York. Either someone was coming to our house, or Mom and Wally were going away. They made it a point of going to Disney World at least once each year. There they would book a room at the Polynesian Hotel for several days. Wally enjoyed going to Disney and seemed to enjoy indulging my mother.

I continued to spend much of my time out of the house. Between working and socializing, I might have been in the house to sleep every night, but that was it. I don't remember eating many meals at home. I could have, but it was my preference to grab something out with friends. It was of no real concern to me who was coming to stay at the apartment. That was Mom and Wally's business, although it was never kept secret from me. I was, for the most part, disinterested, and simply went about my business.

One sure way of telling that we had company coming was the

tablecloth. Our dining room table was the furniture equivalent of a mood ring. Depending on what my mother had placed on the table, I was able to tell whether or not someone was about to show up. Company always got the good tablecloths and table settings. Or upon my arrival home after work, I could see that Mom was getting things together, straightening up the house. She did a lot of that type of busy work once Wally had gone to bed. It was "her time" to clean without interruption.

So this one particular time, I didn't think much of Mom doing her busy work. The next day, I had no work, so I slept in. When I finally awoke and made my way to the living room, I was greeted by a house guest—the same house guest that had stayed with us in New York many years earlier. I thought to myself, *ugh—what is he doing here?* Rather than being hostile, however, I simply said hello, went into the kitchen, and fixed myself something to eat. I avoided him as much as possible—which was not at all difficult, since I was usually gone with friends.

Upon returning home that evening, I went straight to my room. It wasn't long before I realized I had nothing to drink with me. I always liked to bring a drink of something to the bedroom with me, either hot tea, water or a soft drink—something. I went back out after a drink, and the house guest appeared behind me in the kitchen, almost as if he had descended from the ceiling. "Hey. What are you up to?"

"Just getting a drink."

"Yeah. I thought you might be around more when I came here. I didn't see you much today."

"Nope, I go out a lot. No point in staying home—nothing to do here."

"Yeah. I know what you mean." Before I could make my escape, I heard, "Hey, do you remember years ago when I stayed at your apartment in New York? Do you remember when I came into your room?"

"What did you say?"

He kept talking, with no hesitation, "Yeah, I remembered that just the other day. Was that wild, or what?"

"What—it was *what?* Don't ever speak to me about that again! Don't bring it up. Don't think of it yourself. You leave me alone! Do you have any idea what that did to me? I'm not kidding—leave me alone. What the hell could you be thinking?"

I quickly made my way into my room and locked the door. I had asked the question, but I knew good and well what he was thinking. He was thinking he would just waltz into my room and do it again. What an ass!

When I awoke the next morning, I dressed and left without eating or speaking to anyone. I stayed gone until our house guest departed. My mother and Wally commented to me about how rude they thought I was. I thought about telling them, but then I talked myself out of it. Talking about it only made it real. No point in that!

I kept my door closed continuously from that point on. Wally and my mother didn't much bother me anymore, but it was just the idea; I didn't feel I could relax enough to actually fall asleep if the door was open—or even unlocked.

For some reason (and I honestly don't remember what it was that I had done), something happened, and Mom and Wally felt that I had somehow violated their privacy. They were quite angry. To exercise their authority and inflict punishment on me, they removed my bedroom door. Now I HAD NO DOOR. No door meant I couldn't sleep!

I was frantic! In a panic, I called my sister, Genie. She always knew what to do to handle my mother.

"They took my door off! It's gone! What do I do?"

"You always get so worked up over this stuff. She's just messing with you. Mess with her right back. Tell you what! They hate smoke in the house. Smoke cigarettes with the window closed, burn incense, and—oh, yeah—hang those Indian beads across the doorway. That will get her! You'll have your door back by the end of the week, trust me!"

Trust Genie I did. In fact, she was probably one of the only people on the planet I did trust. I did exactly as she instructed. I dug out those old hanging beads from the closet and hung them from teacup hooks across the doorway. I burned incense continually and smoked more than usual just to fill the house with the smell. If I had learned anything from Genie, it was how to be vindictive and enjoy it!

Just as Genie had predicted, Mom had a fit! "You know Wally can't breathe well. You have to stop burning that stuff." "Gee mom, I burn it all the time. Guess you didn't notice when I had the door closed."

Wanting to torture them both was still not cause for me to have my social life come to a standstill. I did what I could to annoy them—and then went out. Like magic, my door was reinstalled by the end of the week.

I was told that my punishment was only supposed to last a few days until I got the message. But I always suspected that it was Mom and Wally who got *my* message—via Genie's courier service! Thanks, Sis!

35. Bliss, My Ass!

WORKING AT A movie theatre can be a treat. It is better than a "regular" job (in my opinion). Granted, it doesn't pay any more than any other minimum wage job; but the perks are terrific! As a movie theatre employee, I had access to all movies as they came out. I remember watching the Academy Awards and knowing exactly which movie or actor should win—because I had seen them all!

The crew that worked at the theatre was basically kids, just like me—but from all different walks of life. There was Charlie, who was an army brat. You could see that in the way he walked and carried himself. He stood like a soldier. Then there was Barbara. Barbara looked exactly like Alice in Wonderland. She had long blonde hair, stood about 5 feet tall, and was very petite. There was Gary, our exchange student usher, who had a strong British accent and some very peculiar eccentricities—not the least of which was his propensity for recording concerts and producing bootleg copies of them for distribution!

Then there was Stephanie. She was the closest thing to a salesman I had ever befriended. Most salespeople have a very strong tendency to sell all the time. Stephanie was a great salesperson, but she could also turn it on and off. She was very intelligent and had a great sense of humor and a compassionate streak a mile long. Stephanie would often work as cashier when I was scheduled to work at the candy counter. When the movie was on, we would be the only ones in the lobby. To pass the time, we would tell jokes, eat popcorn and drink Cokes. It made the time pass more quickly.

Stephanie was good at pretty much everything she attempted. She had a Standard Poodle that she had trained so well, she could get him to do all sorts of tricks. Stephanie would have him respond to the usual commands: sit, stay, lie down, and roll over. But then she would have him play dead. She would just point to the floor and say, "Todd, dead!"—and he would hit the floor as if he had been shot! The only difference was that his tail would be beating the floor. She would look down at him out of one eye and say, "Dead dogs don't wag their tails!" In an instant, the wagging would stop.

Stephanie and I were becoming pretty good friends. While I had a 10-speed on which I travelled back and forth to work, Stephanie had a baby blue Dodge Colt that her parents had purchased for her. The family wasn't wealthy, but they were comfortable. They had a house in Orlando and a vacation house in St. Augustine.

The first time we went anywhere together, Stephanie asked me to come to St. Augustine as a favor. "My parents will let me use the house, but only if I go with a girlfriend. Will you come with us?"

"Who is *us*?"

"Me and Joey." Joey was her boyfriend—a disc jockey at a local radio station. Joey was a really nice guy. Stephanie's parents just didn't want her sleeping alone in the house with a boy. I agreed to go. After all, it was a free trip to St. Augustine.

The house was right on the beach. It was beautiful! Stephanie and Joey spent a great deal of time together, while I sunbathed on the deck. But they didn't just take advantage of me by ignoring me and leaving me isolated the entire weekend. I never felt like a third wheel. We had a great time!

From that point on, Stephanie and I were really good friends. We worked the same schedules and made plans to hang out during our free time.

One day, Stephanie announced that she was going to Miami. I had never been and wanted to go with her. "When are you going?"

"After work."

"Tonight?"

"Yeah—I have to be there by 9:00 a.m. tomorrow."

"How long does it take to get there?"

"Not too long; you can sleep while I drive."

"OK—I'm in!"

We worked until about 11:30 pm. Packing was done in such a hurry, that it's a wonder either of us had anything to wear at all! I bought some beer, which we drank. And then we took off. Stephanie drove all night. She drove fast, but well. We made it from North Tampa to the Miami Convention Center in exactly 4 hours. I believe that was some sort of record!

There was quite a crowd when we arrived. I asked Stephanie, "What is it that is going on here?"

"It's a festival," she said.

"What kind?"

"It's Guru Maharaj Ji. All those who follow him—those who have the Knowledge and those who are pursuing Knowledge—are here to see him."

"Huh?" I had no idea what she was talking about. It sounded weird. But we were in Miami, the weather was beautiful, and the crowd seemed tame enough. Best to just let things be and enjoy.

The Convention Center was packed full of people and activity. We walked around for quite some time in the morning, looking at all the different areas of people. Some were sitting in circles listening to speakers; others were putting together stage displays. Everyone seemed to be doing something. There were adults and children of all ages. It was all very relaxed and free. There were people selling tee-shirts and things, but nothing too elaborate.

I looked around, but didn't see any food. I asked Stephanie about this, as we hadn't eaten since the day before and had had only a few beers on the way.

"Oh, I should have mentioned this—everyone here is a vegetarian."

"You're kidding."

"Nope. But you can get a salad or something to eat. We'll get something in a little while."

As the day progressed, different activities were announced on a public address system. Stephanie was very interested in taking advantage of this one particular event—Darshan. She asked, "Would you mind if I go through the Darshan line?"

"No, I don't mind. I'll do it with you."

"Oh, you can't."

"Why not?"

"You haven't received Knowledge. It's only for those who have received the Knowledge."

"So—I won't tell them."

Stephanie just laughed. "Oh, they'll know."

"Huh?"

"Just enjoy the Convention Center, and I'll catch up with you as soon as I go through."

"OK."

The Darshan line wrapped around the building and wound around those velvet usher cables used to organize and control crowds. I was surprised at the number of people doing this, whatever it was. I walked around and looked at things for some time, but I was getting hungrier and hungrier. After 90 minutes had passed, I thought, *"OK—enough is enough. I'm starving!"* I looked everywhere, but I couldn't find Stephanie. After 30 minutes of looking, I decided to go up to the stage and ask for some help. "Hey, can you help me? My friend went into that Darshan line and I can't find her now. Can you announce her name on the P.A. system to get her to come up here to meet me?"

"No, I'm sorry. There are no announcements when Darshan is going on."

"What are you talking about, you announced "Darshan"–I heard you."

"We can't do it, I'm sorry. Your friend will be out as soon as she makes it through."

"Great."

I continued to walk around looking for Stephanie. I looked what I thought was everywhere—but where was she? I couldn't find her. Stephanie had left her purse and her car keys with me. I had everything; she had left empty-handed and gone to this Darshan thing. But I didn't feel good about going into Stephanie's purse and spending her money. I didn't drive a stick shift car, so I wasn't going to go somewhere to get something to eat. In fact, I didn't know where I was at all! *Stephanie!*

It would be 4 hours before Stephanie turned up. I was so hungry and so pissed from looking for her, I was crazy. I had accosted several people at the festival, basically yelling at them for their incompetence for not helping me. I was frustrated, lost, confused, and I felt that people were just messing with me for not helping me.

Stephanie just giggled when I told her all of this.

"You think this is funny? I've been milling around this nonsense for 4 hours waiting for you to go through some bullshit line that I wasn't allowed into, I'm starving, and I'm tired. Where the hell were you?"

"What are you so upset about? You have my purse, you have my car keys. It's not like I could have left you. You have everything!"

Stephanie was so calm, that she was downright serene. Meanwhile, I was so wound up, I was literally ready to explode.

All the way home, Stephanie tried to explain what I had been in the middle of—that Guru Maharaj Ji was the leader of this Knowledge and meditation that both she and Joey were into and followed, and that it was all about truth and the spirit inside all of us. But I hadn't had a good night's sleep; I had been on my feet all day; and once Stephanie put some food into me, I was shot. None of what she was saying was making any sense. All I knew is that these people had a glazed look in their eyes and wouldn't lift a finger to help me find my friend! And the more pissed I became even talking about it, the more Stephanie found it amusing.

Bliss, my ass!

36. The Lemon Law

MY CAREER HISTORY began at a place called Anderson Drug Company in Tampa, Florida. My brother was a headhunter working for an agency in the city. When the job order came in for an entry level computer operator, he was certain I could fill the vacancy. It was a great opportunity for me. Computers were new to business, and anyone familiar with computer technology would surely have an edge.

The company hired me as a permanent employee. I was earning about $100 per week. Not a lot of money, but there were benefits. Anderson Drug not only sold pharmaceuticals; they sold everything that could be purchased in a drug store. That consisted of blow dryers, electric rollers, shampoo—any product you can think of!

The computer I was to learn was an IBM System III Model 15. This was no PC! The computer was contained in a computer room and took up the entire area, wall-to-wall. We received orders via tape from drug stores, which we then converted to printed data on computer paper. The information from this was then entered by data entry operators who, when typing the information, produced punched computer cards. The cards were then fed into a card reader, and the order would be sent to the warehouse for processing on the line. It was quite a complex process, and I was learning every facet of it.

The man I worked alongside of was called Stephen. He was a son of the owner, Mr. Anderson. Stephen was quite a character! His cousin worked at another branch of the business in Ocala, Florida. A third branch, located in Sarasota, completed the chain. Stephen's brother worked in the warehouse. When the three cousins put their minds to it, they were unstoppable practical jokers.

Our work area was a long countertop-type work station, where we processed the paperwork from the orders that were being filled in the warehouse. Each item that was placed in the box for a customer had a corresponding punch card, which was attached to the item with a rubber band when the order was complete. We would take those cards and feed them into our own card reader, which would then produce an invoice to accompany the order. Sometimes Stephen would work the first chair position. Other times I would. We got along well. We both worked at the same pace and got the job done accurately.

There was another girl working in this area, Cindy. She had been there a while and was very attentive to her job responsibility. It disturbed her that management had hired me from outside, rather than promoting her from within. Cindy already knew that she was being required to step aside in order to allow me to learn what I needed to run the large computer in the next room. Although there was that friction, she was never ugly towards me. She continued to do her job well and never treated me with anything but respect.

My boss was an older woman—a bit of a spinster—who lived alone in a mobile home. Lorna was very prim and proper. I often envisioned that she could very easily have been a nun. She had a certain air about her that demonstrated a sort of reserved superiority. Lorna knew everything there was to know about working that computer and handling the department. However, she was quick to let you know that she did not expect to have to tell you something more than once. After that, you should know it!

On the days when I worked outside with Stephen, we would make small talk all day. It was a much friendlier atmosphere than inside the computer room with my boss. Stephen liked to laugh and did so often! As mentioned, the family was filled with practical jokers.

One practical joke that I remember vividly was when Stephen's cousin came in from Ocala to attend a sales meeting. He drove a Corvette Stingray, which was his pride and joy. While he was in the meeting in the conference room, Stephen went out into the parking lot, opened the hood of the car, and placed a cow's tongue on the engine block. Nothing was said to his poor cousin, who, after the meeting was over, drove over an hour to return home in 90-degree heat—the cow tongue stinking up a storm the entire way! Every time we thought about that, we laughed. All afternoon, the thought of that poor man driving back to Ocala with that smell coming from the engine block just cracked us up.

According to Newton's Law of Motion, for every action there is always an equal and opposite reaction. The Anderson family was not about to prove Newton wrong! Only two days later, a box was delivered to the office addressed to Stephen. No one touched it. It sat on top of his desk until he arrived. No one thought anything of it at the time. Until Stephen opened it, we all thought it was just a normal delivery—just mail. No such luck! Inside the box was the same cow tongue he had placed on the engine block of the Corvette—only days older and much riper! The shoe was now on the other foot, and Stephen's cousin was doing the laughing.

For a while, the pranksters took a sabbatical—but not for long. This time, Stephen's brother took the lead and did something to his cousin, unbeknownst to Stephen. Now retaliation was imminent! Every time an action was made, it upped the ante. The cousin had perceived the act to have come from Stephen, not his brother—a valid assumption, because in reality, the brothers were usually operating in conjunction with each other. The problem was that Stephen didn't know retaliation was coming.

It was a Monday morning. I was typically late, which annoyed my boss. I worked hard once I got there, but I just couldn't seem to get going in the morning. Stephen, on the other hand, had enough nervous energy for 10 people and was always early. I was just putting my things up, with Stephen seated at the desk. He shouted to me across the room, "I'll take first desk and get started."

"OK."

He no sooner opened the top drawer of the desk than I heard a clatter of noise and his scream, "AH-H-H-H." It happened so fast, I didn't have time to react. Stephen's cousin had placed a live rattle snake in the top drawer of the desk, which lunged towards the opening as he pulled open the drawer to get a pen. It was then that I realized, *these guys aren't* playing—*they're crazy!*

Because I had my own full-time job, I was able to purchase my first car. I looked around, briefly, and found a used 1974 Hornet Hatchback. It was Kelly green with a white roof. The front seats were a split bench with cloth covering. I LOVED this car. Now I had my own transportation and could I could go anywhere I wanted—or at least, anywhere I could afford the gas! Wally had cosigned for the loan, which was $2,400. My payments were $100 per month. I was so proud of that car!

This was my first car and my first major purchase. This meant that, unfortunately, I had no idea what I was doing when I bought it. My mother had no real history of buying cars either. She and Wally had purchased one car together, and it was brand new. Wally and I didn't speak much, if at all, so he offered no suggestions. I picked the car out; he cosigned. That was it.

When I brought the car home, I quickly went over to my friends' apartment to get them to come and see my new car. They all came out one by one and did what guys do when they look at a car. One asked for the keys, the other opened the hood, a third kicked the tires. Everyone was looking it over. One by one, each pointed out some-thing they felt was wrong with the car. Sadly, each one was correct! I had picked the car out and bought it because "I liked how it looked." Mechanically, it was a disaster. This car was a total lemon!

My reserve funds were nonexistent. I had no money for repairs of any kind—and this was surely to be extensive work. I was sick over it. Nick, a friend at work, asked about my new car. "You just bought it and you're not driving it?"

"No, my friends looked at it and said there are some things wrong with it, and I don't want to break down."

"Where did you get it?"

"The dealer —just up the road."

"Bring it tomorrow, and we'll take a look at it."

The next day, I drove my new car in to work. I prayed the entire way down there, hoping I would not wind up stuck on the side of the highway. Nick came out on his break and looked the car over. "Yep, they're right. Look over here . . . and here." It was a mess. He suggested that we go back to the dealer after work. "I'll go with you and talk to them. They'll have to fix this for you."

At 5:00, we went to the dealer. Nick asked to speak to someone in the service department and proceeded to point out the things that were wrong with the car. The man there was polite, but basically blew him off. It was obvious he had no concerns about my car—to say nothing of the integrity of the dealership. But Nick wouldn't let him walk away. Instead, he followed him back into the dealership, voicing his discontent with the transaction (even though it wasn't his transaction). Their voices got louder.

I could see this wasn't going anywhere. I also felt bad that now Nick was inches from a physical altercation with this man, only because he was trying to help me out! I stood behind him in the service area, listening to them bicker back and forth. Finally, I grabbed Nick's arm and said, "Let's go—they don't care. So what if they sold me a car that was no good? They got their money. They don't care!"

I was so upset! I continued to carry on with a verbal attack, declaring that they deliberately sold me a "bad" car and that they took advantage of me being an inexperienced car buyer. As my voice got louder and louder, a room full of customers heard me and were about to lose confidence in the business. The manager came over to us and said, "Of course we're going to fix your car. We care!"

In an instant, the barrage of insults stopped and I stopped myself to regroup and regain my composure. I looked to Nick and asked, "Can you drive me home? I'll leave the car here for them to fix."

"Sure."

We walked out of the dealership, got into Nick's car, and left.

"What were you doing back there?" he asked.

"I have no idea."

"Well, it worked!"

37. What's In a Name?

THE COMPANY EMPLOYEES varied in age from 18 to 65. It was as diverse a group as any I had ever been in. There were many different ethnic backgrounds and personalities. While everyone was cordial, it became apparent who associated with whom by looking around the lunchroom. Later, groupings of people made it evident who associated after hours. These distinctions had little to do with work area, age, race, religion or sex and much more to do with personality.

I found myself falling into several different groups: the computer group, the party group, and the young group. I would enjoy the company of many different people at different times. I was not "involved" with anyone—nor did I care to be. But I did enjoy a good time.

Several people at work frequented the Happy Hour that was hosted down the street from the office at the Howard Johnson's. One day, the company receptionist, Renee, extended an invitation to me to join her and a few others after work. It was a Tuesday—but what the heck!

When I arrived, I saw several people from work sitting around a large table with drinks. "What will you have?"

"I'll just a have beer."

Small talk followed with everyone asking questions about where I was from, where I went to school, and where I lived. While I assumed no one really "needed" these details, I realized that they do provide people with a way of forming a box in their heads to put you in. I started learning some of the details of the others' lives. Renee shared with the group that she had been a stripper in Vaudeville shows until she had her children; five in total. She was a divorced woman raising five children—alone. Renee had stories to tell, one better than the last. She also had a lead-lined stomach. Boy, could she drink!

We sat and talked until about 8:30 p.m., taking advantage of the hors d'oeuvres that Howard Johnson served and enjoying the conversation. I liked knowing these people outside of work. It gave me a sense of belonging.

The next day, I was greeted by a somewhat cold shoulder from Stephen. Apparently, he had some hurt feelings resulting from not being included in this invitation. "I didn't think it was my place to extend an invitation to you. I had never been out with these people, and it was their idea."

"No—that's fine."

"Fine" is probably the most misrepresented word in the English language. Almost all of the time, when people use the word "fine"—they don't mean it! There was not much conversation to be had the rest of that day. It was quiet at the desk. The lunchroom, however, was filled with banter about the night before.

Several days later, that same group suggested we do this again. Most of the members that had attended earlier in the week had plans for the weekend, but were willing to plan something for the following week. By Monday, everyone seemed anxious to get together after work. This was not exactly a common practice among working people—to go to a Happy Hour on a Monday evening. A few of the people from the first trip did not attend, but the majority was there.

From the first order, we were drinking bourbon on the rocks. I had never tasted bourbon before. It was smooth, warming. I found something very comforting about sipping something, rather than "drinking" one bottle of beer after another. It seemed classy somehow—classy and more grown-up.

The first bourbon was classy; the second was nice. By the third, it was *drinking*, pure and simple. Time was ticking on, and we were sitting there having great conversation, snacking on pretzels, and drinking—one bourbon after another. The number of people dwindled down to three of us: Rhonda, another secretary closer to Renee's age than mine, and me. The last of the crowd sat in the Howard Johnson's bar like three stooges until 5:00 a.m. When we realized the hour, we decided to do the only thing we could do—go take showers and get ready for work!

The next day was rough. I wasn't as hung over as I was exhausted. The fact was that I had been drinking until 5:00 a.m., so there wasn't time for me to have gotten hung over! I was still under the influence. By lunchtime, the three of us crawled to the lunchroom and laughed about how tired we all were. We had had a great time and weren't sorry we had done it, despite the effect it had on the following day. Toward late afternoon, we decided that we would all feel better if we returned to Howard Johnson's for one more drink. One quickly became four. We drank until midnight.

It was sudden, but this practice of drinking after work became routine for the three of us. There would always be others joining us at one time or another. But we were the staples of the group. I knew this wasn't the best idea—but I was enjoying myself and chose to ignore the downside of what it was doing to my job and my health.

There was talk in the office about an outing of a large group after work on a Thursday. Renee had good ears for office talk, as she was the receptionist and put calls through on the switchboard to every employee. If it was happening, she knew about it! When I passed her work station headed for the ladies' room, she stopped me and asked, "Hey, there's a group going to the Zodiac Lounge in St. Petersburg tonight. Do you want to go?"

"Sure, sounds like fun."

We went to the Howard Johnson first just to get a drink after work. Then at about 8:00, we headed for St. Pete. Renee and I decided to ride together, since this was a distance away from the job. She drove a Suburban. In those days, SUV's were not common. A Suburban was her choice of vehicle because she had such a large family. It was like sailing a boat, driving that monster down the road!

The Zodiac Lounge was crowded. There were people all over the parking lot; music blaring from the door which was propped open by a bouncer. I looked around to take in the details of the area. Across the parking lot was yet another lounge. This one was called Inferno. I thought it was odd to have two bars right next door to each other.

But—this was Florida. A lot of people vacation in Florida, so there must be enough business to go around, I thought.

Renee and I walked into the Zodiac Lounge. It wasn't immediately apparent to me, but as we walked into the lounge area, I was startled to see a topless waitress with a tray of drinks. "Renee, where are we?"

"The Zodiac Lounge."

"Did you know it was a topless place?"

"No. But, since we're here, we might as well have a drink."

"Oh, Renee, I don't want to be seen in here!"

"It'll be OK. It's dark. I see the group over there. We'll duck over here, grab a table, have a drink, and then scoot out. Nobody will even know we were here."

Before one minute was up, another topless waitress came over to take our order. She didn't seem to think it odd that we were in there. I guess one paying customer is as good as another. The waitress seemed nice, although young. I couldn't help but feel bad. As much as I wanted to make money, I didn't think I could ever work in a place like that. But she didn't seem to mind. We ordered drinks and laughed to ourselves at how stupid we were to just tag along to a bar when we hadn't been "officially" invited.

The waitress brought our drinks quickly. She placed them on the table, took our money, and then said, "You might want to move over to the other table over there."

"Why?"

"The movie is about to start."

"Oh, NO!"

At that instant, a light shined directly on the wall next to where we were sitting, and a movie came on. It was X rated. Renee got the giggles and said, "Oh, crap—it's black sock." "Black sock" was a term given to X-rated movies back in the day, because the men in them always kept their "black" socks on – nothing else.

Now everyone in the bar was turning their seats to face directly towards where we were seated. There was no slipping out discretely now. We were caught! I wanted to crawl out of the place, but Renee wouldn't hear of it. "We have every right to be here." That was true. But I still didn't want to be seen!

We sat, finished our drinks, and exited through the side door. We had been seen by every single man from the office. The next day, we got these weird smiles any time we ran into one of them. They weren't mean about it. Truth was; I was harder on myself than they were.

To this day, I struggle with the fact that the topless place was called Zodiac, while the regular bar was called Inferno. How's a person to know?

38. Kansas City, Here I Come

JOBS SEEM THE best when they are new. You are meeting new people, learning new things—and feeling good about having "won" a job by way of an interview. As time marches on, that feeling of excitement dissipates and a feeling of obligation replaces it.

The more time I spent at Anderson Drug, the more I realized that this was not the job for me. My interest became lessened to the point where I was putting my time in; but I didn't care to be there, and it was obvious. I began showing up late more times than not. This was not well received. As my punctuality dwindled and my interest waned, I was transferred to the order desk permanently, and the girl whom I thought should have been given the computer job all along was asked to step up. Now I was at the desk with Stephen all day, every day. Stephen was a good guy, but we were very different—and the differences did not seem to interest me as much as they did him.

Before long, I was given the option of leaving—and decided to grab it. A new job had opened up for me at an insurance agency. As a customer service rep, I could take calls from customers all day long. It provided me the opportunity to talk with many different people, as well as learning something new. The company was Regal Life, headquartered in Canada. There were about 30 people working in the Tampa office. My department had only a handful of employees: myself, Julia (the supervisor), another girl with a position equal to mine, whom I nicknamed Carlotta and two other clerks who moonlighted as Tampa Bay Buccaneer cheerleaders whom I jokingly referred to as Buckettes. We had a ball! Every day, talking over our cubicles, we would chat about whatever was going on in our lives in between calls. It wasn't a "great" job for me, but it had great benefits and steady hours.

I also continued working at the movie theatre. The second job not only provided a handy second income, but it had become a sort of social outlet for me as well. I had become good friends with Stephanie, and she and I were talking more and more about the Knowledge she had introduced me to via our trip to Miami.

Admittedly, I thought the group of people I had met in Miami was the craziest I had been around to date. But I couldn't get the temptation of wanting to know more about their teaching out of my head. I began to attend meetings with Stephanie, which were held at a hall rented by a group of followers of Guru Maharaj Ji. There were individuals from all walks of life attending and pursuing Knowledge. Lawyers, doctors, rich, poor, young, old—it was quite a mixture. Everyone was nice, and the atmosphere was pleasant, although occasionally it seemed a bit "over the top" to me. They were almost all vegetarian—suggesting that this was recommended. But I loved meat! From that perspective, I was not interested in becoming a member or following this way of life. What intrigued me about these people so much was how *happy* they all were—all the time.

Between working days and attending meetings (called Satsang) in the evenings, my life was pretty full. Besides this, I continued to keep in touch with my friends from the apartment complex. As my involvement with Satsang grew, my association with the friends from the apartment lessened, but it never ceased. I never mixed the two; this pursuit of Knowledge was more of a personal investigation than something I was going to begin recruiting friends into.

As my interest grew and my experience became more enticing, I made a conscious decision to pursue receiving this Knowledge. This became my primary focus. I attended Satsang daily, enjoying it very much. My drug and alcohol intake dwindled to almost nothing. I was focusing more and more on this new pursuit, and my social activities centered on the same.

There were more gatherings and festivals scheduled. As finances permitted, I began to attend them. The first such festival I consciously decided to attend was held in Kansas City. A group of people associated with the Satsang hall in Tampa decided to travel together to the festival in Kansas City, which was held in January of 1978. One of the people in the group had a van, and we all decided to go in it, sharing the expense of the gas.

Interestingly enough, for being a high school graduate, I had no idea of the lack of command of geography that I had had up until this point. Travelling from Florida, we were not so much thinking of snow as just driving for many hours, sleeping, eating, etc. We made our way to the panhandle of Florida and entered Alabama before we needed to refuel. It was staggering how differently people spoke! Their accents were very heavy Southern accents. Mine, comparatively, was a very heavy New York accent. The folks in the van told me, "We'll get the gas—you stay here." I thought it was odd that they did not want me to speak to anyone. Perhaps the difference between the North and the South was more pronounced than I was aware!

From Alabama, we made our way into Mississippi. That year, there was an enormous blizzard that swept across the country. As we made our way into Mississippi from Alabama, the snow began coming down heavily, and we were beginning to see icicles forming on the roof inside of the van. We went slower and slower down the road, until we came to a complete stop. One by one we all began to inquire why the van was not moving.

"What's wrong?"

"A tractor trailer jack-knifed, and we are stuck."

"Oh great. Turn on the CB!" We had a CB radio in the van, which did enable us to keep up with the news. It became clear we were not going anywhere for quite a while.

It is not possible to run the engine of a vehicle indefinitely while sitting still on the highway; we would run out of gas—to say nothing of our other problems. Between the cold and the snow, we were learning quickly that we were not just "stuck"—we were also about to be frozen! So there we sat, getting colder and colder inside this ice cube of a vehicle.

We had a hot plate that we had plugged in to make tea and coffee. But that was the extent of our ability to cope with the situation.

"Make some tea," somebody yelled from the front. The group in the back of the van proceeded to boil water for tea. We noticed that the tea seemed to taste better than usual! How good something to eat or drink is corresponds directly to how badly you want it, or how comforting it is.

After sitting stranded on the highway in the cold, we felt that a hot cup of tea was a luxury. No one else on the road had the ability to get this. As we realized how lucky we were, we began sharing the limited amount of beverages we had with neighboring travelers on the road as well, making them tea or coffee. It was one of those impromptu opportunities that life provides.

We sat on that highway for over 12 hours, freezing. Between the cold, the length of time we were stuck, and the amount of tea I had consumed, I now had to go to the bathroom—which was nowhere to be found! I waited until I could wait no longer.

"Go down the side of the road," someone suggested.

"Oh, great!"

"Wait, I'll go with you."

Two of us proceeded to climb out of the van, wearing everything we had with us and trying to keep warm, with the intention of squatting on the side of the road to pee–and yet not be seen! Odds were in our favor, as it was nightfall and visibility was low in the dark. We walked down the road a bit and went towards an embankment, thinking more privacy would be afforded us there. As we pulled down our pants, traffic began starting up their engines—and turning on their headlights. Just our luck! The blockage on the road was cleared at precisely the time we were going! Regardless of the bright lights, there was no stopping at that point. I had waited to go so long, I thought I was going to bust! I just took care of my business and returned to the van quickly, embarrassed as hell, and finding all the males who had remained in the van laughing hysterically at our predicament.

The snow was quite heavy, and the van had no snow tires. A consensus in the van was that we needed to obtain snow tires or chains for the back wheels before we tried to make it any further. In a storm

of this magnitude, there were no stores left with tires or chains available. We found ourselves in Boca Chita, Mississippi—the last place
in the country a New Yorker thinks she will ever find herself! A very
nice man/store owner offered to put us up for the night in his shop.
"You'll freeze out there if you stay on the road. You kids huddle up in
here and keep warm. I'll wake you up in the morning so you can get
back on your journey."

I was stunned that anyone would be so trusting as to open up their
store and allow total strangers to sleep there! No one would allow
me to speak in front of this man (with my New York accent), but he
was clearly just a well-meaning soul, who didn't care about the differences between people. He was a very kind man—and he probably
saved our lives!

The next day, we were off and running towards the festival. We
still had not obtained snow tires, but the roads appeared to be getting
a great deal of attention from snow plows and road crews, so we were
not encountering much difficulty.

As we neared our destination, we realized something none of us
had even considered: *There are two Kansas Cities!* One is in Kansas,
the other in Missouri—just over a bridge connecting the two. We all
looked at one another dumbfounded. "Which one is it?" None of us
knew. We crossed that bridge back and forth trying to figure it out,
looking for a familiar landmark, a sign—something. It would be an
additional two hours of driving around before we concluded that we
were indeed looking for Kansas City, Missouri!

The festival was wonderful on many levels. As a group, we had
bonded over this treacherous journey. And as an individual, I had
become even more enamored with the teachings of the group. We remained there for three days and then began our journey home, which
was much less eventful than the trip to the festival. We sang songs and
talked the whole way home.

My involvement with this teaching would never really end—
which is not to say that it remained this intense permanently. But
for the next three years, I was completely and utterly devoted to the

pursuit of this Knowledge and everything that entailed. I travelled all over and focused on little else.

The good news was that I was now free from "substances" and a lifestyle that had been becoming progressively more dangerous. Like a fish in a tank in need of extra care, I had not so much been rescued as "netted" for my protection.

39. Logistics

LIFE IN THE pursuit of "knowledge" can be both time-consuming and exhausting. As my emotional commitment grew, so did my financial commitment. Traveling from one event to the next consumed all of my time and most of my resources. Money became very much the instrument by which I could put myself in what I hoped to be the right place at the right time. My quest for the Knowledge was relentless—yet I remained without what I sought. Time after time, I would speak to visiting Mahatmas, only to be told, "You're not ready."

More times than not, I was frustrated, anxious, and disappointed. Yet I would continue to tell myself not to give up. "My day will come."

After traveling all over the country requesting that Knowledge be revealed to me, it would be in my very own home location of Tampa that I would finally be granted this wish. An Indian Mahatma by the name of Mahatma Guru Charanand visited Tampa for a week-end and deemed me ready. The actual Knowledge session lasted the better part of the day, with a celebration held that evening. At last, I had what I had pursued all this time. And yes, it was well worth the wait. Without divulging a confidence, what I can say about it was that it redirected my attention. Rather than looking into my past at all the things that had caused me discontent, I was now looking to Knowledge to take me inward to the very core of my being—and this provided me great joy.

A festival was scheduled to be held that fall in Kissimmee, Florida, just outside of Disney World. Tampa, having an international airport, became the hub of most of the arrivals and departures—particularly of those coming from overseas to attend. I volunteered to help in whatever capacity they wanted. I was put into logistics and asked to aid in coordinating the travel for everyone needing assistance getting from Tampa to Orlando. This sounds fairly simple, but there were, in fact, thousands of people planning to attend from all over. Many of these people did not speak English well. It was quite a challenge, but I loved it! Round the clock, I scheduled vans, cars and buses to take people to Kissimmee. I worked from my office, my home, and from the trailer set up in Kissimmee. The entire effort took longer than three weeks. I recruited help via telephone communication, enlisting drivers to aid in this undertaking. In cases where I was unable to connect drivers with passengers, I took them myself. Many a trip was made between Tampa and Kissimmee.

As the day grew closer to the festival itself, I realized that I had not formally requested the time off from work. Upon putting in the written request, I was notified that I would be unable to take vacation at that time.

"Are you kidding?"

"No, so and so is taking off at that time; we expect to be busy. No, you cannot go."

I couldn't believe it! The biggest event for me to date and I was being told I was unavailable to attend. I went from total frustration to total clarity. "What is important here? A job—or what I believe in?"

I went into work the next day and tendered my resignation.

Coworkers were amazed. This simply was not done! Why would someone walk away from a perfectly good job to attend something taking place over a long weekend? It just didn't make sense to them. Be that as it may, it made perfect sense to me. At this point, knowing I was about to leave left little alternative for my employers but to tolerate my total involvement in the logistics for this festival. I remained at work for my last two weeks, but did little to serve the needs of the company. Rather, my full effort and attention were towards the festival and the needs of those attending. With a short but sincere farewell party, I joined the ranks of the unemployed.

Several more trips between Tampa and Kissimmee were made before my job was done. I had worked my way into a pivotal position within the infrastructure of the festival. Everyone was trying to contact me in some way to gain assistance. I was very connected to people

I did not know and was able to work very well within this system, despite language barriers. From a working standpoint, it was terrific experience for me.

The festival began before it officially began, if you know what I mean. There were so many people arriving continually, that the numbers were growing substantially for days before the festival was actually to begin. We worked from sun-up till way after midnight, requiring very little sleep. It was very fulfilling. If "work" could actually be like this, a career could be a wonderful thing, I thought.

The scheduled duration of the actual festival was seven days. I had anticipated attending the last four of the seven, making it a long weekend. Once my employer denied me the vacation time and I resigned, there was no reason I could not attend for seven days or even longer. I had literally no other place to go. Kissimmee had become a tent city of sorts, with people camping all over. It was, however, quite organized. Because I had been so involved in the preparation, I was very familiar with the layout and could find my way to anything easily.

One drawback, for me, was the menu. Food was provided in a huge tent in the eastern part of the area. However, this was a vegetarian diet—a strictly vegetarian one. No eggs, no nothing. Tofu has never appealed to me on any level. Taking a tasteless substance the texture of your tongue and covering it with spices and flavors does not in any way constitute "food" to me! I had worked my butt off; I was starving. I wanted MEAT!

There was a hotel just outside the property where the festival was taking place. I managed to entice a few other non-vegetarian attendees to come with me and partake of some actual food. We went that afternoon and ate until we could not budge. Until I finished, I didn't realize how long it had been since I had eaten an actual meal. It had been over a week! I had been snacking and grabbing what I could in a rush, getting into or out of the car. This was a feast—and my system couldn't handle it. I had eaten so much, I was left weak. We returned to the festival site, where I went to my tent and collapsed in a contented exhaustion.

The next morning when I awoke, I was unable to speak. My voice was completely gone. The more I tried to speak, the more I would cough. In no time, I had a fever and sore throat accompanying the laryngitis. Now what?

A friend from Tampa made his way to the store to bring me some over-the-counter medicine, hoping to provide some relief. He brought back what appeared to be a sample of every product the pharmacy carried for any of the above symptoms. I settled on Vicks Nyquil. One shot, and I was back asleep in the tent under several covers, sweating the fever out. It would be days before I would be well enough to participate in the events that were scheduled.

I had missed days of the celebration due to my illness and was now on my feet for the first time since it began. I had been given word that one of the people I had assisted in getting to Kissimmee was looking for me. Her tent was located in a particular section on the other side of the property. I went looking. Despite the size of the audience in attendance, I was able to find her without too much effort. She did not speak English. The woman had a poem on parchment with a drawing that she wanted to give me in appreciation for my helping them to arrive safely. It was beautiful! I didn't know what it said—but I knew what she meant.

Guru Maharaj Ji was there the entire duration of the festival. Although he would speak every evening from the stage, it was irregular to see him walking around amongst the crowd. Having never experienced seeing him any other way but on stage, I was not expecting it at this event either.

As I departed the area where I had been given the poem, crowds of people were milling around. I looked to see what they were gathering around, but could not make it out from a distance. I was alone. While there was a great deal of heat and still air, I felt a sort of breeze over my shoulder. As I turned towards it, I saw Maharaj Ji walking towards me, with only a handful of people (I assumed Security) accompanying him. I was mystified. How was it that I had managed to be in the exact spot where he was, when so many others were gathered in a group looking for him? Whatever the reason, I made eye contact with him as he approached. It was as if the rest of the surroundings—people, tents, vehicles, everything else—were gone. I cannot explain it—and I know it sounds crazy—but I felt what can only be described as magic.

My voice returned completely to normal at that instant. It shocked me when I spoke and my voice came out as it had when restored to full strength. True to form, a woman who never stops talking was, at that moment, reduced to one syllable, "Hey."

Maharaj Ji smiled this huge grin and said, "Hey, yourself." Then with one move of his hand, he waved me on as if to say, "Come on." So I did. I walked along with him around the grounds of the festival. Satsang was not something that was offered one-on-one in these environments. That is not to say we were the only two there. All total, there were about 8 people gathered while walking. But it was very surreal. Maharaj Ji talked about the value of service and how doing something elevates us.

Everyone that attended that festival hoped to hear Guru Maharaj Ji speak. Every evening, he spoke on stage to a gathering of thousands. I was fortunate enough to be part of an audience of eight!

At the conclusion of the festival, I realized I had no job. I also realized that my life in Tampa was nothing that I wanted. I had made the acquaintance of some people in attendance from Pennsylvania. "You're from New York?"

"Yes."

"Where are you going now?"

"Don't know. I live in Tampa, but I have no job anymore."

"Why don't you come with us? We'll give you a ride at least as far as we're going."

"Really?"

"Yeah."

I had a knapsack of clothes with me. They were mostly dirty, but that could easily be remedied. I also had my car. I had paid for this car every month for the last two years. With two payments to go before I owned it, I had no confidence that this vehicle would make it all the way to New York. Besides, who needs a car in New York? Not me!

I parked the car on the side of the highway along Interstate 4. Without blinking, I jumped from my car into theirs and headed back to New York!

Stage V

40. Five Stars — Three Strikes

IN YOUTH, WE often do things that as adults we would never consider. My split-second departure back to New York City with a car full of people I had only met minutes before is a perfect example. Abandoning my car with only two payments left before the title was mine is certainly another. But thinking was not in my repertoire back then. I was reactionary—much like a dog picking up a scent. New York? Sure!

This trip was meant to be a long drive that would result in a nice visit with some old friends. It went beyond this, resulting in what was to be the next phase of my life.

We were on the road for over fifteen hours—driving, pulling over, sleeping, driving, stopping to eat, and driving. I had forgotten that the group I was travelling with was all pure vegetarians—a fact of which I was quickly reminded when we sat down in the restaurant! One girl grilled the poor waitress, insisting she investigate if the spaghetti sauce had 'touched' meat in any way. I remember thinking, "Damn, just eat it. It's not like you're allergic to it. It won't kill you!" Then it occurred to me that these weren't just vegetarians—they were fanatics! Despite this eccentricity, she was nice. They all were. We enjoyed conversation around where they were from and where I was from all the way to Pennsylvania.

Once arriving in Pennsylvania, I stopped off unannounced to visit my friend, Renee (from Anderson Drug), who had relocated to that area. I spent a few days at her condo and then headed north to New York.

This trip epitomized the beauty of what I loved about being young—you could literally just jump up and blow like a leaf from place to place, visiting people unannounced, and it was totally accepted. If you did this as an adult, you would appear to be unstable.

The fact is, I *was* unstable, but I was still getting by with it.

By the time I got to New York, I had decided to look up my old friend, Mo. She was living at home with her folks (and siblings). The entire family had relocated to New Jersey. This was good news-bad news. Good because the house they lived in was much larger than the apartment they had previously had; bad because IT WAS JERSEY! Jersey is just not New York, never was, never will be! Still, Mo's family was like family to me, and very accepting of my showing up unannounced. They had eight children of their own, so one more in the mix didn't really hurt!

The first few days were my time just to hang out and party. Mo and I were very much able to pick right up where we had left off and venture into the city for whatever good time was to be had. Friends like that are always the best! You can be away from them for long periods of time and as soon as you get back together, the conversation and behaviors pick right back up as if no time has passed at all. It's very comfortable.

As days quickly turned into weeks, it became more and more obvious that I needed to get a job, if for no other reason than to get some money. I had left on this trip unplanned and had no cash what-so-ever!

Mo's sister, Annabelle, had a job working for an advertising agency, in Manhattan. In addition, there was a friend of Mo's who advised us of an opening at that same agency. In no time at all, I had been hooked up with a job.

Every day, I would get up in the morning and head towards the city to go to work. Mo's dad, Jim, worked in the city as well. He would either accompany me to the railroad train, or invite me to join his carpool of other gentlemen who were driving in. Either way, it was a nice ride, and we would take it together. Jim was always the surrogate father, always looking out for me. He was able to make pleasant conversation with me without making me feel as though he were telling me what to do—even though he usually was! He was a nice man.

The job, on the other hand, was as confusing as anything I had ever done. From the first day, I had no idea what to do, how to do it, or who I was doing it for! It's as if they expected me to come in and just know what to do. I would often find myself involved in conversations about advertising for one product or another. I tried to be an active participant, but I was lost. At one point, several people were gathered around pictures and slogans for a presentation. Everyone was throwing their opinion out:

"This looks terrific."

"Wonderful."

I looked at the slogan and thought, *this stinks!* I didn't say that, however. Instead—trying to be polite—I said, "It's too simple; I don't think anyone will like it. Much worse, I don't think it will catch on."

The slogan: "I Love New York!"

After clearly establishing that advertising wasn't my forte, I tried to limit my activities to simple clerical work, as if that would help somehow. But it was a clique environment, and I wasn't in the clique! I was doing almost nothing and was bored all day. Most of my time I spent on the phone. It wasn't long before my being on the phone all the time producing no work became a flashing light to the supervisor on the floor. I was out!

Leaving The ADD Agency wasn't so terrible. As I said, I had nothing to do there and didn't fit in. On the advice of my sister, I went to an employment agency to get another job.

There was an opening at a company called Stein Trading. This was a small coal and chemical trading company located in mid-town. The people in the office were really nice, and my boss seemed nice, too. This was terrific! I accepted the position, which was an Accounting Assistant. My responsibility was paying all the bills for the company. Paying bills is only difficult when you don't have the money. This job was simply printing checks and mailing them out. That I could do!

Stein Trading was a German company. The head of the division office where I worked was named Heinrich. Coincidentally, he and I shared the same birthday. He was a nice man. His first language was German, but his English was excellent. (My German, on the other hand, was non-existent).

This job, I liked! It wasn't that what I was doing was so interesting; it was more that the people in this office were all so nice to me. The atmosphere was relaxed, but not lazy. There was no punching a time clock, no supervisor tapping his or her foot when you arrived back from lunch five minutes late. The environment was great!

I had been working at this office for about five months when the Holidays arrived. Not having been employed in an "office" over the Holidays before, I had no idea what was coming. First an invitation was issued to "cordially invite all employees to attend a holiday luncheon" in a beautiful restaurant a few blocks from the office. I was excited about this! It was the kind of restaurant I would have chosen to go to on my own. It was quite expensive. I remember dressing up for the occasion. It was even more fun being around these people in a social gathering than it was in the office! Every one of us was so uniquely different; yet we all seemed to mesh nicely, as if our differences complemented the group.

At the conclusion of the lunch, Heinrich thanked everyone for all their hard work. As he spoke, his secretary rose from the table and began distributing boxes to each employee. "These are just a little token of my gratitude to each of you." In the box were these delicious German pastries! WOW! All this and dessert, too! Next the secretary distributed bottles to each employee. Having never tasted this, I did not know what we were being given. On behalf of the company, for the Holidays we were being given a bottle of five-star cognac! This was the good stuff!

Upon rising from the table to return to the office, my coworker, Pete, told me, "This is just the goodies. We get a bonus check, too."

"Are you serious?"

We returned to the office and, as Pete had told me, my boss presented me with a bonus check. It was my first—ever! The amount was 10 percent of my annual salary. Oh, my God! Now it wasn't that I was making so much money, although I was paid well for what I was doing. But the idea of receiving 10 percent of it all at one time, in a lump—that was a big deal! I was crazy excited. I decided that I was going to buy myself something special.

My first purchase with this bonus check was to be a television. It was a 13-inch black and white portable TV, which I had great difficulty carrying home from Manhattan on the subway. But I was so thrilled to be able to afford this, that having to carry it didn't deter me.

What should have deterred me, however, was carrying both the TV and the bottle of cognac. I was fine walking through the streets to the subway, but upon entering the subway and going through the turnstile, I heard, "CRASH." *Oh, NO!* There was my cognac on the subway floor in the midst of broken glass. I literally bent down and put my finger into the glass to try to get a taste of it—knowing it was gone. What a disappointment!

I was sad about the cognac, but still quite happy about my purchase. I walked up the five flights of stairs to my new apartment, plugged in my television, and sat and watched it all night until I fell asleep. I was in heaven!

The next day I returned to work. Everyone was talking about how great the party was and what they were doing with their bonus money; what they were buying for Christmas as gifts, etc. In the midst of the conversation, my boss looked up and said, "Hey—how'd you like the cognac?"

I was embarrassed. My face told the whole story—almost.

"You didn't drink it, did you?" The room went quiet and everyone turned towards me to hear what had happened.

"No, I dropped the bottle."

"At the turnstile?"

"Yes, how did you…?"

"I went through shortly after you and saw it lying there. Too bad!"

"Yeah. That was the closest I ever came to tasting it."

"Well, try this." As he pulled his hand from behind his back, he extended another brand new bottle out to me.

"Heinrich knew you had dropped yours and told me to purchase another one."

"Oh, my. Thank you so much!"

That entire afternoon, I sat glancing over at the bottle, which sat on top of the filing cabinet in the office out of harm's way. At 5:00 p.m., I reached up, took the bottle, grabbed my purse, and headed for the elevator to go home. "CRASH!" This time, I didn't even make it off the floor of the building we worked on. I was cursed! "What is wrong with me that I cannot seem to get this home long enough to have one glass?" I cleaned it up as coworkers walked around me, trying their best not to laugh. It was absurd!

It was all I could do the next morning to make myself come to work. I felt so clumsy to have had this happen to me—twice! And I didn't even want to ask the value of each bottle. I must seem so careless that I had dropped two of them. I hoped they didn't think I didn't like the gift or was unappreciative of it.

As I passed the receptionist, she smiled without looking up, "Hey, girl—drop anything lately?" Oh, how humiliating! This was going to be a day filled with harassment. I just knew it.

All day long, I tried my best to get my work done. There were a few more giggles and comments about Ellen, the klutz—things like that. For the most part, though, it was not nearly as bad as I anticipated. At about 3:00, the secretary came to my office door, "Ellen, Heinrich would like to see you in his office—NOW."

Oh, crap! Surely he was furious with me and was going to say something. Oh, no!

I approached Heinrich's office door very sheepishly. "You wanted to see me, Sir?"

"Yes, come in here. I understand you've had some difficulty with the cognac?"

"Yes sir. I don't know what's wrong with me. I dropped the one bottle at the turnstile of the subway, and the second—which was so generous of you to give me—smashed as I went to push the elevator button. I'm so sorry."

"Yes—I'm sorry, too. Come here." He stood up from behind his desk and walked to a café table in the corner of his office. On it was a bottle of cognac and two glasses. "Here; we sit here. This time, I will make sure you try some."

That afternoon Heinrich and I drank to our mutual birthdays, the Holidays, good business, good fortune—and absolutely the best cognac I had ever tasted in my life! When we finished, he pushed the button on his phone to call his secretary who was still there. "Call Ellen a taxi. She needs to be taken home today." He patted my hand in between both of his. "Merry Christmas, Ellen."

"Merry Christmas, Sir. And thank you!"

41. St. Patrick's Day

NO STORY WITH a backdrop of New York City would be complete without the inclusion of at least one tale about St. Patrick's Day! St. Patrick, the Patron Saint of Ireland, was known for his ability to convert pagans to Christianity. The date set for honoring him, March 17th, is actually the date commemorating his death. Having lived in several other cities, I can knowledgably make the comparison and say with assurance that no city in the South knows how to properly celebrate St. Patrick's Day! In fact, many do not even acknowledge it. In New York, however, it is a HUGE celebration of Irish heritage—whether you are of Irish descent or not.

One year just before St. Patrick's Day, I had the chance to meet someone interesting rather unexpectedly. On March 16, 1979, while visiting with a girlfriend in a neighborhood bar, I was introduced to one of her friends. Shane was a middle child from a very large family in the Bronx. To earn a living, he worked as a merchant seaman. Shane would sail away for months at a time and then reappear as if by magic. Somewhat typical of the boys I had met in the Bronx; Shane was outgoing and liked to drink. And there was something a bit special about him! Through the introduction of our mutual friend, I made his acquaintance that day, while Shane was on an extended leave.

Shane and I engaged in conversation throughout the evening. He invited me back to his apartment to continue our talk. I had only known him a few hours. Still, I agreed to go. After all, he was a friend of a friend; it wasn't as if he were a stranger. We talked for the better part of the night. Shane had a great personality!

As morning drew near, Shane invited me to accompany him to the parade the next morning. The St. Patrick's Day Parade was sure to be a good time! Shane had tickets to the grandstand. (How he had obtained them, I never learned). I had never before met anyone with grandstand tickets—and I had been attending the parade every year for as long as I could remember. The invitation was a welcome offer, and I immediately took him up on it.

St. Patrick's Day in New York brings the green out in everyone. There are tee shirts, buttons, crazy hats, even green beer—all in the name of celebrating St. Patrick. The center line down the middle of Fifth Avenue, usually yellow, is painted green in honor of the occasion. This is done courtesy of some very benevolent New Yorker or business each year. I had no green tee shirt or buttons to signify my allegiance. But I was up for it!

We took the subway downtown early in the morning. As we emerged into the street, the music from the bagpipers grew louder. Throngs of people lined the sides of the street, watching as fire battalions, police precincts (both on foot and mounted on horseback) and school bands marched. The parade route begins at 44th Street and continues uptown to 86th Street along Fifth Avenue. Shane wove through the crowd, seemingly determined to walk the entire parade route. We proceeded to mill through the crowd as if entering the main hall of an enormous party. I remember grabbing hold of his belt loop so as not to be separated from him. He plowed through the crowd and I followed, like the tail of a kite.

Our plan was to watch the parade and then meet up with the rest of his rather large family at a midtown pub. From what I gathered, this was a yearly family tradition. Until arriving at the pub and seeing all the people there, I had no idea just how large his family was. Shane had nine brothers and sisters, who had each brought friends with them—and they were not the only ones! Everyone I met in that pub seemed to be related to Shane in some way, either family or friends. There were Irish dancers doing jigs and customers dancing with the music. The beer flowed non-stop!

I enjoy a party as much as the next person, but after being on your feet from 8:00 a.m. until 11:00 p.m. walking a parade route, and then dancing and drinking in a pub, the novelty wears off. I had had my fill of a good time and wanted to go home.

Granted, Shane and I were not long-time friends, but rather newly acquainted. Still, he had brought me down there, so my expectation was that he would see me home. Shane, however, did not want to leave. The night was young, and he had all intentions of staying to party until he could party no more. We butted heads about this almost immediately. In my mind, if Shane wanted to continue the party until the wee hours of the morning, it was not optimal—but certainly acceptable—that he remain. I would simply take a taxi home and call it a night.

But that idea seemed totally unacceptable to Shane. "We" had come to party, and "we" should remain until the party was over! And I could tell that this party was NEVER going to be over; people were literally going to drink until they passed out. I preferred to pass out at home in my own bed. This discussion quickly became a disagreement. To this day, I think the biggest cause of this conflict was the alcohol involved in both Shane's system and mine.

In the end, Shane surrendered and took me home in a taxi. We spent a few more days enjoying each other's company, and then he was whisked off to sea. Every now and again Shane would reappear. He would never stay for long.

During the 16 hours we celebrated St. Patrick's Day, we never set foot on the grandstand, despite having tickets. Those very tickets—along with a four-leaf clover—remain in a silver frame on my wall. Every time I look at them, I remember that St. Patrick's Day celebration—which almost didn't end! Together they remain my good luck charm!

42. The Lemon

THERE'S AN UNWRITTEN rule with friends: If a girl has a dating interest, and the object of that interest has a friend, the friend will assume second chair so that the two boys can double date with the girls for the purpose of keeping a balance. There is no rule, however, that the person stepping up to balance the group is under any obligation to "like" the companion for the evening! Sometimes this scenario turns out to be a pleasant surprise for the second couple. Other times—not so good.

Such is the case with the memory I have of Mo, Jimmy and Zach. Mo and Jimmy were not what you would call "dating" regularly. But from time to time, they would get together. Mo and I were different in many ways, but what we had in common was enough—we liked the same music, we liked to party, and we were very social.

Mo knew everybody. She rarely met a stranger. Mo was two years ahead of me in school, but that didn't matter. We were inseparable after school. We went to all the bars on the weekend, listening to the local bands play until the wee hours of the morning. We attended concerts. If we weren't spending time together, we either just had been or were about to be.

Mo worked as a cashier for a movie theatre on Fordham Road after school. Because she worked there, I got in free. I would sit day after day, watching the same movie over and over. I had actually gotten to the point where I could recite the movies playing word for word.

Back in the day, phone answering recordings were not considered to be good policy. So the business phone of the theatre was answered by a person. In most cases, that person was Mo. She had a great phone voice, sounding like Mae West. Mo could also talk trash with the best of them! I remember several instances when Mo was at work and received an obscene phone call. Sometimes she would talk such smack to the caller that he ended up hanging up on her. She was a trip!

On this one evening, there was not much going on. Mo and I were just killing time, smoking cigarettes and walking around the neighborhood. Mo ended up running into Jimmy. The "why" is unclear, but Jimmy decided to go get his friend, Zach, to join us.

Now remember the rule described earlier. The "friend for a double-date rule" applies when the two friends are "going somewhere" together. This was an exception to that rule, because we were going nowhere! I could have just gone home or gone somewhere else. No harm done. Nevertheless, Jimmy called Zach to join us.

The four of us took off walking. There was no place for us to go. Lacking imagination (and money), we all decided to sit in the hallway of a building down the block from where we were. None of us lived there; it was merely somewhere to go. We began walking up the stairs. Mo and Jimmy went to the landing between the fifth floor and the roof. Zach and I sat farther down, between the fifth and fourth floors. We made the usual small talk for a few minutes. Then, obviously impatient and ill-mannered, Zach pounced! There was never an understanding or intention for us to be together. So Zach must have assumed that his natural charm was enough motivation to sweep me off my feet.

If there is one thing I would have liked to convince Zach of that evening, it is that there is no romance to be had on a staircase landing in an apartment building. This was no date! This was nothing!

Zach was no prince, but he was no animal either. He accepted no for an answer. However, his disgust was evident, as he shouted up to Jimmy on the next floor, "Hey—you stuck me with a lemon!"

A Lemon? Now I'm a lemon because I don't find you so charming? I wondered what exactly the criteria were for a girl in the Bronx to be swept off her feet. I was not going to get the answer to that question that evening—not with Zach. Mo and Jimmy's interlude was cut short; Zach was not going to sit there with me, when he could be throwing himself at some other lucky girl. We ended up leaving the building abruptly.

It would be several months later when I ran into Zach again. This time, I was spending time with Shane. While I did not see him often, I went out of my way to be sure to look extra nice every time I did. There I was, looking pretty nice—if I do say so myself. And there was Zach, just finishing up an afternoon of playing ball with my friend's older brother. As I was about to be introduced to him, "This is El . . ." I interjected, " . . . the Lemon."

"That was you!" he exclaimed. I heard a gulp in his throat. It was fun to watch the blood drain from his complexion as he looked into my eyes and realized who I was. It was clear from his reaction that he did not want me to recall the details of our first meeting to my friend and his brother!

All things being equal, I enjoyed meeting Zach the second time much more than I did the first.

43. Cold Feet

IN 1979 WORK was good, but my social life was all but spiraling downward. I was meeting one guy after another, none of whom sparked any real connection. I was going out a lot – mostly on first dates, but felt quite lonely. It is impossible for me to assess how I impacted others, but minimally, I was perceived as different—as though I didn't quite fit in and more times than not, difficult.

My childhood friend, Marie, invited me to the country for the weekend. "You need to get out of the city for a while, Ellie. Come with me—I'm going to Tommy's house." There were several people going to this house for the weekend.

Tommy was from the neighborhood. I knew *of* him—but that is not to say that I knew him. Tommy was the in the early stages of building a house on the side of a mountain, on property his parents had had for many years. It was three and a half hours outside the city. Our journey to the house was very much like a pilgrimage, the way all the vehicles were following each other in a line on the interstate.

When we arrived, we discovered that the existing house was just this side of an eyesore. It must have been 100 years old and looked as if today was its last day! "Just find a spot to sleep in, and we'll see you in the morning," was all that was said upon our arrival.

"Where's the bathroom?"

No answer.

"Hey, where's the bathroom?"

One girl answered me, "You haven't been here before, have you?"

"Nope."

"Go downstairs and outside; there you are."

"Shit!"

"Precisely!"

There was no way I was walking around outside in the pitch dark by myself. I decided to just put it out of my mind and wait until morning.

Even though I was only in my early twenties, when morning came, my bladder was about to explode! I found Marie and dragged her with me. "Show me where I can go to the bathroom. You didn't tell me it was like this."

"Like what?"

"No bathroom indoors? Where the hell are we?"

"Here, follow me." She led me up a very steep hill through some trees to a make-shift outhouse. "Go here."

"Oh, my God! Where the hell are we?" I repeated.

"Roxbury."

It sounded like some country music song gone sour. "Who names a town Roxbury?"

All day long, people were milling around. There must have been 50 people there. Some were helping do carpentry work. Others were simply hanging out as if they were the entertainment. More still were planning the food preparation. It was quite an operation, despite the rustic nature of everything. Tommy was proud to show off the plans for his new home, which he intended to have built by the end of the year. I had never known anyone who built a house, so I couldn't tell if the estimate of the amount of time it would take to build this house was accurate or overly optimistic.

Everyone was drinking beer—beer, beer and more beer! The partying was increasing and the construction work was dwindling. It was obvious that alcohol was making everyone lose focus. That was all right with me, though. As afternoon became evening, more people from the town began to arrive, joining the party.

One person in particular seemed to be behind me more often than normal. At first I thought I was being followed. Later I just thought it was a coincidence. I was wrong! He was everywhere I went. "Can you excuse me?"

He laughed, but he didn't move.

"Hey, can I get by?"

Still he didn't move.

"Fine!" I took my beer mug and proceeded to empty it over his head. "There, you can move now—right?" I don't know what possessed me! Clearly, the party atmosphere didn't do much for my mood. Actually, I was usually in a bad mood—particularly in my free time. More times than not, I wanted to be left alone. That is not to say I wanted to "be" alone. I just wasn't in the mood to be friendly.

But the beer soaking that I gave this guy didn't seem to put him off too much. He came over with another beer for me and said, "I think we got off on the wrong foot."

Well, he certainly has tolerance, I thought. *I'll give him that.*

We talked for the rest of the night—about all sorts of things. My new acquaintance was Tommy's next door neighbor, living down the long driveway to the right. "My folks own the next property over. My name's John."

"Yeah. OK."

After talking most of the evening, John invited me to his house for breakfast. As I walked in, I felt I was going back in time. The house was a big farm house made of wood. It must have been 100 years old as well, but better kept up than Tommy's. Also, it had a bathroom! Yea! You just don't realize how important those conveniences are until you are in a position to make do without them.

"Here, come inside." It was a homey place, with lots of little artistic touches here and there.

"Who paints?" I asked.

"Mom. She's pretty good. She also knits and crochets. She does all that stuff. Between all of us, there's nothing we can't do!"

"Huh?"

Breakfast consisted of bacon, eggs, toast—the usual. As we finished, John jumped up and said, "I've got to do the dishes before I leave. I don't want my folks to come home to a pile full of dishes in the sink."

"Really?" I, on the other hand, couldn't have cared less about such things. I had spent literally years leaving my dirty dishes behind—not intentionally for my roommates to do, but just to leave them. I re-member thinking that this was so considerate of John. He must really be a nice guy.

The next weekend, Marie was returning to the country to visit, and I went along. I began to see John regularly on weekends. In a whirlwind three months, he proposed—and I accepted.

I do remember thinking this was quite fast to be jumping up and getting married; but I also knew I hated being out in the world dating, and I hated the idea of being alone even more. It all seemed to fit. I telephoned my mother and told her of the impending nuptials.

Had it been entirely up to me, we would have run off and gotten married—no wedding, no church. However, it wasn't entirely up to me. John wanted a wedding, so that is what we planned. The date was set for February 16th in his town of Roxbury. This seemed like a good idea. It was fun up there. That's where John's family lived.

Trying to keep things simple, I selected a dress that I really liked, yet cost only $250. The finishing touch of my outfit was a pair of white leather cowboy boots. After all, February in the Catskill Mountains was sure to see snow, and I was not going to be uncomfortable on my own wedding day!

I typed the invitations myself at work, keeping within the entire budget of $1,000, which Wally had offered to put up to cover the cost. I appreciated that he and my mother would pay for the wed-ding—but I was taken by surprise that they would not be attending. "Wally can't travel in snow. You know that," said my mother.

"Well, you can."

"I can't leave him. Who would take care of him while I'm gone?"

With no parents coming, I then telephoned my brother. I'm not sure what made me even think that asking him would be a good idea. But I called and requested that he give me away in the ceremony. I was told, "Gee, Ellen, we can't afford to drive all the way up there. We are sure excited for you, though."

Two down; one to go.

During the week I called Genie and asked her if she would be my witness. I wasn't going to have a "bridal party" per se. Only Genie. That would be it.

"Of course I will! Are you sure you want to do this?"

"Yeah."

Since there was no bridal party, there was no need to match dresses. So, Genie being my entire bridal party, I told her to pick a dress she really liked and wear it. "It's entirely up to you what you wear. Just get something pretty." She selected a purple floral dress, three-quarter length, with black shoes and long black satin gloves. She looked good—but nothing like a bridesmaid. Oh, well.

Rather unexpectedly, plans for a bachelorette party evolved. Many of the invitees were people that were associated with Tommy and going Upstate on weekends. These were not necessarily long-term friends of mine. But that was OK. My two life-long friends, Lizzy and Marie, were going to be there, and that was all that really mattered to me. Everyone else was "extra." I decided to cook them all dinner, rather than have to pay for a meal out. I prepared venison. I had thought this would be a wonderful treat, but it was met with some hesitation.

Quickly after the meal, we hit the streets—twenty or so very loud New York women. We traipsed from bar to bar, following the fleeting ideas of our drunken minds. This went on for many hours. We drank, we sang, we danced. We got crazy. At one point in the evening, we actually surrounded a taxi mid-street and began singing to it, refusing to allow it to pass. We were out of control!

It was one of those evenings that is not intended to end. The plan is simply to party until you fall over, and that was a ways off. Clubs in New York typically holler "last call" at 2:00 a.m., and we were just not ready to let that dictate the end of a perfectly good evening. So we decided to head uptown to the after-hours club in the Bronx. Now, after hours clubs are typically more "seedy" than regular bars. They are for more hard-core people—drinkers and card players, essentially. As we arrived at the door, we were met with the bouncer. One-by-one, we began recounting the events of the evening to this man (like he was interested), sharing our adventures with him. "We're not ready to go home—we want to party!" Lizzy and Marie were very assertively grabbing me by the arms to lead me in, as if clearing the way for me, "Hey, let her in—she's getting married next weekend," Lizzy blurted out.

As I looked up at the other people in the crowd, my eyes met with a familiar face. It was Cameron. I couldn't believe it! There he was, flashing his fireman's badge at the bouncer as if that would somehow gain him access to the club.

We spoke for only a moment after our eyes met. "You're a fireman? You actually became a fireman – just like you said." Lizzy pushed him aside, telling him, "Clear the way—she's getting married!" I all but told her to hush! In an instant, I was pulled away from him to enter the bar. Cameron scribbled his number on to a piece of paper and reached through the crowd to put it in my hand. "Call me," he said.

"OK."

The next morning, after struggling with the decision, I went to the payphone to call him. I must have let that phone ring 20 times. He never answered.

Everyone in New York City that was invited intended to come up for the wedding, but waited until the day of the ceremony to make the trip. My closest friends, Lizzy and Marie, were there the night before, along with my sister and me. We were all staying at John's parents' house.

That night, John had the expected bachelor party—which he chose to start having before it even began! He drank like a fish and was quite drunk early in the evening. We ran into him at the truck stop on the way upstate. He was plastered!

"Oh, no. Have you talked to him?" asked Genie.

"Who—John?"

"He's shitfaced."

I remember telling Genie not to worry, but she was correct. He was absolutely ossified!

"You need to rethink this," she said to me. The look on her face was one of panic.

All evening we discussed whether I should go through with this wedding. Discussed is not accurate—Genie practically insisted, "Don't do this! You'll regret it forever."

I was tired, Genie was frantic, and John was wasted. The combination caused me to conclude that the best thing would be to call the wedding off—and I did. I got on the phone and called down to the Bronx to the bar where I knew everyone would be and told them. The one friend on the phone asked me, "Are you sure?"

I wasn't sure of anything, but it seemed like the right thing to do at the time.

The next morning was somber, to say the least. There we were—Lizzy and Marie, my sister, Genie, myself, John's parents, and John. Oddly, John was chipper! It was as if he had no recollection of how drunk he had been or the slightest inkling that there was a problem. Ignorance is bliss! Everyone just made small talk, waiting for me to tell him. I really hated this! I hated the awkwardness of the entire incident. His drunkenness took me back to the days of my father being so drunk and out of control—and embarrassing. I kept thinking, "This was supposed to be such a great day for me—my wedding day." This was not at all turning out the way I had hoped.

I pulled John aside and told him I just couldn't go through with this. "You were absolutely plastered. I don't want that."

"Hey, you're over-reacting. It was my bachelor party! Guys always get drunk at their bachelor party."

"You were in the car on the way up here. What party were you at?"

Clearly, we had very different impressions of what the whole event was supposed to be like. John kept telling me how things were going to be so great—while my sister kept telling me how I had all the evidence I needed of how bad things were going to be in the future. I was exhausted to the point where I had no defense left.

The bottom line was, I began to feel bad—leaving John "at the altar" on our wedding day. I just felt that that was the worst thing anyone could do to anyone—ever. I couldn't do it! That afternoon I recanted and announced that we would get married. My sister then gave out. My friends took the entire event in stride; reassuring me that they would support whatever decision I made.

So my wedding day was officially "on"; as was the biggest snowfall of the year. The reality was that by the time I called the wedding back on, the snow had begun to accumulate. New York was having a blizzard. Those few who were on the road trying to come up were stuck on the New York State Thruway. Others had simply decided to stay home when they heard there was to be no wedding. The wedding was, for all intents and purposes, falling apart.

Additionally, my sister, being a photographer, had planned to take all the pictures for the wedding. However, Genie was so upset that she managed to break her camera and was reduced to taking all the photos with a Polaroid.

The wedding itself took place one hour and forty-five minutes after it was scheduled. My sister, walking up the aisle of the church in front of me, walked backwards, whispering loudly to me, "Let's get out of here—I'll help you pay for everything. Please!" It was like a Woody Allen movie gone awry!

By the time we had said our "I do's," I was exhausted to the point of collapsing. I slept in the van going from the wedding to the reception. Those in attendance were John's friends from Upstate. Most of those I had invited from the city did not make it.

There were sixteen inches of snow on the ground. Everyone's feet were freezing. Everyone's that is, except those of the bride—who was toasty warm in her cowboy boots! As it turned out, that was the only smart decision I made that day.

44. Ready, Aim, Fire

BEING MARRIED IS vastly different than being single for a multitude of reasons—the most prominent being that decisions involve more than just you. First and foremost, I was living in the Bronx and sharing an apartment with a childhood friend, Victor. John was living in upstate New York. Since John was living with his parents and had no job, it seemed obvious that we would reside in the City. John agreed and immediately moved into my apartment. He began looking for work right away and found odd jobs, but nothing steady.

I remained at Stein Trading—and loved it! The office staff threw me an impromptu wedding shower, giving me—among other items— an iron! It was almost a gag gift, in that they were always teasing me about not ironing my clothes. The party was well-spirited and the good wishes made me feel really accepted at the office; something I had not felt in other office environments.

Victor and John were getting along really well. It was a bit strange. Here I was married and trying to get used to it and the two of them would be sitting in the living room watching games together or listening to music together. It was almost as if Victor and John were married and I was the roommate! It was good that everyone was getting along so well. Also, John did drink, but nothing like what went on the night before the wedding. I was beginning to believe that that was actually a one-time event, and that I did not have to worry, as previously feared.

Not long after we were married, many of our friends from the Bronx were all gathered in the corner bar. One by one, they arrived, unplanned. We were all having a great time, listening to the juke box, buying drinks. It was a very "party" atmosphere. Most of the drinks being ordered included drinks for John and me, the new bride and groom. People were sending us one drink after another.

At one point, several people were toasting us, glasses and bottles raised, clanging together with cheers, when a pop, popping sound was heard. The thought that ran through my head was, "Who has fireworks at this time of year?" Instantly, the glasses and bottles shattered out of our hands! There was screaming heard throughout the bar, with others yelling, "Get down! Get down!" Before I could even comprehend what was happening, I found myself under a pinball machine on the side of the room. Everyone was yelling, looking for others, asking if anyone was hurt. "Are you hit?"

I remember thinking, "Hit? What happened?"

Shots had been fired through the window of the bar from the street. Someone jumped up and called the police from the payphone in the back. Ironically, the police showed up almost immediately, as if they had been right outside when the event happened. Although not frightened until it was over, realizing that we had all just been shot at and then learning from the police that it was, indeed, a high powered rifle that had been used scared me to death! "If you were ever thinking about moving from the city, this would be the perfect time for us to discuss this!" I said to John. I loved the city as much as anyone; but getting shot at was not in my plans at all! Within two weeks, we had packed up everything we owned and moved upstate.

John's parents were thrilled that we had decided to relocate back to that area. My parents, however, were a bit surprised. "It's so far into the country. Are you going to like it?"

In truth I didn't know if I would like it or not. I was certain I didn't like being shot at! I began to look for work, and John began to look for a place for us to live. It wasn't too long before we found both. John worked at a sawmill, and I began taking civil service exams, trying to find placement working for the county. We lived in a place called a hamlet – not even a town, I thought. It was like being in some sort of children's book! This little hamlet was very much like a fictitious town that was so far behind anything I was used to I almost couldn't adjust. The house we rented was very small, although big enough for the two of us. It was a cottage. We would drive to work every day and come home every night. It was a simple existence, but a pleasant one. I spent my weekends fixing up the house as best I could.

Television reception in our little hamlet left a great deal to be desired. The few channels we could pick up were snowy and difficult to make out. In fact, I remember one specific occasion when the television drama, *Dallas,* came on so clearly that I had to sit up and take notice. "Hey—check this out," I told John. We can see it clear as a bell tonight." I realized after I had said it that my life had gotten pretty ridiculous when the big news was good reception for *Dallas!*

Only six months after we had found the cottage, we stumbled upon a used mobile home that was for sale. It was a bargain with two bedrooms, one bath, living room and kitchen. And it was cute! John's parents gave us three acres of land at the bottom of their parcel on which we could place the mobile home. Of course, electricity had to be run and sewer line installed. Still, it was exciting planning for this.

That parcel of three acres meant more to me than I ever thought possible. I mowed it every week with a push mower, just thrilled to death at how wonderful it looked after I was finished. Mowing the lawn can give a great sense of satisfaction—of which I had had no idea until then! I planted flowers. We even had a rose garden.

After the first year, we decided to create our own vegetable garden. We planted three rows of tomatoes, 12 plants in each row. In the very center of the tomato plants, we inserted three marijuana plants, thinking we were pretty smooth putting them where they wouldn't be noticed. But John's father, a practical joker, noticed them right away. He took tomatoes and with twist ties, attached them to the pot plants, so that we would know that *he* knew they were there!

Every evening we would all eat dinner together. John's parents were terrific cooks, and eating with them was always fun. At times, we would just stay in the upstairs bedroom at their place, rather than walk down the hill to our own trailer. The practical joking escalated between John's father and me.

John's mother was quite a character. She had lots of pets: A cocker-poo (cross bred dog—part cocker spaniel, part poodle) named Casey;

a cat named Willy; a ferret named Acey Deuce; and a boa constrictor named Stanley. I liked most of the pets, but I was afraid of Stanley. My fear of this animal was unwarranted. Stanley was very tame and had been raised by John's parents from a baby. John's mother would handle him a good bit—more so when she had been drinking. She would sit at the dinner table drinking beer and after a few, she would go into the living room and pull Stanley out of his cage and start waving him around. He didn't mind it; *I* did!

One evening we had stayed upstairs at John's parents'. It was a hot summer night. In the middle of the night, I awoke and had to go to the bathroom. As I came downstairs and walked past Stanley's cage, I noticed out of the corner of my eye that it was empty. Stanley was out! I had to go to the bathroom, but had instant visions of Stanley wrapping himself around my leg as I was seated on the toilet. I was terrified! I began slamming things around thinking that the noise would wake someone up and they could find Stanley. My efforts were useless. After banging around for several minutes, I decided that the direct approach was going to be much more effective. I knocked on the bedroom door and woke up my in-laws. "Stanley's out—you have to find him!" The old man just laughed as he walked around the house looking for Stanley. It took a while, but he found him wrapped around a pipe in the basement ceiling.

"He just wanted a place to cool off," he said.

"Yeah, sure he did!" I just wanted to go to the bathroom in peace. Was that so much to ask?

The fact that the old man laughed about my being afraid didn't sit too well with me. So as I entered the bathroom, I started looking around for ideas. *What can I do to him?* I thought. I sat on the toilet pondering my retaliation. I looked across the room, and on top of the linen closet was a margarine cup that contained his teeth. Every night, the old man would take out his teeth and put them in this cup to soak. "That's it!" I snuck into the kitchen, got the pepper, and dumped as much of it as I could into the dish. "This will fix his wagon," I thought.

The next morning at 4:30, the in-laws got up for work. "Ah-h-h!"

screamed John's dad. His yelling woke me up, and I laughed out loud. *That's better,* I thought to myself. I rolled over, pulling the covers up with a sense of contentment that I had evened up the score.

As it turned out, the score would never be "even" between John's father and me. There was no way he was going to sit back and take this. Knowing how skittish I was about critters, he was determined to get the upper hand. I walked up the stairs one day to the spare bedroom where John and I had slept, only to see a huge lump in the bed. Now, this was an old farm house. I thought, "This lump has to be a rat or something undesirable!" I grabbed my baseball bat and beat that lump, which I imagined to be a rat, until I was certain it was dead. The old man howled with laughter.

I was a wreck! "There's a rat in the bed!"

John ran up the stairs and pulled the blanket back. "It's a zucchini, dummy!"

This city girl was having a time getting used to all this country living.

After a year of being married, we learned that John's aunt had passed away. She was the only sister to four brothers and the first of the siblings to die. The family was very sad, as she was a favorite of all of them. I never had the pleasure of actually meeting her, but had heard many nice stories about her. It was planned that we would all ride down to the city to attend the wake and funeral.

Right before departing, we received a phone call from the doctor. The rabbit had died, as well. I was pregnant. As John's aunt left us, another family member was preparing to arrive. Sad as everyone was, the unhappiness took a back seat to the news that a baby was coming.

45. Labor of Love

AFTER COMPLETING THE Civil Service test in Upstate New York, I found myself in the number one slot for a clerical position. Because of this ranking, I was going to be called for any and all Civil Service positions for which I qualified. Until I declined it, the position would be mine for the taking.

Initially I found myself working at the State University library. The staff there was less than friendly. The majority of the women there in key positions resented anyone new coming in and made that known in no uncertain terms. They would do nothing to help incorporate you into the system, and everything to alienate you. After a very short time, I realized that my tolerating this treatment for the sake of having an income was not worth it.

Because this was a Civil Service position, however, I was instantly awarded vacation and sick time—which I proceeded to take full advantage of while looking for another position. I returned myself to the pool of candidates and found another, more suitable and likable position closer to home. The position was in an out-patient drug rehabilitation facility staffed with a director, two full-time counselors, and a secretary/office manager. Coincidentally or ironically, everyone on staff was from one of the five burroughs in New York City. Birds of a feather! The program did outreach presentations in the school system, as well as counseling. Some of this was mandated by the courts.

In many respects, this was not a dream job. But in a few key ways, it was perfect. The Director happened to be an eccentric, who dabbled in antique dealing on the side. Everyone on staff tended to master trivia in some manner. We could be closing a staff meeting, and the Director would throw out a challenge like, "If you can sing the entire theme song to the Beverly Hillbillies Show, you can have tomorrow off with pay." It was a lot of fun!

John had also found gainful employment working for the County as a driver. He would take Medicaid recipients to and from doctor's appointments when they could not drive themselves, for whatever reason. Both of us together were still not making a lot of money, but we did not have a big overhead either. The situation was perfect. Also, being civil servants, we both had excellent medical coverage, so the pregnancy and delivery were going to cost practically nothing.

I was in excellent shape physically. My health always seemed just short of perfect, with a low resistance to germs. The pre-natal vitamins seemed to be just what the doctor ordered to make the difference. For the first time in my life, I felt invincible. I was never sick—not as much as a sniffle—that is, if you discount the morning sickness, which lasted three months! I really enjoyed being pregnant. It was a bit scary mentally, but I felt better than I had ever felt before. My weight was only 108 lbs. at the start. By the ninth month, I had gained 25 pounds exactly—and a few of those were the very welcome addition to my cup size! It was like a miracle. I had spent my entire teenage life waiting for nature to really kick in and develop me, but it never did. I remained skinny and flat-chested. During the pregnancy, however, that changed.

My due date was July 1st, which came and went without incident. I had spent the better part of the second trimester sewing. I handmade the quilt, comforter, diaper bag, dust ruffle, and curtains for the baby's room. I also knitted a bunting bag and a blanket with the help of my mother-in-law, who brought me pattern after pattern until we found just the right one. I was really quite proud of myself for having become so domestic.

On my actual due date, I stacked three full cords of wood, thinking that the exercise would help things along—and also that I had better get it done before the baby came, because there would be no time afterwards. Day after day, I waited like a bomb ready to explode. NOTHING! By the 11th day, I was overly emotional and crying almost all the time.

It should be noted that my husband, father-in-law and father were all born on the 13th of their respective months. On the morning of July 12th, I went into labor. John and his dad began to celebrate, assuming I would be in labor 24 hours and produce a son on the 13th. Personally, while a son or daughter was fine with me, I was not interested in being in labor for 24 hours! That was nuts!

We drove to the hospital in Oneonta, New York, about an hour from the house. There I found that I was one of many women who had gone into labor that morning. Fox Hospital was a tiny community hospital at that time, and an onslaught of laboring women was difficult to accommodate. They simply didn't have the room for all of us. Being one of the last to arrive, I found that all the beds were taken. I remained in the waiting room with the families of those who were waiting for women already inside.

The nurses told me to walk. "This will help your labor along," they told me.

"OK." I walked, and walked, and walked. I walked so much that I began relaying messages of progress to the families waiting, and then carrying ice chips and good wishes to the laboring mothers. In short, I was like a candy striper in labor! Around 12:30, my doctor called for me to be brought in, at which time he manually broke my water. There is so much that is done to and around you when you are having a baby, the process is almost overwhelming.

We had both taken the natural childbirth classes prior to this date. At this point, I couldn't have cared less about that! The only thing I was concerned about was not asking for any drugs too early, as I was convinced this would prolong the delivery, and then I wouldn't be given drugs later when it got unbearable! So I waited and toughed it out. The laboring process was nothing troublesome for me up until my water was broken. After that, the show was on! I couldn't walk around any longer. I lay on my side, just trying to bear the pain.

Trying to be encouraging, John leaned over the gurney (as they still had no actual bed for me) and began doing the breathing. "Hee, hee, hee, blow. Hee, hee, hee, blow."

The nurse standing at the foot of the gurney said, "You're doing great, Ellen—that breathing will take the edge off it."

In my pain, I lay there thinking, "You are such an idiot! That's him! I haven't taken a breath since I lay down!"

The woman across the hall from me was screaming at the top of her lungs. "Help me! Help me—WHOH!" she would scream. Then she would vomit. It was horrifying! I had listened to this poor woman all morning while I walked the halls, and it was still going on. The agony in her voice was scaring me to death. "Nurse, can't you help her?"

"No. She's sick. She ate a huge meal before she came in last night at midnight. We can't give her anything."

"MIDNIGHT?" Oh gosh! That meant that I would be screaming like that hours from now. *Don't take any drugs yet. Don't even ask for them,* I thought.

My next sensation was that of spontaneous convulsions. My body had taken on a life of its own and was ridden with spasms. "Call the nurse, quick, something's wrong."

John called for the nurse who came immediately with another nurse.

"I'm getting sick and I can't stop."

The nurse said, really calmly, "Let's see what's going on here." I hated that I was on the verge of losing it, and yet she was talking to me as if she were sedated. "You're crowning! We have to get you into delivery—NOW!"

"What?" I sat straight up on the gurney. "I haven't even hit transition yet!"

They all laughed at me. The fact was; I was having the baby right then and there, less than 90 minutes after they broke my water. The nurses came and pushed me into the delivery room, which was down the hall. As we passed the doorway of that poor woman who was ill and screaming in pain, she glared at me as if to say, "What the hell is this? That woman just got here!"

Two pushes and a lot of commotion later, out she came—7 pounds, 6 ½ ounces of pink baby. She was adorable! We named her Marlo—after Marlo Thomas, who I thought was the most beautiful woman I had ever seen.

Sixteen babies were born that day, in four rooms. I don't know how they did it, but the staff managed everything without incident.

Once you have a baby, everyone treats you as if you had just found the cure for the common cold. You're a hero! You get whatever you want to eat; you get gifts. And, despite this elevation to a new status of accomplishment externally, internally I was reduced to that of a nervous wreck. I had never held a baby in my entire life. She was so cute! The nurse continued to check on us, asking if she should take the baby back to the nursery so that I could get some sleep. I had waited nine months to see her. "No, you can't take her to the nursery. Leave her here!" I held on to her in the bed with me and wouldn't let her go. Finally I dozed off.

I awoke suddenly, realizing that the baby was gone. I looked under the covers, under the pillows—nothing. The bed rails were up, and I tried to look over them to see if she had fallen under the bed. "Shit, I've lost the baby!"

I was frantic, looking everywhere, when the nurse came in and laughed at me, "This crazy woman thinks she lost her baby. We took her so that you could get some rest."

"I told you to leave her here! I'm *not* crazy—you didn't listen to me!"

After 24 more hours, we were sent home with a clean bill of health. I couldn't wait to put the baby in the room I had fixed up for her. No sooner had I come home, than there was a knock on the door. John was at work by this time, so the baby and I were there alone. I looked through the glass pane in the door and saw that it was my sister-in-law and her three children, coming to see the baby. "Just a minute," I yelled. Quickly, I shut the bedroom door to the baby's room. I returned to open the front door just a crack.

"Hey . . ."

"Hey, Ellie—we came to see the baby."

"She's sleeping."

"Well, just let us peek at her a minute. We won't wake her."

"No. Come back next week." I really liked my sister-in-law, but I didn't want to let her and the kids come in. I just knew something would happen to the baby if I let people near her.

"What? We're not going to hurt her, Ellie."

"I can't. I just can't." I kept the door locked and hid in the baby's room the rest of the day.

46. Huggies

ONE COMMONALITY OF first-born children is the array of photographs taken. Everything they do warrants being commemorated and preserved—forever. Baby Marlo got cuter and cuter as she grew. She went from being a tiny little newborn to a roly-poly toddler. I took one picture of her after another. Everything she did was a photo op. My sister, a side-line working photographer, joined in taking photos of little Marlo. "She should be a model," she said as serious as she could be.

"Yeah, right," I replied.

"I'm serious! You should get her signed up as a model. Do you know how much that pays?"

Until she said it, I hadn't given it a thought. But from then on it was on my radar. I began to search out child modeling agencies looking for just the right one with which to sign her up. The requirements would have been stiff had I not had a photographer in the family.

"Please submit an 8x10 glossy with all pertinent information on the back to xxxx."

I no sooner sent off her photo to the agency I had selected than I got back an acceptance letter. Shortly after, I received another notification requesting that I bring her to New York City to audition in person. It was on! I made arrangements to take off from work, packed an overnight bag, and left with Marlo in tow.

The drive to the city was just over three hours long. Genie lived in Manhattan and agreed to let me stay with her, despite the size and impracticality of her apartment. Forget child-proofing! Genie's apartment was, in fact, a one-room studio apartment with everything from a canopy bed to file cabinets full of negatives. It was a small space with a lot of items! Still, staying overnight in New York City was going to be quite expensive. We certainly didn't have money for something like that. So Genie's invitation was accepted.

The audition took several hours. It was the equivalent of a casting call in a hotel room—although not as seedy. There were hundreds of children with their moms crammed into this very tiny space. All of them were dressed up in taffeta dresses, hair bows, and tights—all, that is, except little Marlo, who was dressed in a sweat suit and boots. I neither had the ability nor the inclination to make her sit all dressed up in frills for a three-hour van ride and an undetermined amount of time, waiting for someone to take a split second look at her and say, "Eh!" She would, at least, be comfortable.

Sure enough, one child after another became restless and antsy. The temperature in the room began rising as well, with as many people as were there. In short, it was hot as hell. All these poor little Shirley Temple "wanna be's" suffered in the waiting area. Little Marlo just sat there playing with her plastic keys and drinking her juice. She was always good, and this was no exception.

After hours of waiting, Marlo got in. They took one look at her and said, "She's perfect," to which I thought to myself, *no kidding!*

"We'll send the papers over."

"Over where?"

I left and met up with Genie in mid-town. When I told her what was said, she jumped up.

"Holy shit—she got it!"

"I guess . . . got what?"

"That was for a Huggies commercial, you idiot! She's gonna be great!"

I thought to myself, *OK, they'll take a picture of her and use it on the diaper bags, or something like that.*

Oddly, the job location was far more congested than the casting call, in that as many children were all crowded into a room in a hotel, and in an adjoining room, lights, camera and action were happening. Admittedly, I was nervous. I didn't want Marlo to be handled by strangers when she went in. Just because she was going to have her picture taken did not warrant her being passed around. It was a pleasant surprise when a very well-dressed black woman came out and said, "Is this Marlo?"

"Yes, it is."

"Come with me."

I followed the woman into what looked like a photo studio.

"May I?" she asked with her arms extended.

"Yes."

I handed Marlo over to the woman, who was ever so gentle placing Marlo on her lap.

"How are you, little one?" she asked Marlo.

Marlo looked up at the woman and in a second, began to scream at the top of her lungs.

"What's the matter, honey?" the woman asked of her softly.

"Yeah, what's the matter Marlo?" I had been so relieved that it was a woman (not a man) taking her in, it had never occurred to me that Marlo would not be as relieved to be handed off to a total stranger. She continued to scream uncontrollably. At this point, the woman handed her back to me and said, "I'm sorry; we can't use her."

Marlo and I left the hotel and returned to Genie's apartment. I remember thinking to myself, *what was I doing putting her through that? She's just a baby!*

I spent the day visiting with my sister and making the most of this trip—which would clearly signify the end to Marlo's modeling career. We walked all around town taking in the sights, grabbing bites of favorite foods. Occasionally we stopped to take our own pictures.

Genie and I engaged in conversation about that fateful night when she came home from being out and bled so profusely.

"What ever happened to you?" I asked. Genie then divulged the details of how she had been raped by this boy she had gone out with. She had previously been cautioned not to see him by my mother and begged to avoid him by his own sister—whom he had also attacked. I always felt terrible that his sister had found the courage to talk to Genie about it, and yet Genie ignored the warning.

Genie's apartment on 73rd and Central Park West was only a block or so from a triangular island known as Needle Park. As we approached the park on our walk this time, she extended her arm out and pointed, "There's *Asshole*," pointing her finger at a man lying on the ground in the park.

"Who?"

"The guy who raped me."

"Oh, God—he's this close to your apartment?"

"Yes. Whenever I'm feeling down, I walk this way. It makes me feel really good to see him lying in the street like this."

"Surely you're kidding."

"No, Im not."

"What could you be thinking?"

"I'm thinking - I win!"

47. A-Hunting We Will Go

BACK AT THE office, I was the only member of the staff to have children. Therefore, my pregnancy, my condition, and everything that followed were of interest to my coworkers. It was as if the baby had three built-in uncles! Work, although not lucrative, had a very stabilizing effect on my existence.

Being a new mother was not so much tiring as it was stressful. The baby slept through the night from the age of ten days. It was as if she knew I was ridden with anxiety and would not be able to take much. I went to work every morning, driving over the back side of the mountain into town; home for lunch to breast feed; and then back to the office for the afternoon. It was a great life—if you discount the increasingly excessive drinking of my husband.

John truly had a wonderful nature about him. He was a genuinely good person with a good heart. But he found cause to celebrate everything—like it being Wednesday! Not a day went by that he did not drink.

On the weekends, many people from the city would come up to visit. Although they were actually staying next door at Tommy's house, they would eat with us. John was a great cook. The drunker he got, the better he cooked. (I never understood that.)

He was also a marksman shot. He once kicked the door of the trailer open while grabbing his gun, and shot a woodchuck in the field in front of the house. Now, we had a rule: If you kill it, you eat it! That was all well and good. But I—being from the city and having no idea how to cook anything more complex than an egg—had no idea what to do with this thing.

That Friday, as usual, people came up to visit. There we were with this dead woodchuck. I was at a loss as to what to do, so I did what any non-cooking New Yorker would do: I "shake-and-baked" it!

We all sat around eating and drinking. Everyone seemed to like the meal—until one guest commented, "This is good, but the bones are in the wrong place."

"What?"

"You know how when you eat a chicken leg, the bones are always where you know where they are? These aren't. It's like . . . it's different somehow. But it's good."

"That's 'cause it's not chicken."

"What is it?"

I now had everyone's undivided attention as they sat meat in hand. "It's shake-and-bake woodchuck!" No amount of alcohol (or any other substance) was going to smooth that news over!

That evening everyone went out into town. John went with them, at my prompting. I was fine sitting with the baby. He was gone until 1:00 a.m. or so. When he finally came home, he could barely make it in the door without help. Everyone took this in stride, evidently thinking that it was no big deal; they had all gone out and had a good time—some more than most. But for me, the novelty of this type of entrance was wearing thin.

By winter, this had become a common occurrence. I told myself that this behavior would somehow be curtailed after the end of the Holiday season. I was wrong. It actually got worse.

In early January, John went out with the boys as usual. When he returned, he was carried in the door and placed on the couch in the living room. He was virtually unconscious. I went into our bedroom thinking he was "out" for the night and that I should just go to bed. Not two minutes later, I heard a thud. John was wide-eyed, glazed over, and reaching for the gun rack. Grabbing his AR-15, he slapped a banana clip with 30 rounds into it and began searching the trailer. "They're after me!"

"Who?"

"Who do you think?"

"I have no idea. Put the gun down."

"I can't—they'll get me."

There I stood in the hallway of the trailer, dressed in woolen socks, jeans and a tee shirt. John shoved his way past me into the baby's room. Of all places, he concluded that someone was crouched underneath the crib and hidden by the bed skirt. He raised the rifle up, supporting it against his shoulder, and grabbed the trigger. I was sick! I leaned over and whispered into his ear, "Honey, let me get the baby so that if there's a scuffle, she's not in the way."

"Good idea!"

In one sweeping grab, I lifted Marlo and the blanket she was under, scooped her up, and whisked her out of there. Without even stopping to grab my purse or a coat, I jumped in the car in the front yard. It happened to be the county car that John drove for work, and I knew he always left the keys in it. I started the car up and took off down the road.

It was now January 8th. The temperature was 12 degrees and there was snow on the ground. I had no shoes, no coat, no diapers, no purse, and nowhere to go. As I turned the heat of the car on full blast, all I knew was that I was getting the hell out of there!

As I drove over the mountain, I tried to think of places I could go. Two towns away, a girl that worked in the same building as I lived in a large farm house with her roommates. Surely she would let me stay there—at least for the night. I drove to her house and knocked on the door. "Sorry to wake you, but John's having an episode and I had to get out quick."

"Oh, God—Are you OK? Come in." She was really kind. She didn't complain or anything. In fact, she drove to town to purchase diapers and baby food for me, so that we had plenty to take care of the baby. "Don't worry. Stay here as long as you need to."

By morning, the reality of my situation had settled in. I was stranded! I had nothing but a baby and the clothes on my back. John, on the other hand, may have shot himself in the trailer—who knew? I deliberately didn't call the police, because as good a shot as John was, he was sure to take a few of them out before they could apprehend him. By leaving the situation as it was, I figured that only *John* was in danger—and that was the lesser of the evils.

Somehow—I assume by a process of elimination—John found me later that afternoon. He had blacked out and come to seeing bullets, the gun—and nothing else. The baby and I were gone. He had no idea what had happened. "I'm so sorry. I want you to come home."

"I can't live like this—and I won't."

"I'll never touch another drop—nothing—ever again." We went back to the trailer together.

It would be eight months of total happiness in our little trailer. John was sober, charming, and helpful. "Good John" was back! Unfortunately, nothing lasts forever. At dinner with his parents one night, John's mother—having had quite a few herself—began to insist that John have a drink with her. "You have every right to drink. She's just trying to control you, that's all."

I couldn't believe what I was hearing. The conversation went from that to the NRA slogan of ". . . having a right to bear arms."

"I have a right to sleep at night! Doesn't that count for something?"

It was literally a tug of war—and John was the rope. In an instant, I lost. He was drinking again—at his mother's request!

I stood up from the table, grabbed the baby, and said, "I hope you will all be very happy together." I was gone the next day.

I was now on my own with a baby. Without her, I would have folded somehow. But there is no giving up when you are a mother. You *have to* survive; it's your job!

I found an apartment two towns away. It was no frills, but I liked it. I went to the bank and begged them to take John's name off the loan papers for my van. I got a few pieces of furniture—enough for my bedroom and the baby's. John kept everything else, including the furniture I had when we met.

For an entire year, I lived two towns away from John. I thought he would straighten himself out and things could be back to the way they had been. But in looking back, I see the reality of the situation. John was a drinker. He was always going to be a drinker. *I* was the thing that didn't fit into his life, and making just over ten thousand dollars a year, I was never going to be able to do any better than I was doing at that moment—not there. I did not know what I should do. All I knew was that waiting for John to change was the equivalent of doing nothing.

48. Exertion

MY LIFE HAD taken a series of turns, and I was now at a crossroads as to what to do. With the intention of getting away, clearing my head and thinking, I accepted Genie's invitation to come to the city for a visit and a walk around town during the St. Patrick's Day parade. My vehicle was an old, maroon Chevy van. I remember calling it my "answer grape" because it got me where I wanted to go.

Genie's apartment was on 73rd Street and Central Park West. Regardless of the location, Manhattan is nowhere to be looking for a parking spot, even on the average day. St. Patrick's Day is far more congested! By some miracle, I found a spot right across the street from Genie's building. She had been watching out her window and saw me coming down the street. I pulled up next to the spot, thrilled that there was a vacancy. But Genie and I both looked at the size of the spot in relation to the size of my very long van and shook our heads thinking, *no way!*

Now, parking spots do not grow on trees in Manhattan. The fact that I was looking at an opening meant that I was surely not going to find two. There had to be some way I could get into this spot! I was determined. I began inching forward and back, forward and back, repeating this time after time, thinking I could just inch my way in. The spot was almost exactly the size of the van. I could very well have been doing this for hours.

In the midst of my feeble attempt, a group of boys (college age) walked up, beers in hand, and began watching me trying to squeeze this monster of a van into this space—all the while blocking traffic on the street. With a thunderous roar, they cheered and surrounded the van. "We'll help ya!" they cheered. This group, seemingly out of control—certainly out of their minds—lifted the van and placed it into the spot, with only inches to spare on either end!

Inside the van, I was stunned into disbelief. The boys continued to cheer their accomplishment all the way down the street. My sister, though aghast at the sight, wanted to run and get her camera to capture the moment, but couldn't tear herself away. I remember thinking; *I'll never be able to get out of this spot, now that I'm in it.*

Genie just laughed and said, "Don't worry. Once the alternate side of the street parking kicks in, everyone will take off and you can move easily!"

"Terrific," I said sarcastically. "That's two days from now!"

During that visit, Genie and I were on foot visiting every bakery, eatery and novelty shop in the area. That was how our visits were spent, few and far between as they were. We would walk, grab something to eat, talk, and take in the sights, sounds and smells of New York. We would reminisce about when we were younger and living at home—together. We shared memories.

When we were growing up, we shared a bedroom. The room was good sized, with a "double" of single beds; by that, I mean that there was one huge headboard (King Size) in the center of the wall with two single beds attached to it. These beds were on metal frames with wheels, so that when you wanted to make them single, you could simply push them apart. My bed was on the window side of the room. Genie's bed was on the door side. Because I was so much younger than she was, I would usually be in bed first. That is not to say I would be asleep by the time she came to bed; many a night, I would toss and turn—thinking about things I couldn't figure out—and still be wide awake when Genie came in.

Occasionally Genie would play a game with me while we lay in bed. The game was called Exertion. One would extend her arm out so that the other could reach it. Then the other would attempt to make tingling sensations up and down the arm with her fingertips. If the person doing the tingling was unsuccessful at making the other laugh, she would then say "E-X-E-R-T-I-O-N" over and over until the other one broke down in laughter. We would do this for quite a while. It was a silly game between sisters, but I remember it fondly.

During these sessions, we would have some deep conversations about life, God, death—big things that were puzzling us. I remember Genie explaining God to me as this wonderful bright light of energy that would come to us when we die. I asked her, "What if we don't go to it? What if it scares us?"

"Don't worry—you won't be scared. You won't be able to resist it," Genie replied. "Besides, I'll die first; so I'll be there, and you can come to me!"

During one of our childhood vacations to Illinois, I managed to climb up the ladder of a corkscrew slide right behind my cousins. The bad news was that I became terrified once I got to the top. I froze. I couldn't bring myself to slide down, and I couldn't manage to back down the ladder. A long line of kids behind me were getting anxious—which compounded my fear. Genie jumped up and climbed up the ladder, telling me, "Come on! I'll sit down, and you can slide down on my lap. You'll love it!" Down we went. It had been it frightening imagining this, but once I had done it, I agreed that it was fun.

So there were times when Genie was very much the good big sister—protective, mentoring, kind. Other times, however—particularly when around her friends—she could be distanced and cruel. As we got older and our age difference became less significant, the distance lessened considerably, and Genie became "the good sister" all the time.

Genie's friends from the neighborhood were very important to her—as were mine to me. We craved being out of the house, and our friends then became our family in the street. Genie had many friends.

One of Genie's girlfriends who lived across the street, Janet, grew up dating just one single boy, named Adam. They were sweethearts from the first. Adam and Janet dated all through childhood and married once they became of age. After some time, they moved to Florida, and I had a pleasant visit with them one time, after I found out they were there. Adam and Janet had a young son, who looked just like them. I viewed their life together as one of those happy love stories you imagine more than see in real life.

Physically, Janet could have been a model. She was very tall and very thin and had long, blonde hair and blue eyes. She was gorgeous! Janet had a younger sister my age, Beth. Beth was also a beauty. While Beth and I did not hang around together, we knew each other and got along well.

One evening while bathing her son, Janet fell ill; suffering from a grand-mal seizure. Doctors were baffled. Janet had no history of a head injury or illness that would have caused such a thing. She was only in her 30's when this happened. Her condition deteriorated rapidly.

Despite efforts to solve this problem—up to and including exploratory brain surgery—Janet's condition worsened to the point of her being completely unable to communicate or take care of herself. For the rest of her life, she was to remain hospitalized with round-the-clock care, kept alive by machines and equipment. Genie actually went to see Janet after this happened and was shaken to her core. "It was horrible to see her like that. It's like she's trapped!"

Genie got on a kick after that to the point of being obsessed. She would tell me every chance she got, "Don't leave me hooked up to machines like that! If that ever happens to me. Promise me you will take me off the machines. Promise! Mom won't do it, you know that. Tell me you'll do it!"

"OK! Jesus, stop talking like this!"

If we spoke about anything at that time, we ended up having this conversation. It was bizarre.

While Genie's thought process was strange, her lifestyle was stranger. Genie worked at night as a legal proofreader. She would read huge corporate takeover documents and correct them for grammar and punctuation. What a job! How she got into doing this, I am not sure. But she liked it, because she liked the hours and the money was good.

Working at night allowed Genie the freedom to take photography jobs during the day. If she had had her way, she would have done photography full time. Somehow, she was never able to break free and do it. She was a good photographer, though. Most of the pictures I have of myself that I like are pictures Genie took. She had a good eye for framing a picture and knew how to capture the essence of a person.

Because of her weird hours, Genie's schedule was very much in contrast with that of the rest of society. By that, I mean that everyone else seemed to work days, while Genie worked nights. Therefore, to call her at what seemed to be a normal hour for you would make her really mad. "You know I work nights—I sleep from 3:30 p.m. until 11:30 p.m. Why is that so difficult for you to remember?" Every time she was disturbed, Genie would yell at the person responsible. She was angry a good bit of the time.

God forbid if anyone ever made Genie mad; she was not going to just be mad quietly! She would scream at them—even people she didn't know. I remember being with Genie in Manhattan on more than one occasion when this occurred. We looked very much alike despite the age difference, so it was impossible for me to step away from her and pretend that we were not together.

I recall in particular one time when we were waiting for a bus. When the bus came, this old woman inched her way in front of Genie to get on the bus first. Now, there was no pushing ahead of Genie— even if you were elderly! "I can't wait until I'm 90 F- - -ing years old, so I can shove everyone else back. What the hell is this? Am I invisible?"

The woman became frightened, and upon sitting down on the bus, she actually shrank down in her seat as if to hide. Bad luck for that poor woman, however! We ended up seated directly across from her on the bus. Genie wouldn't stop. "Yes, I'm talking to you! How dare you push ahead of me! What, were you afraid I'd take your seat?"

I leaned over to her and said, "Genie, stop—you're scaring the s- - t out of her. Leave her alone!"

"Oh, don't you start with me, now! You're sympathetic with her because you don't live here in this city, having to take it from people every day." There was no stopping Genie and no shutting her up!

Another time, after we got into a taxi and were seated in the back of the cab, Genie lit a cigarette. The taxi driver (who was not originally from the U.S. and spoke very little English) held up an inhaler, signaling her through his rear-view mirror, "Asthma, Asthma—no smoka here."

"What? Are you kidding me? Let me tell you something! You're the driver. That means you work for *me*. This is MY cab, and I'll smoke in it if I want to." Turning to me then, Genie said under her breath, "Can't speak a word of English, but he can manage to tell me I can't smoke! What the hell is this?" Leaning up toward the bullet-proof shield between the driver and the passengers, she began yelling again, "How is my smoking impacting you, when this damn thing could stop a bullet? Tell me that!" The driver appeared frightened, looking to me to get Genie to stop somehow. I just shrugged my shoulders and smiled at him, as if to say, "Oh, well. She's my sister, but I can't control her!" As a final exclamation to her tirade, Genie leaned up against the bullet-proof shield. Pulling the change cup towards her, she blew smoke into it, slamming the cup against the window so that it would open up on the driver's side. "There's your tip! Shut up while you are driving people who are paying you." I thought I would die!

As hostile as she appeared to the total stranger, however, Genie was a total riot to be around. Whatever we were doing, we would end up laughing uncontrollably. There was always something hilariously funny about what Genie was saying or doing—even if she wasn't necessarily enjoying herself. Genie was quite a character.

Genie's apartment was on the first floor of what used to be a hotel in Manhattan, directly across the street from the Dakotas. What it lacked in sized, it made up for in location. Her apartment door faced into a long hallway located on the side of the building. It had the appearance of a service entrance. On many occasions, casting calls were held in the building by other tenants. The line for such events would extend down this hallway, leaving those auditioning leaning up against the wall (and door) of her apartment. The echoes of reciting lines, scales being sung, or chatter would often keep her from entering into the slumber she longed for after a hard night's work. This was nothing to be taken lying down!

In an effort to disturb those hopefuls in the hallway, Genie would take a metal trash can—similar to one that you would find in a classroom—place it on its side with a boom box in it, and push it up to the metal door of her apartment like a megaphone blaring one CLASH tune after another. "Damn if I'm going to have to listen to them ramble on!" she would declare in a huff. "I'll rock your Kasbah!" Somehow the knowledge of retaliation was enough to lull her to sleep with a smile on her face. With the music blasting from her apartment into the hallway, Genie slept like a baby!

49. Black and White

WORK CONTINUED TO be very much a feast or famine environment, in that the workload was either overwhelming or non-existent. The counselors were wonderful people and good friends, but they were terrible at keeping up with their dictation. What would prompt them to bring their case records current was the threat of an audit from the State of New York. Therefore, upon news that there would be an audit visit, the three of them would dictate like madmen and then dump days of dictation onto me to be transcribed in hours. I was a very fast typist—but this was mayhem!

The rest of the time, I did whatever I wanted to entertain myself, which was fine just so long as I didn't leave the office. I would pass the time reading periodicals, journals—anything I could get my hands on just to make the day go faster.

One dreary afternoon I sat there alone reading an article about child abuse and the warning signs. It had been written for teachers as a guide to watching for signs from students. This list included:

- Fear or dislike of certain people or places;
- Problems in school, poor grades;
- Withdrawal from family, friends, or usual activities;
- Eating disorders—eating very little or excessively;
- Hostility or aggressive behaviors;
- Drug or alcohol problems;
- Suicidal thoughts or attempts.

Damn, that sounds a lot like me, I thought. I felt progressively more uncomfortable thinking back to that night so many years ago in my room.

Oh, God—is that what's wrong with me? I had always felt like a bit of a square peg in a round hole, but this was staring back at me in black and white.

As the counselors returned from their days on the road, I began asking questions, without trying to sound *too* interested or targeted on this topic. They discussed this as if it were information you would read on a prescription bottle label—very unemotional, very detached. But I wasn't feeling detached. I was feeling like a leper!

Nowhere in this onslaught of information that was coming at me was there any information on how to "fix" someone like this. *Is this just a laundry list of how you can tell if a person is broken?* I wondered. *And once they are broken, then what? Do you have no choice but to throw them away?*

I had a very lengthy history of anti-social clashes with people, relationships that, upon reflection, seemed more like a series of one-night-stands than dating, and now what was turning out to be a failed marriage to an alcoholic/substance abuser. When the counselors began telling me the tendency of children raised in alcoholic families to then grow up and seek out another alcoholic, because ". . . that is what they are used to." I felt positively doomed! Was the "bad" going to haunt me forever? Was every man in my life just another replica of my father falling down drunk in front of the apartment building calling my name? What was there to look forward to? Even worse, was I now going to inflict this baggage on my daughter? *I've got to get out of here!* I thought.

After much deliberation, including some counseling from a local therapist, I decided that the best thing I could do was to quit my job, pack my things, and move to Florida. Once there, I could divorce John and begin anew.

One of the counselors and I went out for a rare lunch together. There was nowhere in that town to eat, so it was necessary to drive to the next town. The road between the two was a straight, two-lane road with fields on both sides, with the occasional house or store sprinkled in. As we drove, we saw a man riding horseback through the fields, headed in the same direction as we were going. "Man, I'd love to take a ride today and just take off," I said out loud. "I wish I didn't have to go back to work."

"Me too," my friend commented.

On we went, grabbed a bite, and then headed back to the office. As we pulled into the parking lot and around back to the entrance of our office, there stood the man we had seen riding, alongside his horse. We looked at each other in surprise, my coworker and I. The man extended the reigns to me and said, "Wanna take a ride?" I thought my friend would fall over!

I couldn't help but have this huge smile on my face. "No—but thanks anyway."

"Are you kidding? Take it!"

"No, I better go inside." I grinned from ear to ear all the way into the building.

"You should have gone; that's so weird that he was here!" said my friend.

"No it's not," I said. "It's not the ride itself; it's the offer that's special."

Where was that coming from? All of a sudden I am speaking like David Carradine in Kung Fu!

Towards the end of my employment at Drug Abuse, I often found myself talking to coworkers and others from the building. It seems the closer you get to leaving, the more you want to say to people.

One evening, a coworker and I seemed to linger a good while after everyone was gone, just talking. As we stood there, a gust of wind blew from out of nowhere. I covered my eyes to avoid dust going in. As I did, a piece of paper blew against my leg and stuck there. I went to brush it off, but unsuccessfully. So instead, I grabbed it and noticed that it was a cartoon. It was a picture of a cow at a computer. The caption read, "Not to worry, I'm into the feed allotment!" I kept that cartoon—but I didn't know why.

With every possession stuffed into my Chevy van, I, my daughter, and our cat (Mario Zumo) embarked on our next adventure. We left Upstate New York with barely enough money to make the trip. The drive was sure to take 24 hours, and I honestly didn't know how I would do it.

I began to think of places where I could stop along the way. I would arrive, stay the night, and then depart quickly the next morning. The first stop was at the home of Lynda, a former neighbor and friend from Tampa, who now lived in Jersey. I stopped to visit with her and spend the night. Next was Wally's sister's house in Virginia.

The weather was uncooperative. It was steamy hot all the way to Georgia. My van, although mechanically sound, had no air conditioning. Unfamiliar with travel, the cat was not taking to the journey as well as we had hoped, and was repeatedly trying to jump out the window. So we kept the windows rolled up. It was sweltering! We would listen to music and make the best of things, calling at the end of each day to advise that we were safe and how far we had come.

Upon reaching Georgia, we were advised that Hurricane Elena was hitting the state of Florida, and travel was not advised. I had no choice but to check into a hotel. I carried my daughter in with just enough clothes to change into. When I went back to the van after the cat, he was gone.

Now this cat, Mario Zumo, had the coloration of a Holstein cow—black and white markings. He had been named after a boy in the high school I attended in New York. The boy was a rather round-faced Italian boy, a bit heavy. His entrance into the gymnasium at any point in a game would elicit the chanting of the crowd, "Mar-i-o-ZU-MO" made to sound like the marching monkey brigade in the Wizard of Oz. Every time the chanting would start, Mario's face would turn red like a tomato. We weren't even close friends—I just loved his name and the fun we had chanting it.

Anyway, Mario the cat was now missing. We looked everywhere. Of course, I couldn't ask around about him; there were not supposed to be any pets at the hotel. It was so hot! We were so hungry! I really didn't like having to look for this animal that had clearly jumped ship on us. But I wanted to find him so that he didn't get hit by a car. And besides, my daughter really liked him. Mario was her pet.

Just when I thought we had looked everywhere, there was Mario lounging on the ledge of the hotel pool and draping his tail into the water. That poor cat was so hot from the trip that a dip in the pool looked good to him. We snatched him up and threw him into the room.

The next day, enough of the storm had passed through and we were back on the road headed towards Tampa. My mother had been kept informed by telephone that we were on our way and the approximate time of our arrival. It was another long day of driving, but we made it safe and sound.

Oddly, as we pulled in, the expression on Wally's face indicated that he had had absolutely no idea we were coming.

"Hey—you made it!" my mother came out of the house waving.

"Yeah . . . and you forgot to tell Wally?"

"Oh well, you're here now. That's what counts."

No, I thought to myself. *What counts is that now I have gone from the frying pan into the fire and will now be used as a ping pong ball in your arguments.* I really hated being in that position.

My sister-in-law, who was a head hunter for a local employment agency, knew that I was on the way and had been looking for job prospects for me. Upon my arrival, she informed me that I had been set up with an interview the next day. Ironically, the job was at a flour Mill. I interviewed and was hired that day. My duties consisted of managing the flour and feed sales desk. *This is a very strange coincidence,* I thought, remembering that piece of paper that the wind had blown up before I left New York. I instantly flashed back to the cartoon of the cows "into the feed allotment."

They asked when I could start work.

"Immediately," I replied.

I began the next day—Friday the 13th.

Stage VI

50. Separation Anxiety

IT WAS A new day, a new town (somewhat), and a new job—all in a 24-hour period. I didn't relish the idea of living back at home with my mother and Wally, but it beat living in the Catskills worrying if I was going to wake up looking down the barrel of a rifle! I was a 28-year-old single parent with a full-time job making $3.25 per hour.

My first day at the mill was spent familiarizing myself with the surroundings and the people with whom I would be working most closely. I was taken on a tour of the facility by my boss, who was very matter-of-fact about it all. The office was a small room upstairs from the mill and packing areas, which were both quite dusty on their best day. The furniture in the office was "late 60's meets paneling." The more I looked around, the more I realized that wearing jeans might just classify me as being overdressed in this place!

There were three clerks who worked in the main part of the office, and two "bosses"—one a supervisor, and one the Plant Manager. In case there was any doubt in your mind—the clerks were female and the bosses, male. It was a pleasant enough environment. I was clearly the most outspoken one of the group.

That is not to say I was the most talkative. The woman who sat behind me, Joann, was a character! Just 33 years old, Joann already had two grown children and a grandchild. She drove a Corvette, which she covered with a canvas top to protect it from the flour blowing over it—which would damage the paint. Joann was someone who very much wanted to be larger in life than she actually was. She wanted a perfect house, perfect family, and perfect car—the works. Unfortunately, there was no way this was going to become a reality, because she did not begin with the perfect husband! Lyle was what I call a trouser snake. He would flirt with anything in a skirt, regardless of whether Joann was there or not. I hated this for her, but she ignored it.

Behind Joann sat a girl named Tina, who had just filled the position there. Tina was about my age and very Southern. Her accent was as thick as Joann's. Tina and I became friendly and enjoyed many a conversation while we worked. We would just talk over the cubicles to one another. It wasn't private, but it was friendly.

Tina and I got along famously. She lived with her parents, farther away from work than she liked, and I was ready to break free on my own. So together we looked for and found a brand new apartment complex in the north part of town, which we decided to move into together.

I took the master bedroom so that I could have a bathroom right there for my daughter, who shared the room with me. I got a suite of furniture for the bedroom from a rent-to-own place, as well as a single bed for my daughter, which was kept against the wall on the other side. It was perfect!

The next step in my liberation was to obtain a divorce. I began looking for a lawyer. While reading a magazine one day, I discovered this woman attorney who was supposed to be a real barracuda of a lawyer. Knowing full well I wanted someone who would guarantee that I would keep my daughter with me, I called her office. She was very nice. I explained my situation briefly, and she began to inquire: "Do you want to retain the house, cars, property?"

"Property? No. All I want is my daughter." Truth was, the three acres of land was still in John's parents' name—and under the circumstances, I really didn't want to live next door to them. I walked away from the furniture. I had my van; he had his truck. What was to settle?

"May I speak frankly?" the attorney asked.

"Why yes, of course."

"You are trying to retain an elephant gun to shoot a dog."

"Huh?"

"My retainer fee is $10,000. I can recommend someone to you who is very good and will not cost you nearly that amount."

"That would be great!"

The attorney she referred me to was right down the road from my office. I was anxious to see him to find out just how much I would need to get this started. In our first meeting, he informed me that his fee would be $1,500—much lower than the price of an "elephant gun"! Still, I didn't have it. I had nothing. I made an appointment with the local credit union loan officer to see about borrowing the money. The woman advised me up front, "If anything comes back on your credit report, I can't do it." Crossing my fingers, I hoped it would be OK. After much of what felt like begging, I was approved for the loan. I took the $1,500 to the lawyer's office and began divorce proceedings.

With me being in one state and John being in another, I had thought living in Florida was going to protect me and my daughter as residents. Once we had lived there for six months, we would become official residents, and therefore Florida—not New York—would have jurisdiction over the divorce. I also thought it would be too far for John to go to contest the divorce. But clearly I had underestimated his desire to argue this!

One afternoon, my attorney had a teleconference set up with John and his attorney, and they began to talk about things like child support, visitation, and shared custody.

"What? Oh, Hell no! I spent an entire year up there living two towns away and he wanted nothing to do with her. He has not supported her in any way for over a year and a half, but now he wants to exercise his rights? *Do* something!"

My lawyer began talking about negotiating these points. My eyes were crossing, and I thought my head would explode. "Can I say something?"

"Yes."

"Is this XXX on the phone?" (referring to the other attorney—a lawyer I knew from when I had worked at the Drug Abuse agency).

"Yes, it is."

"And is John sitting there where he can hear me?"

"Yes."

I leaned forward to talk into the phone speaker. "LISTEN TO ME!

Either you sign these papers and leave us alone, or I will cancel payment on this check I have written to my attorney, and I will take the money and pay someone to make you disappear. I am quite sure it won't end up costing me $1,500; it will probably be considered a public service!"

As I looked up I could see the color draining from my attorney's complexion. "What are you doing? You can't say that on my phone!"

"I'm doing what I thought I hired *you* to do. You're supposed to be a barracuda—not just some fish!"

He looked at the phone and said, "Well, do we have an agreement?"

The other attorney said, "He's signing the papers."

My lawyer looked at me and said, "What did you need me for?"

I just rolled my eyes and said, "I was just thinking the same thing!"

51. Going Through the Mill

MEETING ON FRIDAY the 13th could have been either good or bad. Superstition is just a silly game we play in our own minds.

Our first meeting was in a group. I remember thinking that he had a strange look in his eyes when he looked at me. Still, we did make a good team. I sold flour, and he packed it. Truth was that Bobby was foreman of the packing crew. He managed the crew and the maintenance on all the equipment—and just made things happen.

Bobby was so quiet; I still can't believe we spoke enough to get to know each other. I must have been doing all the talking. What I remember most about the early days of knowing him was that there was no request I could make that he could not make happen.

My new employer was a flour mill/small pack business that sold flour to businesses like Publix, Dominos, etc. Eager to make a good name for myself with the customers and with the manager, I succeeded in selling more flour than anyone ever had before. It was customer service—and I was good at it. The more customers saw me come through on last minute orders, the more of them they would place. I would call downstairs at the end of the day and spring truckloads of orders on the packing crew. No matter what it was, Bobby would say, "O-o-o-K!" I asked; he delivered. For those really last minute, miraculous orders, I would insist that the customer send me a dozen roses as a bonus—which he/she would do. There were times when I had enough flowers to convince people I was about to die!

Bobby and I worked so well together keeping customers happy that I suppose it was destiny that we wind up together. We would talk about orders all the time, and then personal details would bleed into the work conversation. Little by little, we began to talk. After one very long production run, Bobby invited me for pizza and beer after work. "Sure," I said. The restaurant was very close to where I lived, which would allow me an easy getaway if need be. But there was no need. We talked for hours upon hours, until it was quite late.

Most of our communication somehow surrounded work. Still, there were times when we departed from the work environment and went off to talk somewhere else. We found a spot downtown near the water where the Gasparilla ship[1] was docked. We would go down to the ship, sit by the water, and talk until all hours. It was relaxing; it was pleasant; it was invigorating—all at the same time.

Bobby always presented himself as someone who was alone in the world. He had a "loner" quality about him. Although he was not secretive, I was shocked when I discovered that Bobby was married and had children. He just seemed so alone to me. The fact that he appeared this way made it very plausible that he was not "together" with his wife—meaning that they were two very different people who just happened to live at the same address.

We talked about how things were, what Bobby's family situation was. While we spent a great deal of time together, we were not physically involved. He did say more than once that he was not "there" anymore. He spoke about leaving and starting over, worrying about the children, etc. I did not encourage him to leave. The fact was—he was already gone. He just hadn't packed or changed his address.

On most days, Bobby arrived at work in a truck. Every now and then, he would ride a motorcycle. Upon seeing him on this, I hollered across the parking lot, "Hey, are you here to take me for a ride?"

"You want one?"

"Na, not today. Maybe someday."

With July 4th weekend coming up, Bobby advised that he would bring his motorcycle up my way and take me for a ride. "Sounds good," I said. July 4th was on a Friday that year, making the holiday a three-day weekend. The entire weekend, I sat in the house close to the phone, thinking that Bobby was coming. The weather was clear and sunny. He never showed.

---

[1]INFORMATION PERTAINING TO Gasparilla Day and the commemorative ship can be found at: http://www.gasparillapiratefest.com/history.shtml

The longer you sit by a phone, the more disturbed you become when it doesn't ring. I waited and waited. Nothing. By Monday morning, I felt amply put off. I would have been fine, had he not said he was coming; I am capable of entertaining myself. But after Bobby had said he was coming, I stayed around waiting, wasting the entire weekend. I was not happy!

I came to the office, put my purse down, pulled around my chair, and sat down at my desk, getting ready to plow through the workload. The ladies behind me were talking, "Hey, did you hear what happened this weekend? Bobby was in a motorcycle accident."

"Huh?"

"Yeah, he's messed up—bad."

"Where is he?"

"He's in Tampa General ICU. He may not make it."

"WHAT?"

As many times as I have ever thought to myself, *Oh, he/she better have a good excuse* (for whatever)—*or be dead,* here we were!

I worked all day. The plant was a union plant. Since I worked in the office and Bobby was an hourly employee, fraternization of any kind was prohibited. But I did want to find out how he was. I telephoned the hospital and was put through to the nurse's station on the floor outside ICU. After I inquired what Bobby's condition was, the nurse asked, "Are you a relative?"

I knew he had a family and I knew he was one of ten children. Odds are there would be somebody there who would know I wasn't family. "No, ma'am."

"That's OK—we have to ask. He has not had a single visitor here since he came in."

"No one?"

"No—he's alone."

"Oh, my God!" Not only was he in critical condition—but he was in critical condition alone.

At lunchtime I grabbed Tina and told her what I had found out. "I really would like to go see Bobby, just so he knows someone is asking about him. I don't want to go alone, though. Will you go with me?"

"Sure. We'll go at 5:00."

Tina and I rode in separate cars over to the hospital, but went upstairs together. Because it was ICU, only one of us could go in at a time. "You go in, Ellen—I'll wait out here."

As I entered the room, I heard beeps and noises associated with the machinery and equipment. Bobby was lying flat on his back, his leg suspended by trapeze ropes. There was a huge metal rod above his injured leg, with three smaller steel rods protruding from his kneecap, shin and ankle. His entire arm was bruised badly, his hand blackened and swollen to the point that it appeared to be a black rubber glove filled with fluid. He was conscious, but he could not move. I looked at his eyes. He appeared trapped inside his own body. His only means of communication was blinking.

I didn't speak much. I just patted his hand gently and kept telling him, "You're going to be OK. You're going to get better. Just hang in there."

I remember walking out of the room after the 10 minutes were up, and my knees were buckling as I made it to the hall. "He looks horrible," I told Tina.

"Oh, no! Is he going to make it?"

"I don't know. It's bad."

I now knew what had prevented Bobby from coming to take me for the ride. I also knew without a doubt that had I been on the bike when he wrecked, I'd either be lying next to him or dead.

Bobby was about 220 pounds before the accident. Six weeks later, when he stood up for the first time, he weighed just over 160. But he looked infinitely better standing!

Then I learned the rest of the story: Bobby had announced that he intended to leave, that the marriage was over. A few hours later, when the police notified the family of the accident, his wife responded with, "He's dead to me," and left him there alone. But days later, she decided that this would be the perfect opportunity to try to put things back together. She quit her job and made herself a fixture in the hospital room. She stayed at his side for the duration, only to be told, "I'm leaving as soon as I can walk."

I liked Bobby very much, and I knew he liked me. But it was not until I realized that he could die that I began to get a glimpse of how his death would impact me. It was not even the thought of his death that bothered me so much—it was more the thought of his absence.

Not long after Bobby's discharge from the hospital, he came to stay with me. I remember asking him, "What's your favorite thing to eat?"

"Lasagna."

I then went home and asked Tina, "How do you make lasagna? It's his favorite."

"Are you serious? You don't know how to make lasagna?"

"I don't know how to cook!"

"Here—look! The recipe is on the box!"

"Oh."

Our first dinner was lasagna—the first of many.

52. A Simple Acquisition

THERE IS AN effect that occurs when there is a change to any existing environment. I refer to this effect as a weight shift. What that means is that the weight of the environment must rebalance itself. Most notably, a weight shift occurs when the number in a household changes, either by addition or subtraction. It is not necessarily a bad thing or a good thing—just a change worthy of being noted.

When the household previously occupied by myself, my daughter, and Tina was changed by the addition of Bobby, a weight shift occurred. In many ways, it was a pleasant addition. Bobby took up very little space. In fact, he was one of the lowest maintenance individuals I had ever met! He had very little in the way of possessions; everything he had fit inside the cab of his truck.

Bobby's work clothes were uniforms consisting of white pants and shirts. They were easily laundered. The first time I ironed them, Bobby was so appreciative! I was not one to iron (as a rule), but these items were clearly the type that needed to be smoothed out to look even halfway decent, and it only took a few minutes. Without saying so, I think what he liked about it was that someone thought enough of him to care what his clothes looked like when he wore them. That was—and still is—the basis of our relationship, in a nutshell. The little things mean a lot.

On weekends Bobby and I would visit with his children. There were four of them, ranging in age from 3 to 13. My own daughter was also 3. Sometimes we would all go to the apartment complex swimming pool for an afternoon of play. Other times, we would go to a restaurant to eat, or to a park. Bobby tried very hard both to entertain and to relax his children. It was obvious there was tension, but we tried to work through it.

One of the most pronounced differences between the children

was their possessions. My own daughter had several pairs of shoes to choose from. Conversely, Bobby's daughters had only what they would bring with them—and that was usually quite limited, if anything. We decided it would make sense to purchase clothing for the children so that they would have more variety to choose from when they did come to the apartment. We purchased two outfits for each, with shoes to match.

Bobby's youngest daughter was so taken with her new shoes that she begged to take them home with her, rather than leaving them in the apartment. I remember them vividly: they were Stride Rite blue leather Mary Janes. Every time she would put those shoes on, her entire demeanor changed. It was as if she were Dorothy with the ruby slippers! She loved those shoes. With her making such a fuss about it, we agreed that she could take them home with her, but encouraged her to bring them back when she came next, so that she would have them to wear.

It was no more than two weeks later when the children came to visit. As always, they had brought a change of clothing with them in a brown paper bag. As I was going through things, I asked, "Where are your blue shoes?"

"Mommy took them."

"What do you mean, Mommy took them? Where are they?"

"When I showed them to her, she took them. I don't have them anymore."

I was furious! Aside from the obvious—a $35 pair of shoes was gone—Bobby's daughter now didn't have proper shoes to wear when we went out. We were then faced with a dilemma: Do we purchase yet another pair of shoes and keep them at the apartment, or do we refuse and just let her go without?

Every time the children would visit, there would be some similar situation. One would come with pants and no shirt; another would have a shirt and pants, but no socks. There was always something missing, always something wrong. The battle lines were being drawn across the children's heads.

As concerns about the children escalated, so did our concerns about the job. Because we worked at a union plant, fraternization of any kind was prohibited. We were beyond fraternizing—we were living in the same apartment! In order to keep up appearances, a second telephone line was installed exclusively for Bobby. If his phone rang, only he would answer it. Likewise he would not answer ours. His address reflected a post office box.

As decisions like these had to be made, we would sit down and discuss how we would handle them one at a time. But the decisions were mounting up.

Very early one Saturday morning, the phone rang. Since it was my phone line, I answered it. Oddly, it was for Bobby. As he spoke, I could tell that we were about to be called upon to manage another problem. The children's mother had gone out the night before, leaving them in the care of the oldest child. She had gone to a bar or a club and spent the better part of the evening drinking and dancing. As she and someone from the club were driving home, they hit another vehicle, causing that vehicle to burst into flames. In a panic, they had fled the scene. She was now calling Bobby to find out what to do. Bobby recommended the best course of action, which was to turn herself in to the authorities, and he left the apartment to take her to do just that. Not minutes afterwards, we both realized that this meant the children would be alone again. What should we do? I knew if it were my daughter, I would want her taken care of. I suggested that Bobby bring them to the apartment.

It was only a matter of about 36 hours before the incident had been sorted out and the children's mother returned to collect them. She was angry that they had been brought to our apartment! On many levels, her anger would build from this point forward.

The next weekend we were to visit, we took the children to a park with a zoo. We spent the afternoon going on rides and petting animals. They had a ball! Children sleep really well when they are tired out. Although sleeping on the floor, they had passed out before 7:30 that evening.

The next morning, we all got dressed and headed out for breakfast. I noted that just going out to eat had turned into a production—having to dress so many others and then myself. We had our breakfast, and then the children began asking if we could go to the pool. "OK. Wait. No. We can't. You don't have your bathing suits with you." Things like this were making us crazy. We never had what the children needed when they needed it. Out we went to the store to buy each of them a new swimming suit. By the time we got to the pool, we really felt that we had earned it!

That evening, the children were to go back home. We had had a wonderful visit with them. They all piled into the vehicle and waved goodbye. About 20 minutes later, Bobby called from a payphone near their house. "She's gone."

"What do you mean, she's gone?"

"I mean, I am at the apartment trying to bring the kids back—and their mother is not there."

"Maybe she just went to the store or something. Give her a few minutes."

"No, I mean the door is open, there are people in the apartment as if she is having a party, but she is not here. What should I do?"

"Call the police!"

"What?"

"Call the police so that you have a witness that you tried to bring the children back and couldn't."

Hours later, Bobby returned to the apartment with the children. It was now Sunday evening at 9:30, the children were tired and confused, and Bobby and I needed to get ready for work the next day. "What am I going to do with the kids?" asked Bobby.

"I don't know. But we can't just leave them. I'll call in sick. I get sick days. That's the best answer. This way, I'll stay with them and you can go to work. It would be much worse if you called in; that might shut down the packing line."

"You sure you don't mind?"

"No, it's OK."

I did just that. I called in and stayed with the kids all the next day. Monday evening, their mother called. "Hey, were you going to bring the kids back?" She acted as though nothing had happened. Bobby was furious!

"What are you doing? You just take off when I'm supposed to bring the kids back?"

"I knew you'd take care of them." Those were the truest words she had ever spoken. *She knew he would take care of them.*

For the next few months, the scheduling and transfer of the children got more and more out of control, resulting in our repeatedly having to change plans at a moment's notice. In the meantime, another legal problem arose—one that required money. Money that Bobby's ex-wife didn't have. As usual, she called on Bobby to "fix" the problem. But the biggest on-going problem was the children. They were being left on their own or unclaimed like freight. Worse, we realized that this was always going to go on.

All the while, we were hoping that things would settle down. But all the while, things were getting much worse! We decided to make Bobby's "ex" an offer: There was a rather large bill coming due surrounding a legal matter. She was responsible for this. We would pay her the money she wanted (and needed) in lieu of surrendering her custody of the children. With absolutely no hesitation, the children's mother immediately signed all the children over to Bobby as sole custodian. The document—a napkin from a local diner—was signed by their mother and witnessed by a waitress.

The children arrived the next weekend with everything they were going to be given. Four children, two brown paper bags full of clothing. The cost: $3,200. The "weight" of the apartment was shifting, yet again. There would be no more juggling the children back and forth, no more looking for shoes that weren't there. At the end of the day, we had five children, two adults (Tina had moved out), a two-bedroom apartment, and two bags of clothes. Priceless!

53. Living to Work

SIMPLY MANAGING FIVE children can be quite a challenge. Going from one to five overnight is even more drastic. There is no gradual increase. BAM—five children!

The amount of laundry was staggering. A washing machine became the equivalent of the Hope Diamond. At the time, there was a place for a washer/dryer in the apartment, but I did not have one. That meant that I had to take the laundry down a flight of stairs and across the apartment complex to the laundry room and sit there while it was being done. The upside was this (and there really always is an upside): If I managed to time it just right, there would be 8 machines open at one time for the 8 loads of wash I had to do, so I could do it all at once! Conveniently, the laundry room was adjacent to the complex's pool. Sometimes I would go and lie out by the pool while the laundry was being done. At other times, there was just too much going on at once for me to think about relaxing.

There was also the matter of logistics. Five children went in five different directions. The oldest girl, mentally challenged, was physically 8 years of age, but had—and would retain—the developmental capacity of only a three-year-old. She was also non-verbal. Her condition qualified her to attend a special school on the other side of town, which accommodated the distance by providing transportation on a special bus. The other children, however, had to be taken to their respective schools, the youngest to daycare.

With that many people in the household, the instant I woke up, I was stressed over getting them ready and taking them where they needed to go. And all this had to be done before 8 a.m., when I was to be at work myself. In the evenings, the reverse was true. Gather everyone from their respective locations, get homework under way, schedule baths (yes, when you have 7 people and one bathroom, you *schedule!*) and prepare dinner. I was running like a crazy woman every day.

Of everything required of me to master the care of all of these little people, dinner was the worst. I was never much of a cook. I attribute this to my not *liking* to cook. I like to *eat*. It's much different. I am interested in coming to an already set table, sitting down, and enjoying a meal. Having to toil over planning, preparation, and serving leaves little appetite. But for the sake of the children, I was giving it the old college try.

Every night I would struggle with the notion of what to prepare. Children aren't particularly interested in meals. They are interested in eating. When you ask a child if he or she is hungry, they envision things like chicken nuggets, hamburgers, hot dogs, etc. I, however, have never been much of a fast food lover. (I have eaten my fair share, certainly; but this is not my first choice.) No, I was determined to do this well! I would think of things that I was reasonably certain I could prepare without burning or messing up in some way, and I would begin to cook. I started off simply—things like home-made macaroni and cheese with burgers, or meatloaf and mashed potatoes. Once you have made them for the first time, you are assured you can get through it.

My problem was not so much in the actual preparation of the meal; my problem was figuring out the quantity! I had spent my entire life thus far successfully avoiding cooking. On that rare occasion when I finally did cook, it was for no more than two people. Now I was preparing dinner for seven! I proceeded from a position of logic: Plan, Cook, Serve, Eat—all done in pecking order by age. Bobby's plate would be fixed first, then the children's, from oldest to youngest. My plate was fixed last.

I would fill each plate with what had been cooked—meat, potato, vegetable, whatever—and place it on the table in front of the intended. Sadly, when I finally got to my plate, there would usually be none left! It was very frustrating to have to go through all that cooking, only to have everyone else served but myself. Bobby would try to fix things by telling everyone, "OK, kids, scrape a little off of your plate onto this plate."

"NO!!!"

He meant well, but that was actually worse. Now the kids were fixing my mistake! So I would go into the kitchen and fix myself a peanut butter and jelly sandwich. Not what I wanted, but all I could grab in one minute. I was miserable! Worse—I felt like a failure.

Our next dilemma was with Bobby's handicapped daughter. Every time I would ask for a volunteer to set the table, I would be told rather insistently, "She can't eat with a fork; she has to use a spoon."

"Why?"

"That's what Momma says."

I'm sure I rolled my eyes in disgust, thinking, *Momma isn't here!*

Then I began to look at this objectively. *Why* can't *she eat with a fork? What's going to happen to her?* I asked Bobby about it, and he informed me that the school she was attending advised them to give her a spoon to eat with—to be safer.

"*I* can't eat with a spoon—and I can eat pretty well! How is she supposed to pull it off?" To prove my point, I began instructing the children to place only spoons at each place setting. "If she has to eat with a spoon, we all do!" It only took a few meals for everyone to realize that this was crazy! Eating was becoming more annoying than anything else. So then we gave her a fork—just like we had. Surprisingly, she did much better with that than she had with a spoon.

In no time at all, we realized that life in an apartment with this many people was not going to work. Coincidentally, the manager of the apartment complex advised me that we were going to be evicted. "On what grounds?" I yelled.

"You have too many people living in this apartment. They are not listed on the lease."

"My rent is paid on time every month. You can't put us out in the street. We have children living here!"

"You can't stay."

"Fine!" I said, "You put us out, and I will have Channel 8 News here with cameras telling everyone how despite our rent being paid on time, you chose to put a couple with five little children out in the street."

While they never agreed to wait, the managers never brought it up again.

Bobby and I were hard pressed to find a larger place. We had very little money, yet needed something that would accommodate our sizable family. Fortunately I had a friend who worked in real estate. David was a friend from the apartment complex I had lived in when I first moved to Florida. He was one of those people who wasn't around much, but it was a grand occasion when he was. David was "good people"! He began showing me house after house.

After only a short time, we found a house that was facing a foreclosure. The house had a non-qualifying assumable mortgage attached, which meant that we did not have to qualify for a mortgage loan. We merely had to agree on the down payment with the sellers and take over the payments. Simple! Though we had barely any furniture and not so much in the way of possessions, we now had a home!

The move itself took one afternoon. We informed the children that the boys would be in one room and the girls in another. Since it was "their" room, if they could agree with each other, they could select a color and we would paint it any way they wanted. The boys picked a light blue. The girls picked purple. I remember the paint exactly. It was named "Plum Crazy"!

As I said, we had very little furniture—only what I had had in the apartment. That consisted of the master bedroom furniture and a bed for my daughter, plus a couch and a coffee table that I had purchased used for $50. In short, there were no beds for the other children. For the moment, they were sleeping on the floor in blankets. We certainly did not want that to last long. Somehow, we had to get furniture.

The company vacation policy was set up so that if an employee wanted, they could "sell back" their vacation, or cash it in. This way, the employee would get an extra week's pay, rather than taking the week off. Bobby was entitled to three weeks' vacation. He sold all three. He also worked all the overtime he was able, which amounted to quite a bit. On average, he worked 84 hours per week. All of his money went towards the family.

Bobby was working 12-hour shifts at the plant. I worked 8 hours per day. For each of us, the end of the day was the end of our energy. Still, there was much to do with the house, and we would be at it until very late every evening.

Bobby was absolutely relentless in trying to get everything set up for the children. He would come home from working, change into shorts, and then begin. He spent every evening either painting, fixing, or putting furniture together—doing whatever needed to be done. Then, with only a few hours of sleep, he would begin another day of a 12-hour shift—and then come home to do another room.

Some evenings Bobby would be painting and would continue to paint until late, regardless of sleep deprivation, regardless of aches and pains. I would get so tired just watching, I would cry. "You can't keep going like this. You're going to have a heart attack and then what? I will have to take care of all these kids by myself! *You have to get some rest!*"

Bobby would stop painting for a moment, sigh, and say, "If you will just stop crying and complaining, I'll be able to do this. I can't listen to you and keep this up."

He was Yoda: "Do or do not; there is no *try*."

54. His, Mine and Ours

WE HAD TALKED of marriage several times, Bobby and I. Punctuating every discussion was the looming fact that both he and I had been married before. More to the point, my divorce had cost me $1,500. In all honesty, I didn't want to go through this again. If we wanted to be together, we *would* be. We already were. What was the need for marriage?

While Bobby and I talked about marriage occasionally, the children seemed preoccupied with the topic. My own daughter repeatedly mentioned a wedding. I never did understand what the attraction was for them. We were all there together. Yet at least once a day, I found myself defending not being married—to the children. "You know, most people don't discuss this with their children." After seeing them replay *The Parent Trap* over and over again, it occurred to me that the girls were plotting their own parts in the wedding: bridesmaids in fancy dresses. This was not about us—it was about the production!

I remembered my first wedding—a production of sorts. The expense, while certainly not extravagant, was money that could have been better spent, regardless of the outcome. I just wasn't enthusiastic about this.

What I *was* enthusiastic about was my pregnancy. Bobby and I were expecting a son. Now, I know that back in the day, people preferred marriage to precede pregnancy. But in this day and age, it was not so much an issue. In any case, it wasn't an issue for *me*.

As everyone was settling into the house, however, a strange dynamic was occurring. Within any altercation what-so-ever, dividing lines were being drawn.

"I'll tell my daddy!"

or

"My mother said . . . ."

It was becoming more and more obvious.

By now there were clearly lines of possession being argued over what the children thought were "his" or "hers" in the home. What was also escalating was everyone's excitement about the arrival of a new baby brother; something that became an increasingly more arguable point as time went on.

"He's *my* baby brother."

"No, my mother is having him—he's *mine!*"

In the beginning, it seemed amusing. It quickly wore thin, however. As we drove down the road in the van suggesting names for the baby, another tug of war ensued.

"Mine."

"No, mine!"

"ENOUGH already. He's *all y'all's* brother."

Bobby, still angered by the argument itself, did not see the humor in my asking him, "'*All y'all's*'? Are you serious?"

It became clear that the children needed clear lines of ownership, and that marriage would provide those lines. I then remembered what my good friend, Lynda, had once said to me about this, "It doesn't matter if you can see yourself spending the rest of your life with him. What matters is—can you see yourself spending the rest of your life *without* him?"

I could not.

On a very rainy Saturday morning, I began to look through the yellow pages for a Justice of the Peace or Notary who could marry us. I found one—a very nice man (on the telephone), who said he could marry us that afternoon if we came to his home. I telephoned Bobby at work. "What time are you working till this afternoon?"

"I don't know. Why?"

"I found a Justice of the Peace who can marry us at 5:00 this afternoon. Do you want to do this?"

"Yeah, but let me see if we can get finished (working) by then."

It was that simple. I began to look for something for each of us to wear; called my mother to have her watch the kids; ordered a boutonniere for Bobby's lapel and 6 white roses (one for each child) for me to carry—and we were off!

At about 4:30, the rain stopped and the sun came out. It was steamy hot. We drove to the home of the Justice of the Peace, about 20 minutes from ours. His wife was my witness, and his daughter sat at a piano in the living room and played a wedding march—to which I did not walk, as there was nowhere to actually go! In less than five minutes, we were married. From there we went to Burger King and, from the drive-thru, ordered two vanilla shakes. Then we went back to my mother's house, picked up the kids, and went home.

As conversations about our getting married continued, we informed the children that we had *already* gotten married. We showed them the rings, the papers, etc.

"What? You didn't invite us?"

"No, typically the children don't attend."

They were quite disappointed. But it was done.

55. Something Fishy

FOR CLOSE TO four years, we resided in that first house, thinking we would be there forever. Every weekend, all of us would be out in the yard planting, landscaping, trimming. We loved gardening and had managed to turn it into a family affair. We had the most beautiful yard in the neighborhood. I had lived in a trailer before, but beyond that, had always rented. This was a home in which I had part ownership. It was mine! Every minute I spent either thinking of how to fix up the house or actually working on it. It was a love affair of a project!

Bobby—who worked non-stop every day—came home one evening and during dinner, began to tell me with great excitement how he had seen a huge aquarium and how beautiful it was.

"You have to come with me to this store where I saw it!"

I instantly felt ill with suspicion.

"What's wrong?" he asked.

"You don't go anywhere but work. You don't shop for your own underwear. How did you happen to go into this store?" Clearly, I was so stressed that I was losing it.

"I just passed the store on the way home so often, I decided to stop in."

That weekend we went to the store. It was as Bobby had described—they had huge aquariums for sale, all types and sizes. The two of us fell in love with the idea immediately. "Something so large in our home will have to match everything. We should design our own."

I honestly don't know what we were thinking. We had a house full of children and more bills than we had money. Yet not only did we decide with certainty that we would purchase an aquarium—but that it would have to match our décor! *What décor?* We had used furniture that I had found, picked up at yard sales and Salvation Army discount stores, or been given by neighbors. Granted, I had taken all these pieces and had them upholstered to coordinate together, and they did look nice. But we were hardly living a life that would require something custom made!

It would be six weeks before the aquarium would be delivered— and another six before the water inside could be cycled so we could add the pretty fish. Talk about anti-climactic! We so wanted to put fish in that aquarium that I thought one of us would throw the other in just to watch something swim!

Once the time finally came when we could, we purchased one fish after another to beautify our tank. We were like fish addicts, buying fish every payday! It was the only form of entertainment we indulged ourselves in. And it was a costly one.

Our trips to the local fish store would occur almost weekly. We were learning as much as we could as fast as we could and taking great pleasure in selecting our aquarium community members each week. Sometimes the children would accompany us. Other times, we would take off and go ourselves. It was the only outing we went on other than going to work or running errands. We loved it, though.

One particular Saturday in May, we planned a trip to the grocery store to do the weekly shopping, followed by a quick stop into the fish store to see if any new items were in. With a car load of groceries in the trunk, we headed up the main road. It was a beautiful sunny day, but quite hot. While stopped at a red light in the center lane, we both heard the squeal of tires and brakes screeching against the blacktop. "Oh, crap!" BAM! We had been rear ended. A pickup truck had hit us square in the trunk where the bread was.

My neck was hurting badly. Without thinking, I had turned my head around to see what was making that awful noise coming at us— and found out just as I faced backwards! Holding my neck, I sat in the car while Bobby got out to speak with the driver. The man appeared agitated. I then got out of the car, more out of curiosity than feeling the need to assist. The driver of the other vehicle was rambling on, apologizing to us, pulling cash out of his pockets to stuff into Bobby's hands. "Here! Take everything I have. I have a baby and a wife at home. I need to be with them." I then asked a passerby to call for the police, wanting a report to file with the insurance company to get the car repaired.

It seemed to take an unusually long time for police to arrive on the scene. Once they did, however, the complexion of the event changed quickly. All the while, I had thought the driver of the other vehicle was in shock from the accident. I was wrong. He was drunk! Between being drunk and standing in the extreme heat of the Tampa mid-day sun on blacktop pavement, he was pickled! A very tall state trooper assessed this immediately and placed him under arrest. There was to be no fish shopping that day. Instead, we thanked our lucky stars that we were both able to walk away from this and drove home.

The remainder of that day was inconsequential. Tending to house-hold chores, but taking it easy, we enjoyed the rest of the day with the kids. Sunday morning I was awake only briefly before I realized that I could not move my neck. I called out to Bobby, "I can't move—my neck is swollen." He looked at me and commented, "It sure is."

"I can't believe this! Yesterday we get hit, and today I wake up with the mumps!"

"Are you crazy? That's not mumps; you twisted your neck, I'll just bet!"

Bobby was right. My neck was a mess.

Besides being all but physically incapacitated, we were then met with yet another snag. The company wanted to promote Bobby. This would require a move to a new location. It began with a conversation that raised the question, "Where would you both like to go?"

Bobby and I talked for hours about all the different locations that the company had throughout the United States. With my being from New York, we began to look in the Northeast. There were several options—one in Buffalo and two in Pennsylvania, to name a few. Wanting to be gracious and agreeable, Bobby went back to the managers and made this suggestion, "Ellen and I have talked, and we would like to go to the Northeast."

A day or so later, the managers came back, advising Bobby that they would like him to go to Decatur, Alabama. He relayed this information to me.

"Decatur, Alabama? That's northeast of what—Texas? Are they crazy? Why did they ask us if they never intended us to go where we wanted?"

The poor man was sandwiched between the company and his wife—and it wasn't pleasant.

My neck began to improve with treatment from a local chiropractor, and we sought the help of an attorney who was recommended to us. The truck that had hit us was a business vehicle. The driver was one of the employees borrowing the vehicle on the weekend. An accident can happen to anyone. But driving drunk infuriated me. I also learned that this was not the driver's first offense of this type. He was a repeat offender.

The local victims' assistance agency contacted us by mail providing a questionnaire regarding the incident. In it, we were given the opportunity to voice our opinion of what had happened, how it had impacted us, and what we would like to see happen. I gave a great amount of thought to this before I submitted it to the courts. One part of me felt very angry and desiring some sort of revenge for what had happened. Another part of me was consumed with compassion and empathy. After five years of working in an out-patient drug rehab, I knew for certain that jail would not in any way rehabilitate this individual. If anything, jail would make matters worse. *It has to be more difficult to live in jail than it would be to live a free life with a wife and child,* I thought to myself. Of course, I was imagining circumstances. I didn't know anything about this person.

After much deliberation, my recommendation to the court was that this person be given however many hours of community service as the judge deemed appropriate, but requested that the community service should consist of being given a list of victims that had been killed by drunk drivers. This man would then have to go to the headstone of each of the victims (some of whom were children) and clean the headstone. Somehow I envisioned that getting down on his hands and knees staring at the dates on these placards might make a profound impression on him. I did not attend the court hearing, but was later informed that the judge really liked my suggestion and made it so.

As for the lawsuit against the insurance company of the other vehicle owner, our lawyer handled that for us via correspondence with the opposing attorney. In the interim, we flew to Decatur with the intention of being wooed by the plant manager. The flight was pleasant and not too long. As we were on the approach to land, I asked the gentleman next to me, "What time is it here? I'd like to set my watch."

"Oh, I always tell people, Turn your watch back one hour and twenty years."

Little did I know—we might as well have been going to Mayberry! The roads were clear, the town was small, and there was cotton as far as the eye could see. I tried to be optimistic, but I was struggling.

The plant manager had set up an appointment for me with a local Realtor as soon as I arrived. She and I spoke over lunch about what kind of house I was looking for, and off we went. She showed me one house after another—all of which fit the description I had given her. At the end of two rigorous days of house hunting, we stumbled upon a beautiful two-story, five-bedroom house on a double lot at the end of a cul-de-sac, with a brook running through the property. It was perfect! I took pictures all around the house to bring back to show both Bobby and the children. This was the best house—better than I had imagined! I had been just "OK" with moving, but this house was changing my attitude quickly.

In one short, two-day trip, we had been swept off our feet—Bobby by the company and me by the house. We returned to Tampa to announce the impending move to the family. With the company helping to relocate us, they would pay closing costs and related expenses, but we didn't have enough money for the down payment on the new house until we sold the old one. I remained in Tampa, while Bobby instantly became part of the Decatur staff.

As I had suspected it would, being isolated with the kids—juggling work, their homework, laundry, and whatever else needed to be done—was wearing me down quickly. I would repeatedly ask Bobby if he had found a way to get the new house yet. I wanted to move up there and have us all together. We were in a holding pattern, and I didn't like it. My nagging was taking on legendary proportions, as were our stress levels.

Making matters worse, my neck was improving, but a new symptom with my jaw was arising with a vengeance. At varying times, my jaw would lock open; sometimes while chewing gum or eating a large sandwich. Immediately pain would radiate up the side of my face to the point where in a very few moments, I would be unable to see. I consulted the chiropractor who advised me, "When that happens, jump in the vehicle and come to the office so I can give you an adjustment."

"Are you mad?" I asked. "I'm telling you that I'm blacking out and you're telling me to get in my car! REALLY?"

I then began to receive calls from a manager at the business whose vehicle had struck us. "We'd like to repair your car for you. No charge, of course, "

"WHAT? Let me see if I understand this: You have a business that does what?"

"We customize 4x4 trucks."

"Which means you work on 4x4 pick-ups, right?"

"Well, yes. But a vehicle is a vehicle. We can fix your car!"

"My car is a Cadillac. Somehow I see this as a conflict of interest—to say nothing of the fact that you are not the people to fix the car! I appreciate the gesture, but no thank you."

It was just as Murphy's Law had predicted: Anything that can go wrong—will. Murphy was working overtime!

There are many ways to deal with stress. Keeping busy was certainly an option. When my stress level—be it emotional or otherwise—hit overload capacity, I complained. As the stress became more and more unbearable, I became more and more vocal about my discontent. During one of our later conversations, I remember saying something to the effect of, "You're up there with room service, and I'm down here with six kids and the weight of the whole house on my shoulders!"

Bobby is a tolerant man, but everyone has limits. I believe I made one comment too many. One day, Bobby telephoned as usual at the end of his day, this time to say, "Get the kids together and get up here; I bought a house!"

"You got it! Oh, Honey!"

"No—I didn't get *that* house. I bought *another* house."

"What do you mean, you bought another house? How?"

"Remember that check you gave me to keep in my wallet for emergencies?"

"You bought a house with that? Are you crazy?" For the first time in my life, I realized I might have gone too far.

The move to Alabama was scheduled to take place immediately after my birthday at the end of the summer. With the blackouts occurring more and more frequently, I sought the help of a board certified maxillofacial surgeon recommended by my attorney to address the problem with my jaw and the blackouts. Tests, tests and more tests revealed—NOTHING! I couldn't stand it any longer and confided to the doctor, "I can't take this anymore. I'm going to kill myself if you can't make this stop."

"Well, I don't know what's causing it. But if it's that bad to you, let's schedule a surgery to explore and find out exactly what the problem is."

I advised Bobby of the plan.

"You know, it's going to hurt pretty badly. Any time they go into your bones and start messing around, it hurts. I'm telling you!"

"I can't stand it, though," I told him. "I have to."

"Do you want me to come home?"

"No, it'll be OK. I'll get the kids to stay with my mom. We'll be fine. Don't worry."

I awoke from the surgery in the recovery room and before I knew it, the pain was becoming more and more profound. "GET ME A PHONE!" I uttered to the nurse. I could barely speak. It was as if my jaw would not move at all. I was speaking through my teeth. "Get my husband on the phone. NOW!"

The nurse then asked me how bad the pain was. I could hear ringing with the phone up to my face. "COME HOME," I said and began to cry with pain.

"Are you OK?" he asked.

"It hurts—bad."

"I told you," he said.

At that point, the nurse gave me something which eased the pain tremendously. While still on the phone with Bobby, I realized it was now becoming manageable. "I'll be OK. Never mind."

In no time at all, I was taken to my room. There I was met with a magnificent spray of pine boughs and long stem red roses, a dozen in all. The card read, "Relax. You're in good hands." It was signed by my physician. I thought to myself, *If he fixed the problem, this guy is the best!*

The problem was, in fact, corrected. Invisible on x-ray, the cartilage in the joint of my jaw bones had pulled out and was grinding bone and bone. This had caused a bone spur to form, which was causing the joint to lock. The surgery corrected this.

In 24 hours, I was home to greet the movers, and the packing began. Bobby arrived home on a Friday evening and helped prepare to take the family to our new home. After a grueling eleven hours of eight people and two dogs in a station wagon, towing a Ford Escort, we made it to Alabama.

Pulling up to the house was quite a shock. Not only was it not the house I had originally picked, it was nothing like it. It was one story, three bedrooms, and—not to make too fine a point of this—lacking the charm of the other house.

The children just looked at me as if to say, "Do something!"

56. Pearl Jam

LIFE IN ALABAMA was something I had never anticipated. After all, I grew up in New York City. You don't grow up in New York thinking, "Someday, I'll live in Alabama." It just doesn't happen!

But it was happening now. There I was, in Decatur, Alabama—not in the dream house I had picked out, but in the house Bobby had found and grabbed in an attempt to shut me up. It was the ultimate end to an argument. I was now living in the result of my pushing his buttons!

There was absolutely nothing about this house I did *not* want to change, except for the fact that it was located on a corner. I began looking the place over—sizing it up to see what changes I could make immediately vs. what changes I would make after a while. The kids were enrolled in their new schools and I was at home with the baby (now two and a half years old), decorating and arranging.

I remember being so put out about this house that I went to a wallpaper shop and picked out the most expensive wallpaper I could find, just because I could! It was a marble-like pattern of pale blue, pale pink and grayish white, with sparkles all through it. I thought to myself, "Hang on to your hat, Bobby. I'm doing the kitchen!" I painted the cabinets white, inside and out, and then hung this wallpaper above the chair rail, which I had also painted white. In all honesty, I was going for a shock factor. But it looked pretty good!

If anything, I had managed to punish myself! While gluing the wallpaper, I noticed that the sparkles were getting into the glue—as well as on me—and by the time I had completed the room, I looked very much like a glittery snowman. But *I showed Bobby!*

In three days' time, had I managed to unpack everything, decorate, and set up living for our family of eight in the new house in Decatur. We no sooner took a breath, then we had to jump back into the station wagon and drive to New York for my friend, Lizzy's wedding—for which I was a bridesmaid. I spent 23 hours in a car with the entire family, getting almost no sleep, only to arrive in Long Island just in time for the rehearsal dinner. I was an absolute zombie! I was also a starving zombie. Surgery left me unable to consume anything but liquids. Exhausted, hungry and stressed, I found comfort in the fact that the entire situation seemed to make sense. After all, if all you can do is drink—what better place to be than a wedding?

This was not to be your average wedding. Lizzy and Evan (her soul mate and husband-to-be) had met in Hampton Bays, Long Island while Lizzy was searching for a summer place for her mother. It was L-O-V-E! Their wedding was a huge celebration, including everyone they knew, loved, or were related to—all in attendance for the duration. Most weddings last one day. This one lasted 6. We arrived on Day 2. It was a wonderful festive occasion filled with happiness; a reunion of sorts. It was also a very welcome de-stressor from our move. At last, I could breathe. And I wasn't blacking out!

Lizzy had painstakingly selected the dresses, shoes, accessories—everything—to make her day perfect. In my excitement, I had provided her with multiple issues of Bride magazines to help her with ideas. The dress she picked for us (the bridesmaids) came from one of those magazines. Not exactly what I would have selected, but they were pretty, and we looked fantastic in them. She had paid such meticulous attention to detail that we were all stunned. "Everyone should wear pearls with the dress," she declared. "I want you all to wear pearl necklaces!"

I don't remember exactly how it came about, but we (the bridesmaids) collectively decided that Lizzy would be giving us each a string of pearls as our bridesmaid's gift. Convinced of this, none of us brought pearl necklaces with us to the wedding. At the rehearsal dinner, Lizzy and Evan both gave very touching speeches to their friends and family, thanking us profusely for being in attendance at this most important day for them. They then presented the gifts to the attendees.

As Lizzy handed each of the five bridesmaids her gift, the expressions on our faces began to reflect the shock we felt at the weight of the package. "Oh, my," Marie looked at me and mouthed from the next table. As she put the box in my hand, I understood what Marie meant. This was way too heavy to be a pearl necklace. Instantly, Marie lifted a brass Tiffany alarm clock from her box, which she half in jest held up to her neck as one would a necklace she was trying on. *Oh, shit! No pearls!*

The morning of the wedding, Lizzy woke each of us up bright and early. Lizzy and Evan were very much like camp counselors. "Rise and shine, campers! It's time for the festivities to begin!" With a full breakfast prepared for us, we ate and departed for the hair salon which Lizzy had reserved especially for us—and only us. We drove into town to find this hair salon decorated and stocked with chilled champagne and orange juice for mimosas awaiting us.

I had a plan. As Zoe and I had short hair, our "dos" would take the least amount of time. We would run out and find pearl necklaces for everyone while the others with longer hair were getting fixed.

"Where are you going?" Lizzy asked

"We just have to run to the store really quick. We'll be right back!"

In a flash, Zoe and I flew to the car. Neither of us was that familiar with the area, but we were determined to find something in a hurry. In a local department store, in a 50-gallon drum, we dug till we found five strands of pearls on clearance. The two of us laughed all the while. "Who would think we'd be dumpster diving hours before the ceremony looking for the pearl necklaces that Lizzy told us to get in May?"

Five matching strands of pearls—costume jewelry—marked down to clearance prices. Priceless!

As we departed for the church later that day, I could not help but think back to my own wedding with Lizzy and Marie by my side—along with my sister, who had begged me not to go through with it. Now here we were again, Lizzy, Marie and I, experiencing Lizzy's life event. Musketeers were we. One for all, all for one! No matter what twists and turns our lives seemed to take us through; there we were, the three of us—together.

The wedding ceremony was beautiful. It went perfectly, as planned. The party went on for days afterwards. On Tuesday, Lizzy and Evan departed for their honeymoon—several weeks in Australia and Fiji. Marie flew back to her apartment in Chicago. Bobby, I and the kids drove back to Alabama. We had all come together for this occasion in time, and now we were back out in the world once again, all in different directions.

In the weeks after we returned to the new house, the old house in Tampa sold. There was the down payment for the house I had originally wanted—now that I didn't need it! I took that money and hired a landscaper to create something wonderful in the front yard of the house we were in.

As it was, the yard had one single bush underneath the main window. That was it. There was not another bush, plant or flower anywhere! It was as if all the other shrubs had run away. The new landscaping added three crape myrtle trees on either end of the house, with a swirl of various colored shrubs throughout, including holly bushes. It was beautiful; the landscaping made a world of difference.

Although everything had been placed prior to our departure to New York, decorating the inside took real effort. I literally could not decide which rooms to make into what—to say nothing of what color to make them. I changed things around constantly, trying to make this house a home. The master bedroom featured a wall of purple wallpaper. The remaining walls were a pale green. These colors, combined with the black floral bedspread and drapes, were striking. If nothing else, you would have to say that I wasn't afraid of color!

Bobby, on the other hand, was a "white" kind of guy. He liked white paint only. No matter what color I picked, he would say, "Why is this not white?" He kept referring to my decorating as the psychedelic look. Still, I think he would have tolerated anything just to make me happy—and he did. For the better part of that first year, I went through fits of experimenting with different colors and decorating plans, trying everything I could think of to turn this house into one that I wanted. But it just wasn't going to happen.

Stage VII

57. The Rest of the Story

IN THE MIDST of all my decorating and fixing, I found myself having much time during the day to talk with my sister. Previously, when I was working days, I was often not available to speak to Genie when she was free. Now, although our schedules were not the same, they at least did not conflict.

Genie was always upset about one thing or another. If not that "people" chose to call her at the wrong time (waking her up), she complained that whenever she was on the phone with me, the kids would be interrupting the conversation throughout. She felt she never got to speak to me uninterrupted. Now this was not the case, however. We had all the time in the world to talk. We would talk for hours upon end—about everything under the sun.

One conversation took us back to childhood. Genie began asking me question after question. "Did you ever go anywhere with this person (naming him)? Did he ever bother you?" I felt very strange that she was asking me these things. I felt even stranger that after all these years, this was the first time anything like this had ever come up.

"Did you know he did this to me?" (She described the incident.)

When she asked me that, I got sick. "No, I didn't know." The very individual who had snuck into my room in the middle of the night, putting his hands all over me, had done the same thing to Genie years before! She had never said anything—and neither had I. I had always assumed that I was the only person to whom this had happened. I don't know why I had thought this. Looking back on it, this was a very stupid assumption. But to find out that we sisters had both been abused by the same person—I couldn't stand it! I went from feeling uncomfortable to angry—instantly.

There was so much about this that I did not understand. I was furious! I wasn't mad that Genie hadn't told me before that day. But now that we were both adults, we were comparing notes—and the notes matched! The guy wasn't even original enough to use a different routine; he used the same line, the same gestures, the same M.O. with both of us. I don't know why I was so much more outraged knowing that what this person had done to me he had done to someone else as well; but I was.

Over the next few days, what I began getting really angry about was that my mother had invited this person into our house. Didn't she know he was like this? Couldn't she tell? I was so angry, I was consumed with it. It was all I could think about.

That conversation took me right back to my childhood—to feeling like a victim, feeling dirty. "Now," I thought, "I feel terrible. And I still have to cook dinner for my family of eight, do dishes, and hold things together—while my insides fall apart and my head rattles. SHIT!"

Although Genie and I talked a great deal that year, we never spoke of that situation again. Suffice to say, we had each divulged our secrets to each other, consoled each other, and shared the burden. And that was the end of the conversation about it.

I can't speak for Genie, but these thoughts were burning a hole in me. Not one day went by the rest of that year when I didn't think about that. It was in my mind all the time. Even when I was having a good time doing something else, I was thinking about it. I was beside myself—and we were quite a pair!

At 3:30 one afternoon, Genie called. This was unusual, because she was always looking to go to sleep by 3:00 and had complained on numerous occasions when others would try to call her at that time, accusing them of being inconsiderate. "Don't they know I'm going to sleep?"

I was getting the kids ready for their softball games. The girls were embracing the local way of life—sports were HUGE in Alabama—and had joined softball teams, despite their obvious lack of athletic ability compared to some of the other kids. I answered the phone in the midst of the commotion of getting them out of their school clothes and into their uniforms.

"Hey, what's up?"

I could hear in Genie's voice that something wasn't right. She sounded different—depressed in some way. On any other day, I would have just told her, "I've got to take the kids to the game; I'll talk to you another time." But I could hear it in her voice—today was not the time to do that!

We talked for a few minutes. Game time was nearing. I told the girls, "Run across the street and see if Mrs. Jones will drive you to the game." I couldn't believe I was doing that. Never-the-less, Mrs. Jones took the girls to the game. I intended to follow, but I never left the house.

Genie and I remained on the phone that day for 2 hours and 45 minutes. I was still on the phone when the girls came home from the game, standing in the doorway of the kitchen tied to the wall phone like a hostage.

We talked about everything under the sun. We laughed some, but mostly we talked about serious things. Genie needed a lot of dental work—which she could not afford. I offered to pay for it with some money I was expecting from the accident settlement. She refused. Genie wouldn't take a cent from anyone. Genie talked about some-day moving out of New York (which shocked me). She had been to Kentucky to visit some friends, and absolutely loved it. She knew she would have to learn how to drive, but she wanted to go anyway. We talked about Genie's job. We talked about guys we had dated, music, and photography. We talked about everything!

When the conversation ended and we said goodbye, I had difficulty hanging up. I felt somehow as though I shouldn't stop talking to Genie—that we should talk all night. But my ear was hurting, my arm was cramping from holding the phone. Clearly it was time to stop.

Less than three weeks later, my mother telephoned at about 10:00 a.m. on a Tuesday morning. "Genie's had a problem. It's her heart."

"What do you mean her heart? What happened?"

"She's in the hospital. She's in a coma. It's bad."

"WHAT? How?"

"I don't know what happened."

"Who called you?"

"Her friend called me."

"When?"

"Yesterday."

"YESTERDAY? They called you yesterday and you're telling me today? What were you waiting for?"

"I thought they would call back and tell me they were just kidding." My mother burst into tears. For the first time in my life, my mother was caving.

My mother was literally falling apart—and my mother just didn't fall apart! My mother had taken a beating from my father, yet still had the composure to take down the badge numbers of his buddies so that there would be no mistake that she wanted him arrested. My mother was tough!

No more. My mother was caving in a big way! I offered to coordinate flights with her so that we could go to New York together to take care of Genie.

"I can't go."

"WHAT?"

"I can't leave Wally."

"What are you saying?"

"I'm saying *you* go. I can't go."

I couldn't believe what I was hearing.

I got off the phone with my mother and realized something. *I don't even have the money to get to New York*. Airfare for a ticket the next day would be $800 or more. I had nowhere near that amount—and no credit card.

I called Lizzy. No sooner had I told her what had happened than she booked me on a flight for the next morning. Instantly, I was on my way.

58. Signing Off

ON A MOMENT'S notice, I was boarding a plane heading for New York City. For any other reason, I would have loved to be going up to the Big Apple. Not this time. This was crazy. Genie's friends, Bill and John, were meeting me at the airport and taking me to the hospital.

All the way there, I tried to pick their brains for details. What had happened? My sister smoked, but was in terrific health. She might have been 5-10 pounds overweight, but she exercised. Hell, she was 41 years old! What had happened to her?

We went directly to the hospital where I quickly found my sister in the intensive care unit. Unfortunately, I could not get in to see her. ICU has strict regulations on visiting. Only one person was allowed every few hours, for 10 minutes at a time. Since someone was already in there, I had to wait. The three of us sat there like stooges, dumbfounded, not knowing what to do or whom to talk to.

Suddenly, out walks this woman (unknown to any of us) crying her eyes out. "She's trying to communicate with me."

"Who?"

"Genie. She looked right at me and tried to speak."

"Really?"

"I know she was trying to speak to me."

"Sure she was. Do you know what she was trying to say?"

"No, but I know she was trying to say something."

"I know. She was trying to tell you to get the hell out of her room!"

"WHAT?"

"You heard me."

"Genie is a very close friend of mine."

"Really?"

"Yes, we work together."

"Genie hated being around people when she didn't feel well. She despised it, in fact. If you were such a good friend of hers, you would know that about her. I can tell by looking at you that you are no friend of my sister's. She wouldn't be caught dead talking to you (no pun intended), and since you have convinced yourself that you have had such a deep communication with her this time, that should hold you. Now go!"

Bill and John just looked at me, then at each other. "She's not going to need *our* help!"

A doctor came up to us, asking, "Are you Genie's family?"

"Yes."

"Come with me."

We were escorted into a conference room on the floor. There, along with the doctor we had met, were several of his colleagues.

"How much have you been told?" they asked me.

"Practically nothing. I know there is some problem with her heart. I know she is in a coma. What else is there?"

"Well," they began to explain, "Genie has suffered arrhythmia—which is a sort of stalling of the heart."

"Like when you're driving your car and it just shuts off?"

"Yes. Unfortunately, her heart was not restarted quickly. She was without respiration for over 20 minutes, which has resulted in brain damage."

"How much brain damage?"

"Massive. We have done several tests. Her brain activity is not charted, meaning that it does not register."

"How long can she live like this?"

"Well, this does not affect her life span. The heart function has been restored. She could, technically, live a full life to the age of 72 or longer."

"WHAT? Like this?"

I couldn't believe what I was hearing. It was like a premonition coming true. Genie had been terrified of exactly this—that she would be hooked to machines keeping her alive. And here she was. And here *I* was, just as she had said.

"We know this is a great deal for you to take in all at one time. Do you have any questions for us?"

"Yes, I do. What are your credentials?"

"Excuse me?"

"You are suggesting to me that my sister is hopelessly brain damaged, although not brain dead. We are on the verge of discussing what to do about that. I'd like to know just how educated you are, what your area of expertise is, how long you've been doing what you're doing and how good at it you are."

They looked at each other in disbelief. I guess I was just supposed to believe every word they said—simply because they were wearing the white coats. Perhaps they expected me to be catatonic myself, from shock. I don't know. Clearly, my questions caught them a bit off guard. Their response, however, caught *me* unaware.

"Well, I did my residency at ____," was the first response. "I did my internship at ____ and then I got ____."

I was in the presence of Doogie Howser! This child of a genius didn't look old enough to have done anywhere near all that he was able to claim on his résumé. (I say sincerely, the man looked all of 27!) I was mortified. On the other hand, I believe the doctors got quite a kick out of being questioned—and then watching my reaction when they rattled off all their accolades. These guys were pretty impressive. Johns Hopkins, Harvard—these weren't just random names they were spewing out.

So now that I had established that the doctors were good, I had to figure out what to do.

I asked to see Genie and was allowed in. ICU was a small, rather confining room with a plethora of devices. Beeps and strange sounds I am certain were there to alert nurses were concerning me. I had trouble focusing on Genie. It was as if the instrumentation had more animation than she did. There she laid, a tube taped into her mouth. She looked uncomfortable. I knew she would be pissed! I began to pat her hand, rub her arm. It felt kind of like her—but different. I realized that this *wasn't* Genie. I began looking around the room, as if I would see some shadow of her floating above her body, and then I'd know, "There she is!"

But—nothing.

I leaned over and whispered in Genie's ear, "A promise is a promise—I'll get you out of here."

Bill, John and I went to have lunch. It was 3:00 in the afternoon, and between the flight and the meeting at the hospital, I hadn't had anything to eat. I knew I needed to eat, but I couldn't do anything but pick at the food. I remember thinking I would order a beer, and then I realized, "This is probably the worst time to be reaching for a drink." The beer sat on the table untouched.

Our conversation drifted in circles. We relived funny incidents we had with Genie. Then we discussed options we felt we had if the hospital would not let her go. We sat over lunch deciding how we would let Genie go ourselves if it came down to that. We realized that we would have to get her discharged and take her home. Then, Bill suggested, we could inject her intravenously with air, causing an embolism – which would most assuredly kill her. This was madness!

We returned to the hospital to meet again with the doctors.

"Well, what would you like us to do?"

"My sister was very clear. She knew that something like this would happen to her, and she was absolute. She did not want to live like this. You have to let her go."

"What do you mean exactly?"

"I mean, I want you to end her life." "You guys know how to keep people alive indefinitely. Surely you know how *not* to. She didn't want this. Let her go."

"How would you like us to do that?"

"Give her a shot or something—I don't know."

"We can't."

"What do you mean, you can't? Why did you ask me?"

"We only have certain means at our disposal. We can withhold hydration and nutrition from her, which will cause her death, but it will take some time."

"How long?"

"It varies. We can administer Phenobarbital, which will prevent spasms and keep her comfortable."

"Will this work?"

"Yes—it will work."

"OK."

"Yes, well, we need you to prepare a written statement; all of you. We need documentation of this being Genie's wishes. Tell us how you know that she wanted this."

Bill, John and I all proceeded out of the room and into the hallway, where we sat and wrote statements detailing how Genie had told us of her wishes regarding her death. It was so surreal, writing this! I had always thought we would grow old together. Yet Genie had told me when I was little not to worry about dying, because she would die first. All those conversations came welling up inside me out of nowhere, and now I had to carry out the most difficult request that had ever been made of me.

I tried to focus on the task at hand—not the person. My job was to see this through, not to cry about it. "Be strong," I told myself. I had had a lifetime of having to be strong right up to this point. When was it going to end?

I wrote the statement and turned it in. Something of such a serious nature—and I had written it out on loose-leaf paper! I kept flashing to my mother saying, "My letters are too important to be on plain paper. That's why I use stationery."

Geez! I'm writing out documentation defending my sister's wishes to die—and I'm worried about the paper *it's on? It's like I'm a crazy woman!*

We signed everything, and the three of us headed for the elevator.

Before we left, a doctor approached me, "Are you Genie's family?"

"Yes"

"Well, I don't think you can kill her just because you don't want the responsibility of taking care of her for the rest of your life."

"What did you say?"

"You did sign papers to that effect, didn't you?"

I was stunned, but not to the point of speechlessness. "Tell me, are you important enough to have an office or do you conduct all your business in the hall?"

"Of course, I'm sorry. Forgive me. This way."

We walked in a line—the doctor, me, Bill, and John. We found ourselves behind the nurse's station on the floor. The man turned to speak again, but I put my hand up.

"It is obvious to me that you are a religious man." *appearing to be of the Jewish faith since he has evidenced by the payot (side curls).* "I suggest that you go to your place of worship and pray for her soul. As for any interaction with my sister, I am ordering you to sign off her case immediately! You have no business with her or our family. You do not know her. You do not know of her wishes—and you have no right to interfere!"

I turned and stormed off, Bill and John behind me. Bill laughed and said, "I'm impressed—you certainly told him!"

I began to cry, "He's going to try to stop this. We have to do something."

I ran to a hospital phone and immediately paged the doctor in charge of Genie's case. Before I was even able to get through the details of what had happened, he uttered, "I know who you are talking about. That's not a doctor—he's a nurse." I had failed to pick up on this fact. *Talk about missing the point!*

"I'll handle this." Genie's doctor reassured me.

"Genie's doctor is going to handle it," I told Bill and John. But I knew this was going to get more involved because of that incident. I was incensed! I did not go through all of this to end up fighting with people who didn't even know Genie. The lady coming out of ICU; now this nurse—ENOUGH!

Bill, John and I compiled a list of approved visitors for Genie. It was quite easy, and the list was short. We then requested that the hospital place a guard at her door and admit only those whose name appeared on the list. If there were any questions, I was to be called to approve entry. I was now going to be the equivalent of a guard dog!

That first day was the worst. I set up camp at Genie's apartment. It felt horrible to be there, knowing that she wasn't. I kept telling myself she wouldn't mind. I looked around her very tiny efficiency apartment, remembering times I had spent there before.

Genie's refrigerator was a dorm-size model, which typically had nothing in it. Genie was no cook, and the apartment was not set up for cooking. As we investigated, we discovered that the refrigerator had just three drinks in it—coincidentally, one for each of her guests.

How did she know?

59. Bon Voyage

DURING ANY REGULAR visit, I would be concerned about walking through the streets of New York alone, particularly at night. Strangely, at this time I had no fear, no concerns. I walked with complete ease of conscience—no looking over my shoulder, no worrying about someone jumping out from behind a doorway. This was no ordinary trip to New York. I was on a mission. I was protected—and I knew it!

My sister's apartment was located on 73rd Street just off Central Park West. Every day I walked confidently to and from the hospital—which was quite a walk. Aside from the reason for being there, it was the most relaxed time I had ever spent in New York. Every day I would get up, dress, and walk to the deli on the corner—where I would get a roll—and then, while eating, I would walk to the hospital.

It was a chilly spring in New York. I hadn't prepared well when I packed in such a hurried fashion, so I ended up having to wear Genie's denim jacket to and from the hospital. Genie was always collecting little things—buttons, coins, etc. So I didn't think it so odd when I reached into the pocket of the jacket and felt a button. I did, however, find it peculiar when I pulled the button out and read it: "Gene Lives." I couldn't even imagine where such a thing was made or for what reason. But I put it on the jacket pocket.

I had met with another friend of Genie's, Lee—who was also Bill's sister. We had met many years earlier, when Genie and Bill lived together. Lee had offered to walk with me to the hospital that day. As we walked, we talked about many things—me being back in New York after so long, for one. It did feel strange, but not totally unfamiliar to me.

As we approached the hospital entrance, a vagrant man yelled at me, asking for money. Lee grabbed my arm and told me, "Just ignore him."

"Nope—not this time."

He came right up to me, and I had no intention of dodging him. I reached in my pants pocket and felt that I had bills in there.

"What do you need money for?" I asked him.

"I'm hungry."

"Sure you are. I want you to take a good look at my face. I want you to remember me. Can you do that?"

"Yes, I'd know you if I saw you again. Sure."

"Good, then take this bill and stay away from me from now on. I'm not kidding! I'm giving you this and I want you to leave me alone. Permanently."

"You got it!"

We walked. Lee said, "I guess it's like riding a bicycle."

We brought Genie some flowers to brighten up the room, which was now a private one. We sat and talked, trying to include Genie (if that makes any sense), but mostly talking around her. It was strange. By afternoon's end, we were hungry and tired and wanted a change of scenery. Nonetheless, I felt obligated to sit guard over Genie. But then Bill came up, which allowed me to leave—knowing that some-one was there with her.

We began to set up an undisciplined sort of tag-team monitoring of Genie's room. As the days grew in number, we became more famil-iar with the staff handling Genie's case, as they did with us. We also began bringing things to the room—I think in an effort to personalize it, as though we were bringing Genie her favorite things.

This started off simple, but it got out of hand as time went on. Bill had airbrushed a tee shirt for Genie that read, "I'm not in a coma, I'm ignoring you." I brought a skeleton from her apartment (a life-size skeleton!) I hung it from the IV hook. We then found a picture of Genie giving the finger to the New York skyline, which we taped to the foot of her hospital bed. Cartoons began to collect from either things she had read and enjoyed, or that others had read and thought she would find amusing. This escalated even further to our bringing in her collection of rubber water bugs and placing them all around the room—even on Genie's shoulder—in an effort to shake up the nurse!

This nurse was unflappable, though. She was Jamaican. She entered the room and talked to Genie, saying, "I'm just going to flush your IV. Let me move your water bug over here while I work; then I'll put it right back where I found it. Nothing will be disturbed." She was a cool customer!

Ten days into this process, the room was getting to be quite the museum, with artifacts from Genie's life everywhere. We were getting very used to hanging out with Genie, despite her silence. The drawback for me was that Bobby's oldest son was set to graduate from high school in two days. I had a choice to make: Do I stay here with my sister and hold her hand while she dies, or do I fly home and go to the graduation? My decision was based on the thought, "Genie's life is ending; his is not. Go home and go to the graduation."

I flew back the day before the graduation in just enough time to get things together and have a family graduation party. The plan was to make that an occasion and then depart the next day back to New York with Bobby and the two younger boys, this time driving up. We could not possibly take everyone. The girls stayed with friends. The graduate stayed at home on his own.

We were exhausted after 24 hours on the road. Genie's apartment was tiny, big enough for one, possibly two—but not four. We now had the boys with us. So we arrived in New York with plans to stay with Lizzy. She had just the one bedroom set up, so Lizzy and I slept in the bed, while Bobby and the boys manned the floor in the living room. I was so exhausted when we finally lay down, that I was numb.

Lizzy and I talked for a while about different things. We remembered how Genie had hated her when we were kids and used to throw her out of the apartment all the time. It's funny, things you remember at times like that.

While Lizzy and I lay there thinking about things, we heard noises coming from the living room—one loud, ripping fart noise after another, each one punctuated with laughter. "Listen to this one," and they'd laugh. Lizzy and I both got up to investigate. There was my husband, lying amidst the boys on the floor of Lizzy's condo apartment, teaching our boys how to make fart sounds with their arms and legs. They were three hysterical little boys (including my husband), making the best of a bad situation. I just rolled my eyes, looked at Lizzy and said, "I'm so proud!"

We returned to the hospital the next day. By this time, my mother and brother had arrived in New York to man the post of guard at the door. Up until my departure, I had made every decision, large or small, pertaining to my sister—with the family's blessing. Now that my mother arrived on the scene, however, the lead role transferred to her. I was a bit taken aback by this, although it is apparently protocol. My mother was the senior member of the family. My sister not having a spouse, the decisions reverted to the parent—or a sibling in the parent's absence. Evidently, once the parent arrives, the sibling goes back to the cheap seats.

Anyway, we were all there now. Never had I imagined that this process would take so long. In fact, the duration began to play a trick on me. The longer it continued, the more used to it I became—as if this were never going to end.

Day after day, we all continued to show up at the hospital. This process was going on forever—or so it seemed. I was getting edgy. My family was all over the place. Everything was on hold. And I think the fear of the inevitable was looming over my head. I couldn't stand it!

I went into the room that afternoon and sat alone with Genie. I remember looking all around the room again, as though I would see her somewhere up in the corner of the wall looking down at her body and me. I began to rationalize this with her. "You're going to die. This is what you asked me to do. I did what you asked. What the hell are you waiting for? Just go! Your friends are waiting for you." I began naming her deceased friends. "Go to them. More to the point—let me go back to my life. I don't like this any more than you do, but it's over for you. It's time." I left the room with confidence, feeling as though I had said my piece, and now I was all done.

The phone in Lizzy's apartment rang at 7:00 a.m. the next morning.

Genie had died at 4:30. I burst into uncontrollable tears and could not stop. Bobby heard me and ran in, grabbing me. He rocked me back and forth while I cried in his arms. I don't think I had ever cried that hard in my life. I felt like my heart was going to stop. He kept holding me, trying to console me, to no avail.

Finally, Bobby said, "You're not crying because you think this is your fault, are you? It's not, you know."

"NO!" I stopped. What a strange thought—Bobby was concerned that I felt guilty! But I felt no guilt. I had done exactly what any good little soldier would do. I had followed an order. I just hated it.

Concerned that the heart problem my sister had suffered was the result of an unknown congenital defect and not an allergic reaction to medication, my mother requested an autopsy performed. I agreed. Genie was gone. She was free. What they did with her body was of no real consequence to me. My mother also made arrangements for Genie to be cremated after the autopsy. This was something that had been openly discussed many times among the family, including with Genie, and everyone agreed that this would be acceptable.

Mom wanted very much to have a church service in the Methodist church where she and Wally had been married in the Bronx. Genie had long since disassociated herself from her own upbringing in the Catholic Church resenting the insincerity of it all. She was very vocal about her disgust with people connected to religion of any sect or denomination who (she felt) did not live according to the doctrine of that church. "People get married and get divorced. It means nothing. They take vows and they change their minds. It's all bullshit!" She really hated it. She had vowed to all those close to her that she would NEVER attend another church service of any type.

Much like my sister, I had distanced myself from churches. I had never been a member of the particular church my mother was recommending for the service, but I felt it would make her more at peace with the whole thing – so I saw no harm in it.

60. Leaving the Past Behind

A VERY STRANGE phenomenon occurs when someone you love dies. It's as though magic fills the air around you. I often wondered if that was angels circling the bereaved trying to soothe their pain.

We gathered at Genie's apartment—which wasn't large enough to seat six comfortably. Somehow, we all piled in. In a very small studio apartment, Genie had a very large blue canopy bed. There was little else in the way of furniture. She had her art table, file cabinets containing drawings and things, crates containing some supplies, and boxes. In the corner of the room was a life-size stand-up cardboard of Bruce Springsteen. I love "the Boss" as much as the next fan but there was no room for him there! On any given day, I would have entered this room and told Genie to toss a lot of this stuff. It was junk! However, yesterday's junk became the last hold we had on Genie today. Now it was the contents of a shrine! I looked around the room wondering how I was going to get through this stuff—and where I would put it until I did!

My plans were to take all of Genie's artwork (and there was much to choose from) and to compile it into a book of sorts to publish it. I wanted her voice to be heard, even if it had to be after she was gone. I discussed these plans openly with everyone so that they would know I had every intention of making things right for Genie. Everyone thought it was a great idea—or at least agreed with me as if they did.

We talked about different memories we each had of Genie. There we were, all trying to sit on this canopy bed of hers making ourselves comfortable. My mother was tearing up, although she tried to hold it together. I remember her reaching up her hand towards a Tupperware holder on the wall by the bed and grabbing one of the gold coins Genie had up there. As she spoke, she unwrapped what she believed to be a chocolate, all the while saying, "I know I'm not supposed to eat this (meaning chocolate) but I can't help it right now." As she continued, we all looked at each other aghast!

"STOP, MOM!"

"What?"

My poor mother had managed to pick up a gold circle condom—not a piece of chocolate! We all cracked up laughing. Weeping, my mother declared, "At least we know she was having safe sex."

Genie's apartment in New York was extraordinarily low-rent. For this one room efficiency apartment, she paid $375 per month. In this location, it was actually deemed a commercial property, which the building's owners desperately wanted back in order to take advantage of the higher rent they could have been charging. Genie—who read legal corporate takeover documents as a profession—was no amateur when it came to finding loopholes in things. She had managed to circumvent every attempt they had made over the 15 years she lived there to oust her from the apartment. Now her death was their shining moment to get the property back, and they took full advantage of it! The very day the family arrived in New York (prior to her death); the manager came to the apartment and advised us that we needed to get her things out as soon as possible. I remember telling him if he knocked on the door when my mother was in the apartment, I would cripple him!

My mother insisted that she wanted Genie's items to be shipped to my house. "She was your sister; she would want you to handle them." Genie's death was a really a tough blow to her. Mothers just don't anticipate burying their children—particularly when they are not sick. She had had no time to prepare for this. Although she managed to pull herself together to make the trip to New York and face the funeral, she was stumbling in other areas.

Mom and I were at odds about many of the side issues. One of those issues was deciding whom to tell about the situation–whom to invite to the service. In her infinite wisdom, my mother listed all family, including distant relatives. When the name of one particular individual came up, I absolutely cringed.

"Him? Are you serious?"

"Yes, he's family."

"Oh hell, no!!"

"What's the matter?"

For twenty three years I did everything I could to bury that memory. I couldn't hold it in another second. "Do you know what that asshole did to me? Do you know what he did to Genie? THE SAME THING! Didn't you know? Didn't you even suspect? Tell me you're not going to have him come to this!"

"I didn't know anything had happened. I wish you had told me. But as family, he is still entitled to pay his respects."

"WHAT?" I thought my head was going to explode. My mother was standing here explaining to me the proper etiquette of including someone because he was in the family, regardless of the fact that he had molested both me and my sister!

"Who's making the rules on this?" she asked.

"He's *not coming*—and that's final!"

"You're just upset."

"I've been upset my entire life. Now I'm pissed! Don't make the mistake of letting this man show up. If he does, I will crucify him right in the middle of the service. You can count on it."

The invitation was not extended. I had won the argument.

The entire time we were growing up in New York, my mother had kept us informed about having three plots that she had purchased. We didn't have much money, if any, but my mother was practical to a fault. She knew of someone selling grave plots in Nassau Knowles, the cemetery where my Nana was buried, and she had jumped at the opportunity to purchase them.

"Why three?" I asked her.

"Because that's all they had available."

"But, who will get them? There are four of us."

"Hey, first come, first served!"

It became a sort of joke. Clearly, we had somewhere to bury Genie. However, when making the arrangements the day after she passed, my mother insisted that she would be cremated and that she would take the urn back with her to Florida.

"What could you be thinking?" I asked her. "Genie's going to be some bookend in a garage sale if something happens to you! I can't deal with this. You should scatter her ashes in Kentucky. That's where she wanted to be anyway."

"NO!"

This was not a discussion point with my mother. Genie was not going to be scattered in Kentucky! I never really understood why. It was what she would have wanted, but my mother would not hear of it. I think in some way, she was insulted that Genie wanted to be somewhere the family was *not!* However, to Genie's way of thinking, she *did* have family in Kentucky. The people she knew who lived there meant a great deal to her. She loved them.

Didn't matter. Genie was not going to Kentucky. So now as far as I was concerned, If she wasn't going where she wanted, then at least she would go where it was planned—Nassau Knowles. My mother and I argued pretty vehemently over this point.

"Don't you trust me?" she persisted.

How does someone answer that? First of all, my fear was that my mom was going to die before her husband, leaving me no claim to any of her possessions. *How do you trust someone not to die?* Secondly—and worse—no, I really I didn't trust her. When I told her that, it made her really angry.

"Fine! We'll do all of this your way. That's the end of it."

I thought, "OK, that works." But I realized at that moment that I really *didn't* trust her! My mother was suffering with the death of my sister, no question about it. She had been rocked to her core, and this was no time to pick a fight with her. But there was something about the occasion that merited that things be made right—something I cannot explain. Just like the end of the movie, The Godfather; all family business was settled on that day!

After everything was said and done, my relationship with my mother was severely strained. My entire life I had held in this secret (as did my sister), for whatever reason I did not even understand. Now I realized that my mother wouldn't have done anything about it! I couldn't figure out which pain was worse—losing my sister, carrying the memory of being molested, or finding out that my mother was willing to overlook it.

We notified as many of Genie's friends as we possibly could the date, time and location of the service. Since the date this episode began, news of Genie's impending fate had been circulating. The church was filled with friends, acquaintances and coworkers all coming to pay their respects. Rather than commemorative religious cards, pictures of Genie were placed in the vestibule of the church for anyone who wanted one to remember her by.

As the service was getting under way, the minister read a synopsis of Genie's life—which had, no doubt, been written by my mother. Some of the milestones that were mentioned were things I was certain Genie would never have admitted to, much less brought up in a public forum! Typically, the coffin is placed in the middle of the aisle towards the front of the church containing the "guest of honor." But this time, there was no coffin. I and everyone else in the church began to wonder, "Where the hell is Genie?" You could hear the rumblings of people asking each other.

My mother leaned over to me and said, "Her body was sent to Jersey for the cremation. There was a delay. She's not back yet."

"WHAT? Oh, my God—she did it!" I couldn't stop myself from laughing. This was great! Genie had sworn she would never attend another church service, and she was true to her word. She never did. In fact, Genie had missed her own funeral!

The ride home to Alabama was a long one. Bobby did most of the driving. He was like this pillar of strength; never tiring, never complaining; strong and steady.

The boys seemed unusually well behaved, as though that was their way of saying how sorry they were. They had met Genie once or twice, but didn't so much know her. What they did remember of her was that she was fun to be around. So the little they did know of

Genie, they managed to get right! For almost the entire ride home, Bobby just sat there, keeping his arm around me with his free hand and using the other to drive. Every now and again, he would just pat my arm. "It's gonna be OK."

We had several cassette tapes that I had taken from Genie's apartment to listen to on the ride home. She was always taping music from the radio, making up her own selections of what to listen to. Her taste in music was similar to mine–but she was better at finding and organizing it. One by one we popped in the tapes, wondering what surprise would be in store for us.

One particular tape revealed Genie's voice speaking in a telephone conversation to a neighbor/friend of hers—Gary. I had met him years before and had seen him during the course of taking care of Genie's affairs. They were close. On the tape, Genie and Gary were speaking, "I feel like crap—I can't breathe."

"What do you mean, you can't breathe? What's the matter, sweetie?"

"It feels like someone is standing on my chest. Every time I inhale, I can't breathe."

"Go to the doctor."

"I know. I need to."

"Are you taking anything?"

"SOMA."

"What's that?"

"This stuff she gave me for my neck. Oh, this sucks! I can't breathe."

"Tell the doctor. Let her call something in for you."

This was awful! With my own ears, I heard Genie complaining that she couldn't breathe. She knew she was not well, and yet she blew it off until it was too late.

The cause of death recorded on the death certificate was heart failure. I suspected the underlying cause was an allergic reaction to a combination of SOMA Compound, a muscle relaxer, and Erythromycin, an antibiotic given to Genie after she called her doctor and complained of difficulty breathing. Did the doctor think she was suffering with an upper respiratory infection? It's was never definitively stated.

Even after we got home, I just wanted to curl up in the bed. My entire life, Genie had been my advocate. She ditched me as a kid. But as we grew up, our age difference mattered less and she became a real pal. Genie was always there when I needed her. She understood me. Now she was gone. It was like another vicious twist to my life; as if the gods realized that they had somehow overlooked this aspect of my life that was good and then decided to mess with me yet again by taking her.

Conversely, in my anger I had blurted out my deepest, darkest secret in front of my husband. But he didn't bat an eyelash. He never questioned me about it. More importantly, he never backed away. He officially knew all my secrets—and he wasn't going anywhere!

61. Framed

SOMEBODY ONCE TOLD me, "The best way to get your life back to normal is to actually do the day-to-day normal things."

There was plenty of opportunity for me to get back to normal, that much was certain. I was surrounded by normal! My kids were finally all back together in one house—and so was their laundry. I had a full day of washing ahead of me. And that was OK. In a strange way, I was looking forward to being in the house and doing the laundry. I was back home!

As I sorted through the clothes, doing load after load, I would walk past the phone. I couldn't help but think of calling Genie. If I dialed her number, I wondered, would I get her answering machine? Or was it already disconnected?

Bobby called during his workday to check on me. That was more unusual than it sounds. Bobby was someone who focused on work when he was at work, and he didn't often stop to make a call. But that first week we were back, he called often. We would only speak for a minute or so—just long enough for me to say I was all right and for Bobby to tell me that he loved me. There was no fix for the way I was feeling—but that was close.

It was only a matter of days before the movers called announcing the arrival of Genie's possessions. How I dreaded going through everything she owned! Where was I even going to put it all? There were eight people living in the house as it was. Now I was going to add in all of Genie's things—none of which I had room for. It was going to be a mess! I was also dreading how this was going to impact Bobby. I was no neat freak and Bobby wasn't either, for that matter. But he does like a certain amount of organization to his environment. He dislikes clutter. And we were about to be bombarded with clutter!

The movers brought in box after box after box. In pieces, Genie's bed was placed in the garage, as were many of the contents of her apartment. I decided I would keep four boxes or so at a time in the living room to go through what was in them, thinking that I would examine and discard things very routinely. I had no idea what I was in for!

Genie had inherited my mother's genetics for keeping things and my grandmother's sense of creativity. I think she was one of the original scrap bookers, although she was not in any way leaning towards anything country. Genie kept EVERYTHING. She wrote to radio stations, entering one contest after another. She would win more times than not, and would always write a thank you note after the concert or the show telling them how great it was and how much she had enjoyed it—which would then prompt a response from the artist. She had letters from Chuck Berry and other entertainers—neatly pressed in a book. She also had the ticket stubs from the shows she attended. Genie had a copy of a cancelled check that Mick Jagger had written to Jerry Hall. How she got that I don't even know! It was difficult not to sit and wonder about each item as I came to it. I was making little progress going through all this stuff, daydreaming about how it came into Genie's possession.

What I did notice missing rather early on was her artwork. Among the boxes I had opened, none of her drawings were in there. In fact, the more aware I became of this, the more anxiously I searched. I ripped open box after box looking for them. Not a one in sight. "Where the hell are they?"

I telephoned my mother simply to inquire where the artwork was, as it was obvious it was not included in the shipment. I was somehow hoping that it was shipped special freight because of its value, but my fear was that my mother had done something else with it.

My fear was correct. She began by telling me that she didn't want to upset me. That is the worst opening line in history! Whenever someone says that to you, they know they are going to piss you off! In fact, if they hadn't wanted to upset you, they wouldn't have done whatever they were thinking of doing in the first place—so they *wouldn't* have upset you!

"I gave the drawings to Bill," said my mother.

"YOU WHAT?"

"You have your hands full with all the children, and we decided that he would have more time to devote to putting a book together."

"You took my idea and then gave it to Bill without as much as a word? You all conspired to do this? Take the drawings right out from under me? You knew I wanted to do this for Genie, and you took everything? Don't you have any loyalty? You sided with people outside the family! How *could* you?"

If I had thought earlier that I wouldn't speak to my mother again, this iced the cake! Not only was I not going to speak to her, I was going to ensure that she never speak to me! I called the telephone company and requested a number change—immediately.

Before the change in phone numbers took effect, Bill called. He tried to explain how they had all gotten together and decided that giving him the artwork would be best. I was furious! I wasn't 16 years old anymore; I was grown. And more importantly to me, I was his equal. How dare he or anyone assume that I was not up to something that I had committed myself to do! I literally couldn't speak to him without yelling—which I did, and then hung up the phone on him. In the end, I believed they had all done what suited *them*.

Bill and the others did manage to compile many of Genie's cartoon drawings into a booklet, one copy of which I received via mail from my mother. I glanced through it and put it in my desk, still angry. It was months before I actually really examined it. And, it had turned out nicely. I may have hated what Bill did, but he was one of the best artists I knew and had a great eye for layout and design. No argument there. I just thought that it shouldn't have been his to do!

My mother tried to telephone, but was stopped by the number change. This alarmed her, and then she then realized just how angry I had become. She telephoned Bobby at work, imploring him to "talk to Ellen—get her to understand."

Bobby came home that evening telling me of my mother's call

and how she felt that she "had already lost one daughter." I remember thinking, *that may work on him, but I'm not going for it!* For the time being, I was keeping my distance.

Weeks turned to months, as I continued to sort through paper after paper. I found discipline letters from Genie's former employers, letters to dry cleaners expressing discontent with inferior service. It was unbelievable! As much as this stuff was garbage, it still reminded me so much of Genie, that it became valuable to me. My progress was hindered by my sorting through one pile and forming another. I was *moving* paper—not discarding it. The house was becoming more and more cluttered with debris. I was literally burying myself alive in Genie's stuff!

After we had moved to Decatur, I happened upon a store that sold knick knacks, specialty items and framing. The frames were beautiful! I was so taken with them that I took items that were special to me, one by one, and had them framed. I was framing everything! If the kids won a medal, I framed it. Our wedding picture—framed! Our walls were covered with the important trinkets of our lives together. It may have been frivolous, but it made me happy.

This store was called Judy's Place. It was a business started in the owner's (Judy's) garage, which grew in size until she had quite a prosperous enterprise. I remember a billboard being erected on the corner of the main street near our house with a sign for her business. Bobby used to look up as we drove past it and comment, "I'll bet we paid for that damn sign!"

Now as I stumbled my way through Genie's belongings, I happened upon a portrait of her drawn by Bill. It was a beautiful picture of Genie, done when she was 25 years old and they lived together. Both Bill and Genie had their eccentricities—and Lord knows I was furious with him for taking the artwork out from under me the way he did—but I had never understood why they had split up. It was the perfect love/hate relationship, in my opinion!

The picture of Genie was quite large, done in pastels on a 30" x 32" piece of art paper. Genie had purchased one of those chrome poster frames and hung it on her bedroom wall. I had always thought it was a cheesy frame for such a nice picture. The movers brought it to us intact, but the glass in the frame had cracked. So there it stood, against the living room wall, the immortalization of Genie—with a huge crack across the front!

Bobby came home that evening and looked at the picture. "She was beautiful, you know?"

"Yeah."

"You look a lot alike."

"Yeah—I guess."

"You should take that to Judy and get a decent frame put on it."

"Are you kidding? It's a big picture—it's not going to be cheap!"

"I know. Just go ahead and do it."

It took a few weeks, but Judy outdid herself! When she telephoned to advise that the picture was finished, I was so anxious to see it, I drove there immediately. As soon as I walked into the shop, I saw it propped up against the wall.

"Oh," was all I could say.

62. Ghosts of Sisters Past

MY SADNESS BECAME numbness with regard to losing my sister. The more time passes, the more unreal a situation seems. Your mind tends to play tricks, popping in thoughts of, "The phone will ring and it will be her—or she'll just show up at the door." But tricks are all you get. It never happens.

My days were spent busily sorting through Genie's items, as well as trying to keep up with housework and errands. Six children and their activities require a great deal of scheduling and transportation. I was always on my way somewhere. As much as I missed my sister, there was no time to dwell on things. Life had officially returned to normal, and I had to try to keep up with its demands.

I find that people are prone to certain things—for whatever reason. I am a dreamer. I dream of things that I wish to have come true. And most nights, I dream when I sleep. Now, it is a rare occasion when I have a frightening dream. Most often, my dreams are pleasant. I sleep well. In fact, throughout my entire life, I can recall times in the middle of the night when I was awake and frightened—but not so much when I was asleep. In sleep, I usually find peace.

Bobby and I share a queen-size bed. He sleeps on the right, I on the left. We both roll from side to side during the course of sleeping, but no matter which way either of us is facing, Bobby keeps one hand on me at all times. So should he be lying on his right side with his back to me, his left hand will be draped over behind him reaching for me. It is one of my favorite things about Bobby—he never lets me go.

Most evenings, Bobby and I would lie in bed until we fell asleep. The television would be on to suit whoever stayed awake the longest. I was usually the winner. Bobby would no sooner lie down, than he would fall asleep, remote control in hand. I would then slip the remote away from him and take back what I felt was rightfully mine—control!

There was nothing particular about this one evening that made it stand out from any other. By nature, I am a creature of habit. I'm certain I watched the same shows I always watched. The room was very still—with the exception of the TV volume, which was turned down. I was completely asleep.

I was dreaming, yet it seemed very real. I was standing alone in the middle of nowhere. It wasn't necessarily light or dark out, but I could see well. A figure approached from the distance. When close enough so that I could see who it was, I realized it was my Nana— deceased since 1966. I had dreamt about her once or twice before in my life. Each time, I had resisted touching her. This was very clear to me. I loved Nana. But she was gone; passed over to the other side—where I was *not*. I always felt that should I touch her, I would be taken.

In this dream, Nana smiled at me and I smiled back. We exchanged a long look at each other in a loving way. I was very glad to see her, and she seemed pleased to see me all grown up with a family. No one spoke.

As I began to move away, I turned slightly—and instantly saw Genie! Before I could even think, I grabbed her as tight as I could and pulled her close to me. I wanted to speak, to say something—anything. I wept. I cried so hard I couldn't stop. I thought to myself, *I will NEVER let go of you—NEVER*. I cried and cried so long and so hard, it was as if she and I melted together. I could actually feel her blending into me. Then her voice surrounded my head. She said, "Thanks, Sissy. I knew you would take care of me. You're the best!" I continued to cry, holding on even more tightly.

I would have stayed in that standing hold for the rest of time. I had Genie back and wasn't about to let her go. But I awoke to find my arms wrapped tightly around my own body, tears streaming down my cheeks. My first thought was, *NO-o-o!* It had felt so real. I had *had* her; right in my arms I had held her. I know she was here.

But there I was sitting upright in my bed, with my arms around myself. I was so sad.

Bobby was awake. With his one hand pressed against my lower back he said, "She was here!"

"What?"

"I looked at you—but I saw Genie. She was here, wasn't she?"

Stage VIII

63. Window of Opportunity

NOT THAT I needed something additional to occupy me, but Bobby had had a bug for quite some time to start a business. We were coming into some cash, by way of the accident settlement, and decided that it was "free" money—so why not try this? Between the two of us, there was no actual business experience. What we had going for us was that we were both very hard working. We thought this would assure us success, but sad to say, it was not enough.

Bobby and I had both fallen head over heels in love with saltwater fish and aquariums. Our passion blinded us into believing that everyone would feel as we did. Our hobby became the cornerstone of our business. I found a location very close to our house and began to look into connections for fish and supplies.

What I should have looked into was financing! Neither one of us had ever had extra cash. We lived payday to payday. So when we came into a lump sum, we thought we had more than we did. In retrospect, we probably should have taken the settlement to a bank, shown it to them, and said, "Here—this is all we have. We would like to start a business and get a business loan." Then we probably would have gotten one. But we did it ass backwards: We took the money and stretched it as far as it would go. Then when the money was running out, we tried to get a loan. No can do!

From the first, we did not have enough money. In spite of that, we managed to build the business by working seven days a week. Bobby continued working for the mill, while I manned the shop accompanied by our youngest; not yet in school. It was a long day, but in many ways fun! I loved fish and so did Bobby. Just ordering them and getting them into the store was enjoyable. Our customer base was small, but growing. I believe where we went wrong was that the business was never quite large enough to support the family. It was just supporting itself.

After three years of really trying, we realized that it was hopeless. We were falling behind on house payments and not able to afford much else. It was inevitable that we throw in the towel. In desperation, I telephoned a local employment agency inquiring about temporary work. I was willing to do almost anything. I tested well on all of their business skills tests, and before I knew it, I was placed in a bankcard center issuing gold cards! *Isn't life ironic?* I spent hour upon hour looking at those cards trying to think up some way to grant myself such a privilege—without success; I didn't even have my account at that bank. Still, it was a job.

The assignment was to last approximately 4 weeks. Day after day, I performed data entry for hundreds of customers, issuing gold cards to them. It was a regimentally strict environment. Not much laughing goes on in a bank. This may not be true of all banking establishments. But for this one, the more rigid and standoffish you were, the more liked you were by personnel from the Human Resource Office.

At the time of this assignment, there were five other women hired to perform exactly the same task—all temporary. Each woman was very different. Not to boast, but I plowed through stack after stack of information cards, matching their production by almost two to one. Yet on Monday of my sixth week, mid-afternoon, the supervisor came up to me, smiled, and declared, "You're done!"

Stupidly, I refuted, "No, ma'am. I have this whole stack left here."

"I'll take those," she snapped, as she thanked me for coming.

Before I could say "assignment over"—it was! I had been led to the door and relieved of my duties.

I tried to no avail not to cry on my way to the car. Tears streaming down my face, I went over and over my actions while working there. *Did I curse in front of someone? What have I done that caused these imbeciles to let go of the fastest data entry clerk they had? Are they devoid of any kind of logic?*

My home was just a hop, skip and a jump away, with the drive lasting literally less than two minutes to get me there. Still crying,

I walked into the kitchen, to be greeted by my mother—who was visiting from out of town—and my six children, all screaming about whatever they felt was urgent. I was about to have a meltdown! All I could think to do was to focus. *Call the job counselor and get another job—NOW.* I called and just hearing the ringing started my tears flowing again. *How is it that I am unemployed? What just happened?*

The call to the agency was answered, and I was quickly reassured that no, I had done nothing wrong. The company that had contracted for my services were simply going to let everyone go by the end of the week anyway; since I had mentioned that my mother was in from out of town, they had thought I would appreciate being first, so as to be able to visit with her.

"My mother doesn't give a shit if I visit with her—she gives a shit if I have a job!"

To this day, I still don't believe that story. I feel confident that to get ushered out on a Monday afternoon, you have to have pissed someone off in a definitive way!

"Take it easy," the woman at the other end of the phone said, very composed.

"You have to find me something else. Right now! I mean it; I'll do anything!"

She reiterated that she would get back to me just as soon as she heard of anything opening up. In less than an hour, the phone rang. The counselor advised me that a job order had just come in for a temporary assignment for a clerk in an accounting department. The duration was expected to be about 90 days. "But they're fussy. They want an interview, drug screen—the whole bit."

I jumped up and said, "Not to worry. Just get me in first. I'll get it!"

This was a pivotal moment in my life. I realized that while the others all sat their desks thinking how lucky they were to get to stay while I had been shown the way out, I (and no one else at that bankcard center) had the opportunity to apply for this new job! And it would last for 90 days.

It was true! *When one door closes, a window opens.* And the window was mine!

The interview itself became a bit of a twist, in that I was scheduled to see someone named Shawn. Upon my arrival at the plant, I found a very nicely decorated—but locked—lobby, with a desk phone and a massive directory, organized by last names. I remembered that most business phones require you to dial 9 before getting an outside line, so I tried that. I telephoned back to the employment office and asked "Shawn who"? I was then given the last name, as if to say, "Oops!"

Oops—I now look like a complete idiot! How am I going to get a job if I virtually cannot get anyone to announce that I am even here! In reality, what if THIS is the interview process—to see if I'm smart enough to figure this out and get in. Then do I get the job?

Luckily for me, a very sympathetic employee/administrative assistant came back from her lunch break and eased my nervousness, declaring, "I hate that they have done this; we miss having a receptionist!" *Me, too!* I thought. In two seconds, I learned that there was only one Shawn on site (a woman), and this other lady was kind enough to find her and tell her that I was waiting.

Shawn was a woman and a half, "out to here" pregnant expecting her first child. She would be my supervisor. We spoke for a while, discussing some aspects of what appeared to be a very straight-forward assignment. Coincidentally, we shared a birthday, which—for whatever reason—was considered a positive sign. I was next handed off from a 20-minute conversation with Shawn to her supervisor.

Chase, the supervisor, was a very personable, Midwestern looking man of respectable height, very thin. He began by asking me, "So what do you think of living in the South?"

I interpreted this to be a question intended to trip me up. I could feel my face contorting, as if I were asking him in retort, "I like it here?" There was great significance to this exchange: it was the only time I withheld my actual opinion, solicited or otherwise, for the duration of my career at this location! The next day, I found myself submitting to a drug screen—eagerly.

My assignment, not to exceed 90 days, required me to process all accounts payable in the M-Z portion of the alphabet. I was given a wage of $6 per hour and advised, "We need a work horse!"

"I'm your horse!" I eagerly responded.

I worked diligently performing data entry on a computer in a room I shared with one other woman. Phyllis was a permanent company employee who, although quite knowledgeable and nice, was also very moody. Thus when I would ask a question, the answer would depend solely upon whether Phyllis felt up to talking that day or not. Sometimes I would get instructions promptly. Other times, I would ask and be left to feel as though my voice made no sound in the Universe what-so-ever.

Still, I had a job. And I was thrilled!

As time passed, the 90 days I was to be employed were replaced in my mind by the number of days I had remaining. *I have been here 60 days; therefore, I have 30 left. OMG!* My inner hope was that somehow, some way, I would be picked up as a permanent employee and be given "a job"—permanently! That was all I wanted—then.

After a while, my office mate, Phyllis, became a bit more engaging towards me and would occasionally initiate conversation. She had been employed there for a very long time. Her husband also worked in the plant, for a contract company employed on the site. In my mind, they had it made—both of them working, making pretty decent money (although I had no idea how much money that was). Every now and then I would disclose my concern that my time was growing short. She repeatedly reassured me, stating very matter-of-factly, "In ten years, you'll be sitting right there and I'll be sitting right here."

As my workload decreased and the end of the project drew closer, I was instructed by Chase to "be flexible" and make myself available to whoever might need assistance in the department. As luck would have it, an analyst who had left a rather important assignment until the last minute needed help and came looking for me. The task was to reconcile the billings of an in-house contractor. It was due first thing the next morning, and it was now 3:00 in the afternoon. "Can I take it home?" I asked. "Sure. Do whatever. Just have it back here at 8:00 tomorrow."

I worked on this all evening, scrutinizing each and every line of this report in order to make an impression. Upon returning the next day, I proudly handed my work over to the analyst, feeling certain that he would take full credit for doing the work. I was wrong! When asked for explanations as to why he had done this or that, he told the truth. "I'm not sure—Ellen did this."

"WHAT? Why?"

"Hey, you told us all to use her if we needed help, so I did."

"Get her in here!" I was called before the man who had hired me some 65 days earlier to explain my notes.

Within days of that meeting, I was reassigned to track production and yield for the plant. I had managed to pry my foot into the door!

To perform this task required me to physically move my work-space into another office. I was to co-habit with an analyst; a woman who had worked at the company for a considerable length of time. While knowledgeable and skilled at her responsibilities, she had some rather unique eccentricities with which I became familiar rather quickly.

The woman's name was Leona. She was a university graduate; mother of two girls, widowed—and as Southern a woman as I had ever met! Her accent was very heavy. She also spoke very loudly and with a lisp. Now the "loud" was not something that I was not accustomed to! I, myself, have been known to be quite loud (although I had been seemingly more subdued at this job since beginning a few months earlier, so as not to offend anyone). At any rate, there we were, sharing HER office. In an 8x10 space stood Leona's desk, type-writer return, credenza, file cabinets, coat rack, and bulletin boards. I, on the other hand, was told to sit at a smaller desk crammed up against the front wall, so as not to impede any of her personal work space. Five more pounds of body weight, and I would not have been able to slide into the office chair—that's how small the space was. I remember asking if Leona would move her desk back just a bit to make room for me.

"I need all this space to do my work!" she declared, waving her arms about without even looking up at me.

I remember thinking to myself, *OK; I'm in—even if I have to use a shoe horn to do it!*

64. Burnt to a Crisp

FROM ALMOST DAY one, I observed that this was the most food-friendly workplace I had ever encountered. There was food every day—somewhere. Filled with employees all earning a pretty good living, this workplace created an assembly of people who liked to socialize and could afford to do it at will. And food is a very social indulgence! In addition, the company made such a comfortable profit, that it was often a practice to order something in, rather than having the employees go out to lunch. So not only was this a very social/eating environment, the company was footing the bill for much of this.

I, on the other hand, was brown-bagging—bringing lean cuisines, soup or some other less desirable snack to get me through.

On this very deserted Friday afternoon, I had missed lunch, having brought nothing from home, and was for all intents and purposes starving! Phyllis recommended that I check in the kitchen or the break rooms for any leftovers from meetings. "If it's in there, you can have it—it's Friday!"

My scavenger hunt began. I explored one room after another, searching for something to satisfy my hunger, when—there it was! A HUGE bacon cheeseburger with fries from Steak-Out!

Now Phyllis had told me point blank that if I found it, I could have it. But to me, it felt as though I were stealing this cheeseburger. It wasn't mine! So I grabbed it, tucked it in on my side and checked the hall, looking both ways before I entered, with the evidence of the Steak-Out box in hand. Seeing no one in the hallway, I decided the coast was officially clear. Who was I kidding? The administration building hallways were a barren wasteland on Friday afternoons! I could never figure that out! How could everyone be off, every Friday?

Oh, well. I had mine and was on my way to cook me up a little something! I took my prize to the microwave, which was in the mailroom, across the hall from Phyllis's office and two doors away from the one I shared with Leona. I had used the microwave before. Typically, I would throw whatever I was cooking into it and then return to what I was doing, which would give me a comfortable five minutes to allow the cooking, cooling, etc. and for me to multi-task.

This Friday, however, was different. I was getting to know my way around, beginning to feel that I belonged, and the place was nearly empty. I stayed in the mailroom. Then Luther, a visitor to the administration building (who worked in the lab), rounded the corner and entered. He began to entertain me with all of his latest, greatest jokes.

Luther was quite the comedian. He had started his career in the mailroom years earlier, working his way into a much better paying position. Anyway, there we were, Luther telling me his latest jokes, me talking about how much I liked working there, etc. And then a popping sound began to overtake the conversation. "You making popcorn?" he asked.

"No, I swiped a burger from the kitchen."

Pop! Pop – POP!!!

"What the hell is that?" I walked towards the microwave, becoming totally mesmerized by the sight of what appeared to be a meteor; a burning fireball inside the microwave. "Luther, shit—it's on fire!"

"Oh, I got this," Luther said in a very confident but mechanical voice. He walked to the closest fire extinguisher in the hallway, returned with it, and took control. Pulling the door of the microwave open, he proceeded to douse the flames with a long, continuous burst of the chemical extinguisher.

I was stunned at my inability to do anything once I saw the fire burning. Even worse, there went my cheeseburger!

The following Monday, almost first thing, Chase called me into his office. "Please close the door," he said solemnly.

Oh, no! This isn't going to be good, I thought.

"I understand there was a fire?"

My face began to shrivel up like a five-year-old caught doing something wrong. Clearly, it was all over for me—so denying it was pointless.

Chase looked at me and said, "We like to try to learn from incidents around here—so I'd like to go over what happened with you and perhaps discover how this could have been avoided."

One of the rare moments in my life where I found myself speechless, I thought to myself, *is he kidding?*

We sat there and went over everything as it happened. It was apparent that had Luther not run into me and been telling me jokes, I wouldn't have even been in the room to hear the popping. I would have been two doors away at my desk, and who knows how much of a fire would have developed in the interim? We wrote up this experience of "shared learnings" together, and rather than feeling chastised, I was feeling that I had actually contributed to the future well-being of the place, listing all the things I should have done. It had begun in a scary way, but ended with me feeling pretty good.

That changed quickly. Chase then advised me that of all the locations in the building that I could have chosen to cook the burger, the mailroom did not have a "company owned" microwave. Rather, the microwave that was in there had been brought in by Leona. Since it did not belong to the company, and since I had caused the fire, I would have to reimburse her for the damages.

So my "treasure hunt" that fateful day resulted in my learning several things:

1. You can't put foil in a microwave, even if surrounded by a Styrofoam container.
2. Once you use a fire extinguisher on a microwave—it's toast!
3. Nothing is actually "free."

The "free" burger that I never actually ate ended up costing me $125.

65. There Really *Is* a Santa Claus!

ONE CHARACTERISTIC OF the ladies I was working with is that whether they actually were, or not, they lived well-to-do. By that I mean that their nails and hair were always "done" and their clothing was always beautiful. Clearly, this luxury came with years of working at this company and having steady income and a generous benefit package. Also—more characteristic of the South than this particular office—their choice of clothing was very colorful. In New York (or more aptly, larger cities) business clothing choices were limited to black, brown, gray and navy. I was never sure if these dark colors were worn so prominently because of their slimming nature, or if it was thought to be a more sophisticated choice. Regardless, they did not seem to be on the menu here. In this small Southern town, the color palette came directly from tropical fruit such as watermelon and berries. It was just as they were: always cheerful.

During the Holiday season in particular, these women would appear each day donning brand new holiday sweaters, a different one each day. It was so very festive; I couldn't help but enjoy it. But enjoy it from a distance was all I could do. With such a large family to support and limited funds, there was no room in our budget for such luxuries as "holiday" sweaters; even if it was the season to be jolly! Out of habit as much as necessity, I appeared every day in denim jeans and a sweatshirt or sweater. Casual was the order of my day. After all, with six children to get ready each and every morning, I was not aiming for "stylish"—I was aiming for dressed!

Once again I found myself to be the square peg in the round hole. Although no one ever said such a thing, I looked upon myself as the smudge on a beautiful holiday table; the one black dot in the midst of all the festive trimmings of poinsettias, holly and pine. I didn't mind being different. I had been different my entire life. I even rationalized being different in my own head as, "If I were to find myself in a holiday sweater, it would not be quite so colorful. I would choose something more subdued."

Leona didn't go overboard with the whole Christmas theme. She tended to dress on the more casual side of life as well. So in my immediate area, I didn't stand out quite so much.

It was more noticeable in the hallways. There were also a fair amount of holiday decorations going up around the building, both in and out of people's office spaces. As with any other grouping, there are those who put up Christmas cards from vendors and friends on his/her door, and there are always one or two who insist on creating a winter wonderland right in their office. It was a very accepting environment in that nothing, or over the top—and everything in between—were all accepted equally. It was entirely up to what people wanted to do. The company itself would string lights throughout a very large pine tree in the front yard of the administration building, as well as put wreaths on the outside of the building and the entrance gates.

To demonstrate to my coworkers that I was indeed "in the spirit" of things, I wore a string of bells around my neck. They were rather colorful by comparison to what I normally had on, a Kelly green string with red, silver and gold bells at the bottom that jingled ever so slightly when I moved.

Every now and again, I would compliment someone on her choice of sweater. It was interesting to me how many totally different holiday sweaters there were—and that no one seemed to have selected the same one. Not that it would have been a problem, but for so many individuals to be shopping in the same town and none to have purchased the same sweater was really surprising to me. This simply reinforced just how unique everyone is!

Day after day, I came to work, in the midst of my coworker elves, in my habitual black, brown or navy attire. In truth, I was just glad to have a job! Glad that with my husband, we were managing to support our family. It wasn't so terrible; not dressing like everyone else.

In fact, it wasn't "dressing" that mattered. I did take notice, though, of other people's ability to indulge themselves in articles of clothing that clearly one could only wear for a 30-day window during the year. The fact that they did not repeat their choice during those 30 days made it even more obvious how privileged everyone around me was. *Must be nice,* I thought!

One Thursday morning close to Christmas, I arrived at work to find a beautifully wrapped box at my desk. The tag simply read, "To Ellen- Love, Santa." I remember fearing it was some sort of joke being played on me. I turned to Leona, who was already seated at her desk, and asked, "Did you see who put this here?"

"Yes," she replied, "but I'm sworn to secrecy."

I looked the box up and down for several minutes before gathering myself and the courage to open it. Receiving gifts was never high on my list! I love to give; not so much receive. (I'm not sure why, exactly.)

I began to open the box. Leona continued to work as if it were none of her business, though I'd be willing to bet she had one eye on her work and one on that box! As I pulled the tissue paper back, I could see what it was: My own holiday sweater. It was a red sweater vest with a white turtleneck, both decorated with black and blue nutcrackers. They went all the way around the turtleneck part and were knitted into each side of the red vest. The gesture itself was touching. The choice was amazing!

While ice skating as a child, I performed in many a holiday show. One year in particular, I was costumed in a red satin jacket with epaulets on the shoulders and a large black fur top hat with a big red plume of a feather. *I was a nutcracker, on ice!* Since then, I received the occasional nutcracker from my mother reminiscing about that performance. Whoever this "Santa" was, however, he or she was someone who knew nothing about that.

This was a total surprise! It was one of the few times in my entire life that I have ever been completely surprised. And it was good! I took the box and walked to the ladies room to try on my new sweater.

It fit perfectly. I wore that sweater all day long, and several other days during that holiday season. Although I never was able to discover who played Santa that year, I love that sweater and what it represented to me. I was lucky enough to have a job—and I was clearly working with really nice people. It was a jolly Christmas!

66. An Old Dog Learns a New Trick

ONE FRIDAY AFTERNOON, I was called in to the supervisor's office for an unscheduled meeting. Upon responding to his call, I was instructed to close his door and sit down. He smiled a bit and informed me that he was able to offer me a "temporary" position working for the company. Now—to clarify this offer—I would not be working for temporary agency any longer, but rather working for the company itself, though I would remain a temporary employee. This would afford me all the benefits of a full-time permanent employee, with just one exception—no dental insurance.

Fear overtook me as the offer was being made. I do not know where or how I knew this, but I felt sure that being a temporary employee directly for the company would mean that I had one year from that date to secure a permanent position—or be cut loose. So there would be a sort of clock ticking in the back of my job, and time would now potentially run out.

Seeing the look of concern on my face after the offer was made, the supervisor asked, "What's wrong?"

I informed him of my concerns.

A look of disbelief came over his face, as he insisted, "Take the job!"

I was quickly drawn into the whirlwind of events that accompany accepting a job: paperwork, photo id, announcements, etc. It was a very exciting time! For the moment, I had found a position and received an increase of $2 per hour, bringing me up to $8. While those numbers may seem small and insignificant, imagine getting a 25% increase. The fact was that I was in heaven! I continued to work in the accounting department, but constantly looked for opportunities to improve my skills and my ability to make myself a more viable candidate for permanent employment.

By this time, everything was done by computer. Every employee in a clerical capacity worked on a computer, not a typewriter. I had, of course, exaggerated my skills and ability in this area, stating affirmatively that I did, indeed, have computer skills. The truth would have been more accurately portrayed by stating that yes, I can turn on a computer and type! So now I was determined to familiarize myself with the various software choices contained in the Microsoft arsenal of weaponry.

Regardless of the subject matter, the best way to excel at anything is by doing it, over and over. So I took full advantage of a workload crunch that hit the accounting department and volunteered to create and assemble the entire QPR presentation.

QPR was an acronym for Quarterly Performance Review, which consisted of the business unit sending down all leaders in our location to discuss the state of the business. The presentation was informational segments put together in PowerPoint—a program I had NEVER used before. What I did not realize until after I had made this offer and it was accepted was that this QPR presentation typically had 50-60 slides, ranging from charts and graphs to bullet items with pictures. It was baptism by fire! Although I had little knowledge of what all the information meant, I completed my crash course in PowerPoint and passed with flying colors. I had managed to come to the rescue of my department mates and, at the same time, to contribute to my much needed education.

As I settled into my surroundings, there was a particular man I got to know, who worked in another department. His name was Maurice. I was told by others that Maurice had worked for the company for many years as an Environmental Engineer and was now back working for them as an independent contractor.

Maurice and I had been running into each other while working on various projects, and through conversation, we discovered we were both from New York. One day Maurice inquired of me, "What part of New York are you from?"

"The Bronx," I replied.

"Me too—Whereabouts?" As we exchanged more specific details, we began talking about schools.

"I went to St. Nicholas of Tolentine," I told him. "Where did you go?"

Maurice smiled, "Oh, I didn't go to a Catholic school; I went to Bronx High School of Science."

@%$@!!!!

Immediately those twenty-five years disappeared, and I was instantly as angry as I had been then, arguing with my mother for weeks in the kitchen about not being permitted to go to Science. Staring back at me was the person I could have been; with the career I could have had—not to mention the income level. On the other hand, what are the odds that someone born and raised in New York City would run into someone much later in life, IN DECATUR, ALABAMA, who attended the very school she wanted to go to?

As I walked back to my office, I couldn't help but cry. There is no worse feeling in life than to know with certainty that you have missed the boat! I had been so angry that I did not get to go to the school I wanted to go to that I threw what education and opportunities I did have into the wind. And here I was today—a clerk.

Day by day, both my past haunting me and my present disgusting me welled up inside like an illness. I was so miserable; I could not make myself happy. I imagined what could have been—knowing full well that "what could have been" wasn't.

For months, I continued to search the company website for job postings, trying to envision myself being exactly what they were looking for. But nothing really suited me. Then—low and behold—an announcement was sent out to all staff members that the company would be hiring new operators for the plant by selecting viable candidates from the "Work Keys" test results.

I had never pictured myself as an Operator, but I was very interested in this, particularly because the pay scales which stair-stepped up from a starting salary of $15+ topped out, after a five-year period, to in excess of $30 per hour. Operators worked 12-hour swing shifts, regardless of weather, holidays, illness or anything else. But the pay and the benefits were out of this world! I was now on a mission.

I was advised by the HR representative that I would be granted an interview based upon my test scores. Now, I had spent close to 15 months at this facility and had put my networking skills to task—meeting, greeting, and making sure that everyone knew I would pitch in and get done whatever job needed to be done. At this time, that networking seemed to be paying off. After inquiring who would be interviewing me, I was informed of the members of the interview team: Mary, Donald, and Andrew. Oh, Happy Day! Mary was an engineer who had been quite pleasant to talk to and had befriended me in conversations concerning my unending quest to secure a permanent position with the company; Donald and Andrew were assigned to one of the units, and both were "good-ol' boys" who liked to pal around and cut up when having to come up and deal with accounting issues. I considered all to be friends. I was in, I thought. Short of my throwing up during the interview, I was very confident that this was a job I was going to land.

Well, I have always been told not to count my biddies before they hatched. This was no exception! Virtually five minutes before I was to begin my interview, the unit had an upset calling both Donald and Andrew away. Mary had fallen and injured her back and was now on sick leave. My interview team—my "sure thing" interview team!—had disintegrated.

I graciously offered to postpone the appointment and wait for a more convenient time. HR would not have it. They had a schedule to keep, and keep it they would. In the blink of an eye, a new team was assembled, consisting of a different engineer, a maintenance tech, and the HR rep himself. Not what I was expecting!

I was questioned for two hours about everything under the sun. Upon hearing the declaration that this would be the last question, I exhaustedly declared, "Seven."

"What?" they asked.

"My shoe size; It is the only thing you haven't asked me." I was

trying to be funny. Although they did laugh, I felt that this may have
been a liberty I should not have taken. Nonetheless, the interview
ended on a positive note, and I returned to my work station.

After weeks of waiting to hear without so much as a word, I sat
trying to focus on my work, while wondering what it would be like
to make some of that high pay that was offered to Operators. I also
wondered what it would be like to juggle my life, my husband, my
six children, dogs, cats, grocery shopping—all the while working a
12-hour swing shift. Well, that question was never to be answered.
As I imagined all of this, the twelve "new" operators paraded down
the hallway of my office towards the HR Department to have their
photo IDs and paperwork completed. Not the announcement I had
envisioned, but I got the message: I didn't get the job.

If there is one thing that could be said for this company I worked
for, it thrives on initiatives. Every time you turn around, someone higher up has introduced a new initiative which will optimize, capitalize
on, and streamline whatever process it involves. It has long since
been my belief that these initiatives are instituted not so much out of
concern for improving the process they address, but rather to pad the
résumé of whomever has thought up this particular brainchild.

In this instance, the initiative was that of adopting selected por-
tions of the "SAP" accounting software program into the day-to-day
operation of the company. I now found myself working towards in-
tegrating the SAP system into our accounting procedures—a process
made more difficult because it was decided that only *some* compo-
nents of SAP would be included (to be more "cost effective"). The
process was referred to as a roll-over, and doing the testing, trouble
shooting, etc. took several days of concentrated effort on this—and
nothing else.

There were several consultants who came on site during this time
to assist with this implementation. One of these consultants, Marilyn,
worked with me diligently to ensure the integrity of this process.
During one particular evening we were working late, Marilyn divert-
ed her attention from the SAP migration and began to speak with me

about my future career plans with the company. She asked such questions as "What do you see yourself doing in ten years?" I was taken aback, as my roles have typically been clerical in nature, and the conversation placed me in very unfamiliar territory. Long story short, Marilyn confided that she had been asked to speak to me specifically about my future by the supervisor who had hired me. "He thinks you have a great deal of potential—and also thinks it would be a really good idea for you to go back to school."

"Are you serious?" I blurted out, half in jest.

"Absolutely," she said. "You demonstrate a great deal of skill, and people who have observed you working feel that you are very intelligent. It would be in your best interest to go back to school. It would make a big difference in your future."

Afterwards, I remember thinking to myself, "Everyone who has a college degree thinks that everyone else should have one. What's up with that?" Little did I know, I was about to find out!

67. Gidget Goes to Rome

VERY EARLY INTO my tenure with the company, I had taken the advice of those more senior in their careers and invested 20% of my salary, small as it may have been, into a 401(k). I invested the funds after tax, so that should I need or want anything, I could make a withdrawal without a penalty. So I had a savings. As I observed and listened to others who had taken full advantage of their two transactions per month free of charge, I decided to try my hand at investing. After careful consideration, I decided to move my funds from the company stock to a higher yield account to maximize my earnings. I followed the directions, which were pretty easy to understand, and then anxiously waited for my money to skyrocket.

If you have never heard this advice before, listen closely to what you are about to be told: When dealing in stock, news trumps EVERYTHING. If you haven't heard any news, it just might be because you are not listening closely enough.

So on one particular day, I had moved my funds out of the company stock. When I arrived at work the very next morning and logged in to my computer, up came the company home page with the opening stock price—which had shot up over $10 per share IN THE FIRST 10 MINUTES OF THE MARKET OPENING. I actually thought someone had tampered with my computer in an effort to play a joke. Sadly, the joke was on me, but I had played it on myself. The company had announced an impending merger, and the stock was shooting up. I, however, having moved my funds in an effort to make a quick buck, lost $10 per share in minutes. What a shrewd move, eh?

Now, as if it were not enough of a blow to lose $10 per share in my very first stock move, it also occurred to me that a merger would bring about many changes—not the least of which was causing a ringing in my head: *Last hired, first fired*. I became overtaken with fear and emotion. The last time I was this anxious about anything was so long ago, I could not even remember. But I was anxious now.

A reasonable period of nervousness was followed by resurgence towards securing a new, permanent position. Again I found myself checking the job postings. On this occasion, I observed a new position listed as available: Administrative Assistant for the Capital Projects Group. *What exactly is a "capital projects group"?* I thought to myself. Then I realized, *WHO CARES? If they need an Administrative Assistant, I can do that!*

I began to position myself in the mindset of selling myself as the best darn Administrative Assistant they had ever seen! This time my interview was conducted by two men, both of whom (unbeknownst to me at the time) were applying for the position of Manager of that area. The interview went very well, and it was only a few short weeks before I discovered that I was their choice for the position. *HELL, YEAH!* I was now in!

This was very much like marrying into a huge family. Everyone had tips on what to do, how to do it, and great things to take advantage of as an employee. I was informed of my starting date and salary.

My former position continued to require my full attention, but did not get it. Instead, I drifted in and out of adding up just how much money I could make and save if I worked in my new position the rest of my natural life. My salary was somewhere in the neighborhood of $9.30 per hour. But it might as well have been a million dollars! The excitement of this new job and the prospect of what might be surrounded me. It was all I could think about.

Despite my lack of skill when it came to stock investing, once I left it alone, my savings did grow—and quickly. I was now in unfamiliar territory—having a savings, or financial cushion. I began to think of all the things I had thought about wanting and pushed aside due to lack of funds: a new car, furniture, a new wardrobe. It was during this time that I discovered a trip opportunity through the local Catholic Church. It was a group tour going to Rome for the Millennium. The cost would be $2,600 per person, a bit less if there were two travelling together.

I thought back to my childhood and the trip to France my class-mates were offered in sophomore year. I could remember my mother telling me, "No, I don't think so. You will go when you're grown up." All well and good, but now I was grown. I had never gone. In reality, I had never been anywhere outside the United States.

Then I thought about all those people at the company whom I had met who had travelled around the world. There was something different about them. It's not easy to explain. But, it's almost as if they possess a broader perspective of the world because they have been to other places. They are not limited to only knowing what is here. I could see a difference—and I wanted that for my children.

I spoke to Bobby about it, suggesting that we send the girls to Rome.

"Are you serious?" he asked.

"Absolutely. I want them to go."

"Are you sure they *want* to go?"

"Oh, I'm pretty sure."

The plan was on! I became giddy with excitement. I loved plan-ning surprises, and this was going to be a great one.

The girls were 15 and 16. There were many people planning to travel. To facilitate the group members getting to know each other, dinner parties were being held monthly during the year prior to the actual departure. I wanted it to be a surprise, but I didn't want them excluded from those dinner meetings. My plan was to surprise them at Christmas with the trip, enabling them to attend the dinners in January, February and March prior to departure.

Coworkers got involved in the preparation, having been overseas themselves. One provided me with three Italian coins for each girl to throw into the fountain to make a wish. I purchased passport wal-lets. Then I thought, *I know what I'll do: I'll get a copy of the movie, "Gidget Goes to Rome." I'll wrap that up with the passport wallets and give it to them Christmas morning. Perfect!*

My husband, advocating for everyone else in the family, said,

"You *are* going to do something for the other kids, right? I mean, we can't give the girls a trip to Europe and give the boys socks and underwear." Oh, I was way ahead of him! We shopped and purchased a go-cart for the youngest boy. Our middle son, now driving, got a check to pick out rims for his car. Anna, older than all of them but limited in her ability, got a brand new television for her room. It was going to be a GREAT Christmas!

The anticipation was maddening! I played their surprise over and over in my head. It was almost impossible to contain my excitement. When Christmas Eve arrived, Bobby and I announced, "You kids are all older now. You know there is no Santa Claus. So, we're going to open our gifts on Christmas Eve—as long as nobody will mind not having anything on Christmas morning. Is that OK?"

Well, what kid is going to argue that logic? Even if they mind, they are too close to the "promised land" to back away. "Oh no, Daddy, we'll be fine."

There were several gifts given to each child, of a more generic nature. Clothing mostly, with a few extra items such as cologne, hair accessories, and the like. They seemed relatively happy, but certainly not blown away. The kids enjoyed staying up late, playing games and making hot chocolate. Bobby and I took full advantage of their ages and went to sleep!

The next morning, we entered the kitchen. One by one, each child awoke and came into the room, asking what we were going to have for breakfast and when. We then told them, "Well, we do have one more present for you to open."

I walked to the dining room where the tree sat in front of the large picture window facing the road. I pulled a festively wrapped box from the back and handed it to the girls, stating, "This is for you to share." They smiled at each other and began ripping the paper off. As the box top was removed by one, the other reached in and said, "Look—wallets! Mine is black, yours is brown." Just then, one of the coins fell out. They both looked down at the floor and yelled, "Money!" At this moment, one of the two girls (the honor student) picked up the coin and exclaimed, "Oh my God! It's Canadian! WE'RE GOING TO CANADA!!!"

Bobby and I both looked at each other with total confusion. "What are you talking about? Girls, that's not Canadian money; it's a 'lira'. It's Italian."

Again the honor student looks at us with disgust and says, "What are we going to do with a Lira in Canada?"

Bobby and I both put our heads on each other's shoulders and sighed! "They're not smart enough; we can't let them go," he said to me.

"Girls. You don't use lire in Canada. Lira is used in Italy. You're both going to Rome with the group in April."

Screams came instantly from both girls. They could not believe they were going! For that matter, neither could Bobby and I after what we had just witnessed.

Instantly, the boys chimed in, "What are you saying? They get a trip to Europe and we get clothes?"

"No. You each have one box as well," we told them.

Both boys grinned from ear to ear as they opened their boxes and saw their prizes. "I have my own personal vehicle," the little one said. Bobby and I just shook our heads.

The saying is true: It is better to give than it is to receive! That Christmas was the best one our family ever had.

68. Net-Working

AFTER DOWNSIZING THE number of employees in the department, Human Resources needed to shed some of its responsibilities. Subsequently, an all-user e-mail was sent to the workforce announcing that the plant newsletter needed an editor. Anyone willing to take on this responsibility (in addition to his or her regular duties) should respond to this note. What was implied was that "if you want to do it, we'll let you—but you will get nothing added to your pay for doing it."

I don't know why, but I thought it would be really interesting to be able to take on a newsletter. So I volunteered. I was the only person who did. With no competition, the job was mine! Quick and easy. My supervisor, however, was not as delighted with my acquisition of additional responsibilities. It would have been preferable to him that I remain in my own area, keeping only unto them. But I thought this was a perfect opportunity to get to know everyone who worked out there, what they did, what went on, etc. I would be the "Rona Barrett" of the plant!

As I became more and more familiar with members of the plant staff and met more and more people, I found myself crossing into many different circles. One day, an engineer named Anthony approached me in the hallway. He asked if I was aware of the men's Industrial League basketball team that the plant had organized, of which he was himself a member. Yes, I had heard this—but did not have much information beyond that it existed.

Anthony's primary interest was in my allowing announcements to be placed in the newsletter. As we travelled through the hallway walking and talking, however, he did not try to conceal his secondary agenda—that of securing a coach for the team. My first reaction was that I was being "punked" by some sharp, young engineer who wanted to get the better of me. But I quickly learned how serious he was, "We could really use a coach. It'll be good. Just give it some thought."

If there was one aspect of this of which I was certain, it was this—I would not take this on and associate myself with this team without it turning into a win! My belief: "If you're going to do something, do it right!"

I thought about whether I would do it—but I admit that my mind was made up early on. I met with the team—a mixture of men: ages early 20's to late 40's; white, black, Latino; company employee and contractor. I asked them one question, "Are you here to play, or are you here to win?"

The vote was unanimous: "WIN!"

"OK, then—practice will be several afternoons each week until the season begins. Do not miss practice and expect to play in a game; it will not happen!"

Of the few who thought I was perhaps "kidding," they quickly learned that I was not. "No smoking during the practices or games, and most importantly—watch your behavior!" We were all now representing the company in the community and as such, needed to represent it well. "No fights, no mouthing off during the games. Just be nice!"

Well, it was a "nice" thought!

I believe I was the only coach in this league—and definitely the only female. Do not let my description of the team and the two terrific seasons we spent bonded together be interpreted as an indication that I was this knowledgeable coach who led her team to victory! Our success was more the result of Anthony's wisdom, together with my eagerness.

The only difference between ours and the other teams was that our team *had* a coach! All the other teams were self-coached. What this meant was that, on any other team, all the members would be speaking at the same time, all thinking they knew what was going wrong—and all suspecting that the only change that did *not* have to be made in order to correct things would be their own removal from the floor!

Not so on our team. I may not be a genius, but—unlike the situations on the other teams—at least I was not suggesting that "you sit out so that I can take your place." Consequently, we argued less and observed more of what was actually going on, enabling us to correct things to our own advantage. It was genius on Anthony's part!

The team had a mixture of experience levels, but everyone had *some* strength and more than not, had actual talent. In fact, one man who worked for an on-site contractor had been a walk-on for Alabama University in his day. Bart played center.

Then there was Jim—agile, fast, with the coordination of a finely tuned machine. Jim simply did not give in! He could drive the lane, shoot from outside, and set picks and screens like a pro.

Oddly, Anthony didn't play much. While possessing the physical stature of a basketball player, he lacked the absolute conviction to win that the others had. This was something he was doing for recreation. He was a welcome addition, but not a starting member.

Rodney, an engineer from my own projects group, started out as a back-up center to give Bart a break when needed, but then found himself in the game in a more supporting role. He rarely shot inside the key, relying on his ability to hit a three with no one on him.

The line-up would not be complete without singling out Joey. Joey was the shortest member of the team—and in most instances, the quickest! The problem with Joey (and it *was* a problem) was that Joey envisioned himself in a park-side pick-up game with one or two other players, rather than one of five team members on the court at the same time. Once Joey got his hands on the ball, Joey kept the ball! Now, Joey was lightning fast and would drive the lane, but often he would get tripped up over his own feet or ball-handling, thus losing possession of the ball. So much of action in the earlier games consisted of Joey grabbing the ball, tearing ass down court, and then blundering the score.

By early on in the second game, I had had as much of this practice as I could take. My entire team is running themselves ragged trying to get open to get a pass that is never going to be thrown, while Joey is killing himself without point one going up on the board! I could take no more.

"TIME OUT!" I screamed.

Bart put his hands in a T for the ref to see, and the time-out was called. The team came over to the bench, disgusted, with Joey portraying the temperament of a Jack Russell Terrier, panting from running through the field.

"What do you want us to do, coach?"

Without hesitating, I took the ball and told Joey, "I want you to take the ball and score as many points as you can, and I want the rest of you to sit down and rest."

The guys on the bench stood up ready to replace the others, and I corrected them. "No, you sit down, too. Joey's going to do this."

Joey looked sheepish at this point. "I don't understand, Coach."

"No, Joey—I don't guess you do. Did you even realize that there were four other guys out there that can score for us? Did you consider giving them the ball when they were screaming at you that they were open? If you can do this by yourself—do it! If not, you sit out and watch them."

My grammar-school aged son, attending the game and sitting behind the team in the bleachers, listened to this ass-chewing that Joey was getting. He pulled at my sweatshirt and said, "Mom, stop! He's gonna cry."

I said, "No son, *I'm* gonna cry—if we lose this because of one ball hog!"

The team went back on the floor, minus Joey. The look on his face was one of anger, disappointment, and a hint of confusion. But I moved down on the bench to make sure I was right next to him and talked him through one play after another, as the team was now passing and scoring. After almost five minutes of sitting, I sent Joey back into the game with just one piece of advice, "Pass that ball—or step back out!"

To Joey's own surprise, he passed! They set picks and fed him the ball. Now everyone was working together and scoring. It was terrific!

The core group gelled from that day on. Oh, we had our moments with the tertiary members of the team. But the focus was one for all and all for one. We began having team meetings in the projects trailer every game day, spending our lunch time reviewing game film and eating steaks. This was done to build morale and to review any weaknesses that we had, so as not to make mistakes over and over again. Let's be honest—we were having a great time! This was my way of making sure that the esteem of the group was being stroked.

I began announcing games via e-mail to invite employee support for the games in the stands. My efforts were sincere, but more times than not, unappreciated. The stands remained sparsely populated, with only members of our own families. Staff support was not visible.

At the end of the first season, we had come in third in both the league and the end-of-season tournament. Not a "bad" finish—but not what I wanted. I wanted to win!

By the start of Season Two, I was already gearing up a more focused strategy towards building this team into a winning machine. I requested a meeting with the plant manager to discuss the team and our needs. The plant manager at this time was a man by the name of William. The idea of going to the plant manager's office was a little intimidating, but William's personality made that a bit easier. He was a real "people person"—always with a smile on his face. He spoke to everyone at every level, and you could tell by looking at him that he liked being in his own skin.

I was given a window of about 15 minutes. William was quite congenial, sitting at the table speaking with me—rather than looking at me from behind his desk. He began by telling me how he was keeping up with how the team had done last year and that—although it was a bit unconventional for a men's industrial team to have a woman coach—we seemed to be enjoying ourselves and doing quite well. I felt better to me knowing that William had looked into our record, as it would help in the discussion.

"Let me get right to the point, sir. The men wear their own shorts, sneakers, etc. and use only the game jerseys given to us by the Recreation Association. But the shirts are from the former company. We don't even have the correct company name displayed on the shirts! The shirts are also quite tattered, and since the men are doing so well, I thought you might see your way to allow me to purchase new jerseys for them to wear with the new company name and logo." I could feel my face shrinking up like a five-year-old again—as if to say, "P-L-E-A-S-E??????"

Without blinking, William replied, "Sure—that wouldn't be but how much? $40 each?"

"Even less," I quickly replied, pulling out my notes with the quotes I had obtained. "In fact, it would come to about $25 each."

At the end of our meeting, I had managed to get permission for new jerseys and two practice balls.

During our second season, we won game after game. Other teams were either very friendly or very adversarial—but they *all* knew who we were! And as our popularity and record improved, so did the attendance in the stands. We won all but one game in the second regular season, placing us second in the league for the season. Then the tournament began. The guys played their hearts out, beating everyone they opposed.

The final game was the reality that I had been striving for all during both seasons. The stands were packed. The guys were pumped. And I was a wreck! I remembered asking them all two years earlier if they wanted to play, or if they wanted to win. "Win," they insisted. Now—gymnasium packed to the rafters—we were about to get our chance!

The game was fierce from the first minute. The lead was won and lost every few seconds, as we fought to retain control. It was entirely a one-point game from beginning to the middle of the fourth quarter. Now, keep this in mind—this wasn't just a basketball game; it was a basketball game being played by men who had just worked off their twelve-hour rotation. They were battling fatigue. My pep talks were becoming more pleas of desperation than anything with any wisdom. We tried everything—zone, man-to-man, full court press, fast breaks, creative charging. And the guys were exhausted! All I could think of to tell them was, "Don't let them take this from us. This is ours!"

The men went back out there and scored one, two, three lay-ups—then a three! They hit every foul shot. With ten seconds left, I realized, "We're gonna win this!" And win we did.

Victory was ours, and we were all thrilled—so much so that we stood on the court basking in all the yelling and cheering for more than a few minutes. Until we each began looking around as if to say, "OK, so where is the trophy?" We knew there was usually a trophy awarded to the winning and runner-up teams for the Tournament, as well as for the season. So in fact, we had two coming. But after waiting for what was an eternity—long enough to allow the gym to become quiet again—we realized that no trophy was being given out, at least not then.

Before heading home, we went to a local bar/restaurant to celebrate. I paid for this with some Reward and Recognition gift checks that I had been holding for a special occasion. Clearly, this was a most special evening. No trophy that night, but I was able to offer some rewards, nevertheless!

69. Saving Grace

BETWEEN MANAGING THE project budgets and supporting the engineers, I was always busy. That is not to say that I was unable to steal moments to direct my attention to this new project of my own—the newsletter—whenever I could.

The trailer office space we were in, isolated from the main Administration Building, was laid out in one huge square, with offices on either side of a walkway. My office was adjacent to the supervisor's office, which was a corner office.

On this one particular occasion, although engaged in my writing, I noticed one of the engineers talking to the supervisor at his doorway. I became increasingly aware that the supervisor was not answering him. Once the engineer walked way, I rose from my desk and went next door to speak to my supervisor myself. I made several comments, but got absolutely no response. There he sat, frozen in his chair, feet up on his desk, hands clasped on his chest. I approached him more closely to see if he was wearing a medic alert bracelet or anything that provided any indication of a known ailment, but I saw nothing. I tapped his arm, called his name. Still no response.

It was lunchtime, so there was almost no one else around. I knew I needed to get help, but had no idea what to do. When all else fails, run back home! I quickly went to the Administration Building to seek out my former supervisor to get his help. By the time I entered the hallway of the building, I was feeling more urgency and began to run. I ran all the way to my former supervisor's office, finding him on the telephone and pacing back and forth. I quickly gasped, "Help—I need to talk to you now!"

He simply looked at me as if to say, "Can't you see I'm on the phone?" and closed his office door in my face.

I was stunned. I continued on to the next hallway, seeing one empty office after another. After all, it was lunchtime. But I had to find someone! Thank goodness one of the members of the Safety Department was walking in, and I grabbed him. I barely knew what to say. "My boss is unresponsive—I think he's having a stroke."

Quick on his feet, Alex called 711 (the emergency number for the plant) and activated the emergency response system. Accompanied by several members of the fire brigade, the plant nurse responded to the call and was at my supervisor's office before I could even make it back. They realized what was wrong and called for an ambulance, but meanwhile began administering glucose. Only after he was revived was I informed that my boss was an insulin-dependent diabetic, and he had not eaten on schedule—which caused him to slip into a coma.

After this emergency was past, the real question for me was, *How is it that I have worked here for as long as I have and yet have no knowledge of how to respond to an emergency?* The answer: Because I was hired as a temporary clerical employee, I was never given the basic safety training that all employees get on their first day. And because I spent so long on site as a "temp," when I actually got hired into a permanent position, it was assumed that this training had been provided me! So I had slipped through the cracks.

Between having a door closed in my face when I really needed help and the awareness that I had no knowledge as to how to handle an emergency like this, I was feeling quite vulnerable. I had the nagging suspicion that my new boss might die on my watch if I didn't figure out some way of dealing with this in a more responsible manner. And what kind of performance evaluation am I to be given if at the end of my first year in the position, my supervisor is dead?

A new position was announced, opened up for bid, and ultimately filled by a new-hire named Thomas. Thomas was a certified EMT—and hands-down, one of the most methodical employees to set foot anywhere near our Human Resources Department. He was rather austere on the surface, but as you got to know him and penetrate that distant exterior, he was found to be warm, friendly, a man of great humor, and someone extremely protective of anyone he considered to be his people.

Thomas sent out an all-user note to the staff inviting anyone interested in becoming a CPR Instructor to sign up for a two-day training session. This was perfect! I had no ability to wave a wand over my own head and become a nurse, but this would be the next best thing (in my opinion)—and would certainly aid in assuring me that my new boss would be kept alive long enough to give me my first raise! I volunteered immediately.

Surprisingly, I was met with a bit of resistance. I was told that others in my work group were not exactly embracing the idea of sharing my services with any outside interests. So the man who was the very inspiration for my taking this training balked at the idea. The Irony was mind-boggling! Here sits a man across from me whose life could literally be saved as a result of my training, and he has no intention of making any kind of case defending my taking the class. *Who better than me? Didn't he get this?*

I insisted (like a teenager pleading his or her case to go out on a Friday night) that I could do this, and that my training and subsequent duties would not detract from my primary job responsibilities. Finally he acquiesced and signed the document authorizing me to participate in the training.

While my boss did not want to "spare" me long enough to train and then fulfill the obligation of training others afterwards, apparently the same was not true for a second clerk from my department. The irony was that this woman did not even work in the same engineering trailer as me and my supervisor; her office was in the separate administration building. So that if there was another incident in which my boss needed assistance, she would not be there to respond to the need—no matter what kind of CPR training she had! Now our very small department was represented by filling not just one, but two of the fifteen seats available for the CPR training.

I found the class to be a welcome departure from the usual boundaries of my own department. It was, yet, another chance to meet employees from other parts of the plant site. I could feel myself expanding.

The training materials consisted of volumes upon volumes of bound materials describing circulation, stroke, diabetes, epilepsy, etc. When I was a young child, there was much talk about how in the future, we would live in a paperless society. Everything would be electronic. As I sat in this class I kept thinking to myself, *are we behind schedule with this? I'm covered up in paper—and there is no end in sight!* By the way this class was organized, it was evident that Thomas *loved* paper! Documentation was his life, and there was no question that did not require its own paper form with each individual's answer. We studied, collected, organized, sorted, and learned all that first day.

Day Two consisted largely of each student giving his or her own 5-minute presentation on one aspect of the training course. The plan was that we each become expert in one particular segment to share with the others during each training session. This was meant to form us into a team. Now, I did think it a good idea for each of us to become expert on one segment of the training and share this knowledge with the others. That way, each person would not have to know every single facet of the presentation; instead, each person could contribute a piece to the whole body of knowledge for the team.

The assignment was nerve-racking, however, because under no circumstances were we to speak for less than 4 minutes and 45 seconds, or for more than 5 minutes and 15 seconds. *OH, YEAH! Sure!* I had visions of an anvil chopping off my tongue at the 5:15 mark— which was about the only way I could imagine hitting that goal! It's a known fact that I cannot shut up. With me, just speaking about not being able to shut up could go on endlessly - (That's how ridiculous it is—I can talk incessantly on any topic. FOREVER!)

My palms were sweating before I was ever even called upon. The beauty of it was that everyone felt so intimidated by this time limit that we all felt as though we were comrade victims rather than adversaries! To my surprise, I was able to confine my presentation to the allotted time. In a robot-like manner I recited the information that was supposed to last exactly 5:00 minutes—and it did!

In the end, the plant had 15 certified CPR instructors ready, willing and able to train not only the entire plant workforce, but also any members of the community who made a request to the company for this service—free of charge.

The occurrences of my boss battling diabetes were coming more frequently. In fact, at least once every 60 days, I was called upon to revive him. While this would appear troublesome, the fact is that the more times I was called upon, the more familiar I became with what to do and the better I got at it.

Realizing that his lack of food intake after his morning shot of insulin was the culprit, I began preparing a 10:00 o'clock snack for my boss to fend off the deficit. The trick here was to locate him! Oftentimes, he would be in a meeting at 10:00 and would prefer not to have to leave to grab something to eat because he would disrupt the meeting. I remember thinking, *isn't going into a coma in the middle of things going to be disruptive*? I would fix a quick something—a sausage muffin, cheese and crackers, or the like—and bring it to him. Then, knocking on the door of the meeting room, I would poke my head in and request, "Can you come outside for a quick moment?"

This strict monitoring of my boss' diet proved to be somewhat beneficial, with difficult "incidents" less frequent. But they were still occurring. At the end of my first year, I had revived him more than 5 times and had tracked him down to feed him more often than not! I was feeling rather strained. During an in-depth discussion at year's end regarding my performance and salary, I was asked, "Do you have any questions, or is there anything you would like to say?" I remember thinking *I've pulled you out of a coma 6 times and fed you like I'm your momma. I think that about covers it."*

Instead, I replied, "No. Thank you."

When all was said and done, at the end of the fiscal year, I was given a raise of about 8 percent—which was considered impressive. What was *not* so impressive, however, was that this significant boost then placed me within the actual pay grade for the level at which I was already working. I realized that for 13 months, I had been *below* my assigned pay grade. My euphoria was beginning to wear off.

Even worse, the other clerk in the department, to whom I barely spoke, decided to share with me her disgust with the amount of the deductions taken from her check by showing me her check stub as we walked down the hall. "Look at this—this is ridiculous!" With one glance, I found myself careening into the wall. I tried very hard not to blink, but I was shaken. This woman was making $2.90 more per hour than I was; yet we were at exactly the same pay grade level—and I had been with the company 6 months longer!

I waited a full year to bring this discrepancy to the attention of my boss, thinking time would calm me and I would present my case in a less emotional fashion. Not a chance! The year had allowed me to cook in my own juices, like a stew! *Now,* I thought, *I've saved his life an additional 7 times, done my assigned duties, produced the plant newsletter quarterly, and trained staff and community members in CPR. Surely I am going to be compensated for my efforts.*

With a straight face, my boss told me how pleased he was to award me my raise—which in no way even brought me to what the other clerk had been making the previous year!

I am now so stunned I can barely speak without my voice cracking. But this time I was going to say something! "I am doing my job and doing all these extra things in addition. I'm a bit surprised that I am not being given more compensation."

"You knew when you took those extra jobs on that they were voluntary. They do not factor in. In fact, you're doing so many things that many members of this group have expressed some discontent with having to share your services with others."

"I'm interacting with the entire plant. This is providing good will and forming positive relationships with other departments! They have provided you very positive feedback on the work that I have done for them. Surely this is viewed as a good thing. Is the work I am doing not valued?"

"Of course they like you—they get you for free!"

"OK, let me put it another way—I am working three times as hard, and yet I am not being compensated as much as others in my pay grade. I would like that corrected."

"Now, you can't expect to make the money that other people who have been here 25 years or more are making—that wouldn't be fair."

"No, but wouldn't it be fair if those other people had been here *six months less?* I have seen her pay stub! Now that you and I are both in the same conversation, would you like to explain this to me?"

70. Money Isn't Everything

AS MUCH AS I had been focusing on tending my career, my family was requiring a great deal of my attention and energy as well. My husband had taken work out of town, which left me to head the household alone. I was managing the logistics of getting everyone to and from school, activities and social engagements. I was running the household. I was coming apart! The stress level was overwhelming.

While stress can be a negative, it can also be a positive. The fact was that I was becoming more adept at managing multiple responsibilities at one time—and delivering on all of them. It is said, "That which does not kill us makes us stronger."

It became second nature for me to take care of multiple tasks at once, continually, throughout the day and evening. The company gave many of the project group members cell phones to ease communication efforts, and I was included in that. My phone quickly became my most valuable tool in my arsenal of attacking the workload. I was gaining self-esteem as I was gaining responsibility. That, combined with the satisfaction I felt every time I completed a task either at home or at work, added to my sense of pride and accomplishment.

Conversely, I was slapped with the reality that my self-esteem was still quite vulnerable every time I looked at my paycheck. I was giving my all to my job responsibilities—and getting back less. All I wanted was to be treated fairly, to be given what everyone else was getting for their efforts. Yet it seemed obvious to me that I was not.

I approached the Human Resource Manager, who was presented as a very fair and reasonable person. Robert had been with the company quite a long time, but at our location only a year. He listened to my concerns, but simply responded with the company standard line, "You are being compensated fairly for the grade level you are in."

After several more months had passed, I found myself in a

conversation about this same issue with the plant manager. He assured me that he would look into it. Of course, that meant he would go to his trusty HR contact, Robert. So the circle looped back around, taking me and my hopes with it.

After two years in that position, Robert was transferred and replaced by Kevin, his second in command. Kevin was a pleasant individual, whom I didn't know other than to say hello to in the hall. But I was so overwrought with distress over this issue that I could not suppress the urge to address it one more time with him.

With no appointment, I appeared at Kevin's office and voiced my complaint about my salary discrepancy. The conversation lasted only a few minutes. I was a clerk at this level making X. Another person was a clerk at the same level making Y. I had been with the company 6 months longer, which should have at least classified me to receive equal pay. In retrospect, after over two years, the amount of money I calculated that I had been shorted would easily equate to the cost of an in-ground swimming pool! All I asked was that this be corrected. All Kevin said was, "I'll look into it." I left the office thinking I had been blown off yet again.

My next performance review left much to be desired. My boss seemed less than pleased that I had gone above his head to address what I clearly felt was an injustice. He very matter-of-factly discussed my previous year's accomplishments as "tasks" and began explaining the new increase I was to get—almost as if he were defending it. "You are all ranked in a pool. Everyone clerical is ranked at the same time. There are so many fives, so many fours, so many threes, etc. It's called the bell-shaped curve. You are considered an above average performer, and as such, we are ranking you a four—which means you will get a 4 percent increase."

"So someone who is a "three" would get less of an increase?"

"That's correct."

"But if the lower performer is already making more than I, then that 3 percent still translates into a bigger raise by virtue of the math. I mean, if the company is trying to send a message, I'm not sure I'm getting the message you're sending!"

"You can't look at it that way."

"Huh?"

Every time a policy of this type was "explained" to me, my head would get twisted into a knot, as would my stomach. "If I'm being rewarded, how come I don't feel like it? Would you prefer I was ignorant to this and didn't question it?"

The answer was yes, but he never said as much. As time went on, I became very conflicted. I hated that I felt this way. I preferred the happiness I had experienced when I got the job and felt lucky. Now I felt used and looked down upon. The more I pondered this, the angrier I felt.

There's a scene in the original *Star Wars* movie when Obi Wan Kenobi is with Luke and they approach a storm trooper. Obi Wan waves his hand in front of the storm trooper's face and says, "We don't need to see your identification." And the storm trooper repeats it back as if he had meant to say that anyway. As they pull away, Obi Wan tells Luke, "It's very easy to influence the weak-minded." That scene has always resonated with me. My whole life, I have felt that if people said something to me, they expected me to just believe it—just because they said it.

I had a dentist appointment that afternoon. As I sat in the waiting room, I picked up a magazine to read and pass the time. In it was an advertisement for the University of Phoenix. *WOW!* I thought. *That's a new idea! Going to school on-line; that would certainly address my problem of what to do with the kids.* I couldn't even consider going to school if I had to leave them alone to do it. Who would watch them in the evenings? I hadn't known you could do such a thing (get a degree on line)!

The entire time my teeth were being cleaned, I thought about this. I remembered the consultant, Marilyn, telling me that my boss thought I had potential, and that I should go back to school. *I might have to look into this,* I thought.

I returned to the office and began to look up benefits on the company's employee web site. The company had a very attractive tuition reimbursement program, paying 90 percent of tuition and books. *90 percent!* I sent my information in to the University, and almost as quickly as I hit the send button, my office phone was ringing. A counselor proceeded to give me all sorts of information, as well as agreeing to fax some forms to me for signature.

What had to happen next was that I needed to go to HR and have papers signed by a company representative confirming my eligibility for tuition reimbursement. Surely when I went down there and suggested to them that I wanted to go to school (to the tune of $12,000 per year!), they would give me a salary increase and call it a day! Heck, they'd be getting off cheap! But I no sooner went to Kevin's office with the papers than he pulled out his pen and said, while signing them, "So, you're going back to school. That's great!"

"WHAT?" I took the signed paper from him and walked out the door thinking to myself, *This is not the way this played out in my head at all. Oh, crap!* In less than 30 days, I was about to return to school—full time—while working full time and raising 6 children. Shrewd move!

During the next three weeks, I developed what I was certain to be an ulcer just thinking about what I had trapped myself into. There was no way to back out. I had effectively bluffed—and had my bluff called! I had no choice but to see this through. In addition, as part of the program, grades are to be turned in to your supervisor, the Accounting Department and Human Resources. So at the conclusion of every class, I would be marching down the hall with my report card, handing it to Kevin, Leona, and my boss.

I did the only thing I could do in a situation like this—what I usually did: I began to line up help! Fortunately, if I was going to return to school as an adult, this was the optimum way to do it. I was surrounded by very educated engineers, one smarter than the other. Engineers confidently boast of their intelligence and education. Nothing pleases them more than to demonstrate their intellectual prowess. If this had to happen, I was in the best place for it to happen! One by one, I solicited their help and expertise. I had 16 tutors at my disposal!

The workload was overwhelming. Still, all I kept hearing was, "It'll be OK—just stay with it." So I did. I was not about to surrender. Not with so many witnesses!

And, although it took an entire season, at the end of three months' time, my salary was adjusted to the proper rate. In a strange twist, I was furious. Now I was convinced that I had been right all along! So why had everyone else just ignored the situation?

In the end, I had gotten both the pay I had felt entitled and the benefit of tuition reimbursement. The increase in my income was a noticeable and welcome change. What was most significant to me was my new mindset. I relished the satisfaction of the wrong having been made right; confident that this would now have me on the right track.

71. Diamonds are a Girl's Best Friend

WHEN DAYS WERE long and the workload overwhelming, something that always provided me with strength to carry on was looking up at that picture on my bulletin board of our girls throwing the coins into the fountain in Italy. Instantly, I was reminded why.

With the projects group members working long hours themselves, the needs of the project found them traveling to and from Houston and other places often. I was not only an Administrative Assistant; I was a travel agent. I prided myself on getting the best flights, best deals and all the award points available for any and all travel they were required to do. I felt they deserved it. Between airlines miles, points on the corporate credit card, and hotel stays, these perks were adding up to a considerable nest egg for most of them. One engineer in the group not only travelled for the project, but found himself traveling all around the world to perform safety audits. He would go to Europe, Asia—anywhere he was needed. And, since he was one of only a handful of employees that did this type of work, he was called upon quite a bit.

One trip he took overseas had to be booked rather quickly. Availability was at a premium. Consequently, I had liberty to book him on whatever airline I could to be able to accommodate the schedule. I found a flight for him on British Air. What attracted me to this especially was a promotion they were running at the time. If you flew business or first class (which he would) and you agreed to participate in this survey once you completed your trip, you would be awarded two round trip tickets anywhere British Air flew—essentially, two free tickets anywhere in the world you wanted to go. Not being able to pass up a good deal, I signed him up.

It would be months before the trip and the survey were concluded. However, upon its completion, this engineer came to my office door one day and presented me with an envelope. "Here—I got my voucher in the mail at the house yesterday."

"What voucher?" I asked

"British Air. The two airline tickets anywhere—from the survey."

"Excellent. That was some deal, huh?"

"Yeah, it's great. I want you to have them."

"What?"

"You set it up. You've always wanted to go, and instead, you sent your girls. I think you and Bobby should take a vacation."

"Oh my God! Are you serious?"

"Yeah. Have a good time."

I had waited 25 years, but it was finally going to happen. I was going to Europe! I spent weeks on the internet planning what stops we would make, trying to make the most of the free travel. If we were only going to be able to do it this one time, I wanted to make it count! Without the use of a tour guide, travel agent or knowledgeable traveler, I decided on London, Amsterdam, Paris and Rome. I very excitedly told Bobby that we were going on a vacation to Europe.

"I haven't even seen much of the US. Why don't we go somewhere here," he asked?

I thought I would kill him! Since sophomore year in High School I have yearned to travel to Paris. Now, I'm inches away from it becoming a reality. "We're going!" I insisted.

I intended to pack this two-week period full of every possible experience. Bobby, a heavy smoker, was encouraged to quit smoking both for the betterment of his health, as well as to accommodate his not being able to smoke on such a long flight. He had never spent 8 full hours without smoking. One trip to the doctor's office provided him with a prescription for a drug known at the time to aid in smoking cessation—Zyban. He began taking it immediately, and it did just as it was supposed to do—eliminated his wanting to smoke. In a matter of a few days, his smoking was reduced from 2 packs a day to 1 or 2 cigarettes.

What worked out rather well, in spite of my not planning it that way, was that our travel itinerary gradually introduced us to areas that spoke less and less English. That is not to say that people do not speak English everywhere. Europe is much different than the US in that way. People there usually speak their own language *plus* English—and in many cases, even other languages on top of that. As Americans, we speak our English and expect everyone to accommodate us.

Our journey gave us more tales than are able to be told in this one forum. We met countless people and for the most part, had very pleasant experiences.

In the interest of brevity, I will say that we were robbed when we arrived in Amsterdam. We were each handling three suitcases— a large, a medium, and a train case with small items. Bobby's train case disappeared as the bell hop from the hotel insisted that he take the bags into the lobby for us. I went to the counter to check in to the hotel and five minutes later, his one little bag was now nowhere to be found. I insisted on speaking with the manager, certain that this bell hop had a "business" on the side. A security tape revealed another man in the lobby taking the bag from the stacked luggage while no one was watching. We were not to get it back.

The good news was that all our credit cards, passports and urgently important things were in the bag I had in my hand. The bad news was that the stolen bag contained my day planner with all my names and addresses of those to whom I wanted to send postcards; my favorite hairbrush; all the liquor bottles I swiped from the flight; and Bobby's Zyban. That meant whoever stole that bag was going to have themselves quite a party—even though they didn't get any cash!

While concerned about the missing Zyban, realizing our inability to obtain a replacement prescription in Europe, I was determined not to have even this spoil my dream of a lifetime vacation. We spent a few days in Amsterdam, visiting (among other things) the Anne Frank house—which was fascinating.

Then it was time to depart for Paris!

Paris was my prime target location. This was the city I had wanted to go to my entire life, even though I didn't know why. We boarded the train and found seating. This train ride was scheduled to last 6 hours or more. There was comfortable seating to accommodate passengers having to sit for extended periods of time. There was also a bar car where drinks would be served. Not long after the train departed, Bobby and I decided to get ourselves drinks. After all, we were on vacation. We both went to the bar car together. There were many people crammed into a very small area, with many languages being spoken simultaneously. We had currency from Amsterdam, but had not yet gotten any French currency. (That was something we planned to do upon arrival.) Then again, we could always use plastic! The bartender accepted any currency.

We decided to take our drinks and head back to the seats, which we did. I began to look around the car. There were so many people of different nationalities! I felt very continental; very world traveler. My trusty cell phone, a Motorola Timeport, was set up to accept and make overseas calls. Unfortunately, I could not figure out how to set the phone to enable this type of use. There was a method; I just didn't know it.

One by one, I took notice of the people surrounding our seats. There was a beautiful black woman sitting across the aisle from my seat, with a young boy next to her. I assumed he was her son. Behind them, what I assumed was a Frenchman in his mid-thirties. Next to him, a Chinese man, with another older man to his right. Bobby and I continued to order drinks, each taking turns making the trip to the bar. While he was gone, I began to talk with those around me.

"You're American?"

"Yes"

"On vacation?"

"Yes. We've been to London and Amsterdam so far. We are headed to Paris now. But I don't speak French and don't know where our hotel is. Are you French?"

The man in his 30's smiled and said, "No, I'm not French."

I must have had a strange look on my face. Clearly, I was puzzled. He *looked* French. At least, I thought he did.

"I'll bet you can't guess what I am," he insisted.

"You want me to guess?"

"Yes. I don't think you can."

"OK. Spanish?"

"No."

"Italian?"

"No."

"I don't know."

"Come on, guess."

"Well, you're not an Arab, are you?"

He laughed out loud, "I'm from Kuwait."

"Seriously?"

At this point, he reached for his wallet to show me his driver's license to prove it. There it was—Kuwait. I don't know what I expected someone from Kuwait to look like. I guess I was more surprised that someone from a country in the midst of a war would be casually traveling to Paris for the weekend.

"Why are you going to Paris?" I asked.

"Going to see my girlfriend. She lives in Paris."

I remember thinking, *boy; people over here really get around!*

With that, Bobby returned with our drinks. Bobby, not much of a social butterfly, returned to his seat and spoke only to me. "What were you saying to that guy back there?" he asked.

"Oh we were just talking. He has a girlfriend in Paris that he visits. He's from Kuwait! Can you believe that?"

"We're from the US. Everyone is from somewhere," he insisted

Bobby had such a basic way about him. Here I was trying to embrace the excitement of such a global community on the train with us, and he was very matter-of-factly thinking, *eh.*

As the train ride continued, the 30-ish man got on his cell phone to make a call.

"Hey, do you know how to set my phone so that it will work here?" I asked him.

"No, sorry. I have this type," he said holding his phone up to show me.

With that, the Chinese man next to him motioned to him. With absolutely no English, French, or any other language at his disposal besides Chinese, he signaled as best he could to ask if he could use the 30-ish man's phone to make a call.

"Sure," he said

"Are you crazy?" I blurted out. "He's Chinese. Just who do you think he's gonna call? And more importantly—where?"

"I don't care," he replied. "It's OK." He smiled without a care in t he world. I, on the other hand—now feeling myself to be this man's friend—am very concerned that the Chinese man is going to run up one heck of a long distance bill!

"You should watch that he doesn't stay on long."

"Don't worry," he kept saying.

All I could think was *it must be a company phone that somebody else is paying for. Perhaps he's a spy!*

As the train pulled into another station, an elderly man boarded our car. He took the seat across the aisle from me directly (next to the black woman and her son). He smiled "hello" at everyone, as if he were now joining the group. Not long after boarding, the man pulled his cell phone from his pocket. It was the exact phone I had.

"You have a Timeport!" I declared

"Yes."

"Can you help me? I have one. I am from the United States, and I can't set my phone to receive calls here."

"Oh, certainly. Give it to me."

In seconds, he set the phone, connecting me with the rest of the world. Now I could call home. I could call anywhere. This was perfect!

"Thank you so much!"

"You're welcome." He smiled back.

Next, the 30-ish man's phone rang. I turned around when he answered it only to see him say, "One moment." He then handed the phone to the Chinese man next to him. THE CHINESE MAN WAS

NOW RECEIVING CALLS ON THIS MAN'S PHONE!!!!

"I told you not to give him your phone. You didn't listen to me."

The man giggled without a care. "It's OK!"

With the Chinese man rattling back in Chinese to the caller, the call seemed to go on for quite a while. Every now and again, I would roll my eyes at the man. "You should have listened to me." This conversation became rather contagious, as others could not help but overhear what was going on.

Bobby and I continued to alternate our trips to the bar car. We were well into four or five drinks. I was having a marvelous time mingling with the multi-national group that I had managed to infiltrate. Bobby, conversely, was sitting quietly.

With the chatter amongst us getting louder and louder, we had become quite boisterous. The group members took turns interacting with one another. We were all getting quite friendly. The older gentleman next to me decided to join in. He leaned over to me and asked, "Are you on vacation?"

"Yes."

"You are American?"

"Yes. We're from Alabama. Well—originally, I'm from New York."

"Oh, yes? I travel on business to New York frequently."

In fact, he was from Belgium. In fact, he was a diamond dealer.

"You deal diamonds?"

"Yes. Sssh," putting his finger up to his lips as if to instruct me to keep quiet.

"I don't want people to know. I'm an old man. I might get robbed."

"Tell me about it," I said to him remembering my recent experience in Amsterdam. "It's likely!"

"Are you interested in diamonds?" he asked

"I'm female! It goes with the territory."

"I would show you the diamonds I have—but I don't want people to know I have them."

"No problem. Why don't we go into the bathroom? You can show them to me in there."

At this point, I turned to Bobby and asked, "Hey, do you want to come with us? We're going to the bathroom to look at his diamonds."

"NO!"

What he said was "no," but what he meant was, "Hell, no—and what are you doing going in the bathroom with the old guy?"

Euphoria had gotten the better of me. Well, that and the 5 drinks I had consumed. We walked to the bathroom in the front of the train car.

The bathroom was extremely small, the size of a bathroom on an airplane. We could both barely get in the door and close it. Fearing that he would lose them, I took off my jacket and placed it across the sink so that nothing would go down the drain. Instantly, the man began pulling little folded up pieces of paper from different pockets in his clothing. He had diamonds EVERYWHERE! He showed me how to look at them through a special eye piece. "Always look at them against a white piece of paper," he said. "You can see any imperfections that way."

So there I was, on a high speed train barreling through Europe, in the bathroom with an old man I didn't know, examining diamonds! From where I was sitting, Life was perfect.

Not so perfect was life for Bobby, however, seated in the car of the train alone, surrounded by people he wasn't speaking to nor had any interest in getting to know. Additionally, the absence of the Zyban prescription that had been taken from him days ago was having a withdrawal effect on him. He hadn't been smoking, he wasn't getting his Zyban, and his wife was in the bathroom with an old man! He was pissed!

We emerged from the bathroom laughing and talking. The entire car seemed to be filled with the banter of the passengers. I didn't think much of it since that commotion had been going on since long before.

"You have made a fool of me," Bobby snapped!

"What are you talking about?"

"You think everybody on this train doesn't know you were in the bathroom with that old guy? They're laughing at me."

"First of all, we don't know these people and won't ever see them again—so who cares what they think? Second, they're all carrying on from before when the Chinese guy was using the Kuwait guy's phone. They don't care what I was doing in there."

"They think you were screwing him in there."

"Oh honey, seriously. Do *you*? Do you honestly think I would have gone in there with him and done ANYTHING and come out without a diamond?"

I thought I had stated my case clearly and concisely. But Bobby saw no humor in it. As for those passengers surrounding us who had seemingly had no interest in what I was doing, they erupted into laughter at that comment, proving Bobby's point.

We did not speak for the remainder of the train ride.

Upon arrival in Paris, the Kuwait man agreed to show us the way to the hotel, which was right near where his girlfriend lived. This made matters even worse as far as Bobby was concerned.

"We don't know where we are or where we're going, and he does. I'm going to let him show us."

Bobby grumbled.

We parted company from the Kuwait man one block from our hotel. After a quick check-in at the desk, we entered a shoebox-sized elevator that crept up two floors to our room. Bobby was in no mood. I, on the other hand, had arrived in Paris! He slammed the luggage into the room and stormed into the bathroom, leaving the door open.

"I can't believe you did that," he snarled.

"I can't believe you did *that*, either," I declared. "You just pissed in the bidet!"

72. Serious as a Heart Attack

ATTEMPTING A RETURN to school when you are over forty is much different than attempting to complete a course of education at a younger, more suitable age. Now, I'm not taking anything away from those people who do this the customary way. But graduating at 22 or 23—even with a GPA of 2.9—is generally considered an accomplishment. When you are over forty, however, it is presumed that much of what you are going to encounter you should have gotten a handle on simply by living! No one is going to applaud—at least not with the same enthusiasm. It's like the punishment you get for not doing it right the first time.

You are now responsible for you, a household, a job, and your homework.

My household was quite crowded on any given day. I would get home from the office at about 6:30 or so, grab something for dinner, and then sit down at the computer and try to get through reading some classmates' posts—with a few responses of my own to be counted as class participation. With on-line schooling, you have no verbal participation; everything is done in writing. There is writing, writing, and more writing. At least one paper is due each week.

After several weeks of trying to find my groove, I discovered that I could read and post to the main classroom folder for participation after work, but any paper required more concentration than I had at the end of a long day—especially amidst the confusion of a noisy household. I would compile whatever notes I had towards an assignment and then call it quits at 10:00 pm. Then I would sleep until about 2:00 a.m.—at which point I was rested enough so that I was fresh. In addition, with my entire family asleep in their beds, the house was dead quiet. It was then that I could best write my paper.

With any luck, I would be able to grab yet another nap from 4 until 5 a.m. Next I would get up and do an hour of yoga with a TV workout program that came on each day. Then it was time to shower, get myself dressed, and get the kids up for school and off to work. After a very short time of doing this, it became routine (or habit).

My life, albeit filled with commitments, was very much like a continuous walk on a treadmill. The more you walk, the more comfortable you become with the journey. The flip side of that is, of course, that the increasing speed of the treadmill is something you are able to adjust to—provided you can stay on! Jump off, and you'll have to run twice as hard just to get back on. I never let that happen!

As I approached the two-year mark, the plant management team determined that it would be necessary to hire additional staff in the area of Operations. No sooner was this news made public, than I began to receive calls from some of the players on the basketball team who were contract employees, wanting me to help secure permanent positions for them. In particular, Bart, the gentleman who was the "center" of the team, had been working at the plant for five consecutive years and wanted very much to secure himself a position. Although I was not in a position to hire, I was in a position to help. Together we worked on his résumé. I also went to the Human Resource Department in person and gave Bart what I felt was a very strong recommendation. He had been doing the very job he desired for five years. On this basis alone, I felt he was a shoe-in.

The criteria for the position had been upgraded from that of previous applicants. A two-year degree was required. Bart had been a walk-on at the University of Alabama. To be sure, I had asked him, "Didn't you say you went to the University of Alabama?"

"Yeah—I went for two years," he assured me.

As interviews were scheduled, I kept in close contact with Bart, asking almost daily, "Have they called you yet?"

"Nope—not yet," he would say. Each time his voice would sound a bit more discouraged.

After learning that no more interviews were to be offered, I went down to the HR department, again in person, to inquire why Bart had not been given any consideration. "All applicants must possess a two-year degree," I was told, with no wiggle room to include him.

With a heavy heart, I met with Bart to break the news to him, confirming what he had already suspected—that he was being passed over. "I thought you went to Alabama for two years?"

"I did," he insisted.

"But you didn't get a degree?"

"No, I was enrolled in the four-year program. I just didn't finish."

As we talked it through, it finally clicked in my head. They would not approve Bart—even though he had had 2 years of college—*because he did not have the 2-year degree.* This literal hair-splitting of needing a two-year degree versus attending the university for two years was now biting Bart right in the behind. I was angry—but I understood.

I couldn't help but project Bart's hitting this obstacle onto my own career. When enrolling in the University of Phoenix program, I had committed to a four-year degree—a bachelor's degree. What if I applied for a position and the same hair-splitting was applied to my case? No 2-year degree, no position? *Not going to happen–not to this old girl!*

That afternoon I telephoned my school counselor. "I need to take whatever courses I need to earn an Associate Degree."

"But you're enrolled in a Bachelor's program; you don't need it."

"Please don't tell me what I need! The company is paying my tuition. They need a milestone to see my progress, and an Associate Degree will serve that purpose. Make it happen."

In an instant, my educational plan hung a hard right and I signed up for two additional courses, ensuring that the two-year degree box on my résumé would be ticked.

Shortly after being denied the interview, Bart left the plant to work as a permanent employee at a steel mill less than one mile up the road. I hated that he had to leave, but I understood his wanting more for his family.

Every now and then, in the middle of a morning, my phone would ring. "Hey, coach—what are you up to?"

"Working—what else?"

"You doing anything for lunch?"

Bart was much better at keeping in touch than I was. It was never that I didn't want to; I was just covered up—buried in all my commitments. Still, he would call, and the time would make itself available. We would sit and talk, sometimes in a Subway lunch shop, sometimes in my office. The conversation would range from kids to work to pay scale to memories of winning moments on the court. We would laugh a good bit. Occasionally, we would round up another team member, Jim, whose office was down the hall from my own. Those visits were always fun—and always initiated by Bart.

At 8:00 am on a Monday morning, Jim came to my office and knocked on the door. "Do you have a second?"

"Sure, come on in."

"Did you hear about Bart?"

As I shuffled papers around my desk without even looking up, I mistook what he had asked and replied, "No, I haven't heard from him since you and I had lunch with him here a few weeks ago. Why?"

"I said—did you hear about Bart?"

"No—what?"

"He died."

"What? How?"

"Just a little while ago, this morning. He was at the job; sat down at the break table and fell over. They said he had a massive heart attack."

"How can that be? He's an athlete. He's in great shape! He's only in his late 30's! Are you serious?"

Just then the phone rang. It was the plant manager. "Ellen, can you come to my office. I'd like to have a word with you."

"Sure. I'll be right there."

Thinking out loud, I said to Jim, "I have to go."

I entered the plant manager's office in an altered state. He began speaking, asking me about some information that he wanted, but I wasn't hearing him. All I was hearing was the sound of his voice. The words meant nothing. I felt more and more empty as the moments passed. Before I knew it, I was crying.

"Are you all right, Ellen?"

"No—I'm sorry. No. My friend just died."

"Do you need a minute to pull yourself together?"

"No, I don't think a minute will do it. Oh, damn!"

Instantly, his assistant was bringing me tissues.

"I'm not a crier. I'm sorry!"

"That's quite all right. You take your time."

As I tried hopelessly to regain my composure, I uttered to him, "You know, this will cause quite a scandal—my sitting in your office crying! People will think you have really laid into me for something!"

"Well, won't that be interesting!" he declared.

It was at that point that we both gave a smile and I was able to shake it off.

Life really is just like Dorothy said in *The Wizard of Oz*: "People come and go so quickly here!"

73. Walk Like a Man

EVERY SINGLE DAY for four solid years, I was either working, going to school, or both. Suffice it to say, when those four years were up, I was deliriously happy—and very proud of myself. The University provides for on-line students to "walk" in a graduation ceremony with others if they so choose. I was discouraged about this, having neither the extra money nor the energy. But my husband prodded me to do it. "You've earned this—you should walk!"

"OK," I thought.

There were graduation ceremonies from the University of Phoenix taking place all over the country at various times during the year. As it turned out, there would be one held in Tampa very close to the time I was set to finish. The ceremony was on May 6th, and my last day of class was June 5th. As long as you were within a few credits, you could attend. Actual degrees were mailed after verification of credits and fees. I ordered my cap and gown and planned for the family to go to Tampa—where my mother lives. I thought it would be convenient for her to attend the ceremony in her city.

The conflict was that the ceremony was also in the city where my brother, his wife and daughter lived. My mother was a stickler for me inviting or including my brother—always. But my brother and I had little to talk about. He was not a happy person, to say the least. During many a conversation throughout my life, I recall him yelling, ranting and carrying on, acting superior to everyone, condescending to most. I had had my fill. The difficulty here was that there seemed to be no way to invite my sister-in-law and niece without inviting my brother, too. I was in a quandary! After much deliberation, I gave in. This was surely not the first occasion in my life in which I had to include him and risk his pissing all over the event because of his mood and demeanor—and I feared it would not be the last! Still, I extended the invitation, and it was accepted. My entire family drove down (in separate vehicles).

The Tampa Convention center is in mid-town. There were so many cars and people on foot as we neared the center that I was shocked to see the size of what this would turn out to be. The size of the graduating class topped 2,000 receiving varying degrees.

Graduates had to separate from their families prior to the ceremony in preparation. Bobby met with the children and took them all in to find seats, as did my mother. The auditorium was HUGE! I had no idea where anyone was. I was so excited; I barely knew where *I* was. For the entire hour, I sat in my seat, shocked that I had indeed completed the course of study! My whole life I had been angry about *not* doing this. That was no longer true. It was not only as though a huge weight had been lifted from my shoulders, but I felt different inside—confident, more self-assured.

The usher came to the end of our row and signaled that it was time for us to rise. One by one we walked out, down the aisle, and up the stairs to the stage, where we had a series of school officials ready to shake our hands. I could feel myself smiling from ear to ear. I walked across the stage as my name was called, and a roar came from my children. I kept thinking to myself, *for God's sake, don't fall as you walk!* Down the stairs on the other side, pausing for a photo and then heading back to my seat, I held on to that rolled up paper like it was a piece of gold!

Within minutes I heard whispering behind me, "Nannie, Nannie."

"Hey, munchkins—what are you doing up here? Where's granddaddy?"

It was my grandchildren, Dani and Cyrus—both beaming with pride. "He's right over there," Cyrus pointed to him in the aisle.

I turned the other way to see Bobby, who had walked up behind me. As he bent over where I was sitting, I heard him say, "He's not here."

"Who?"

"Your brother."

"What?"

"He didn't make it."

"What happened?"

"The car broke down on the way. His wife and daughter are here. He stayed with the car, waiting for a tow."

I just looked at Bobby. I couldn't believe it. *Finally!* I thought. I cannot remember a time when as a family we had not acquiesced and invited or included my brother, only to have him furious about one thing or another, putting a damper on the occasion. I was dreading this as being yet another occasion when history would repeat itself. Not this time! God had given me a graduation present—he broke my brother's car!

I returned to work the following week, proud as a peacock, knowing full well that I still had a month of school left. The BIGGEST mistake I ever made! School required every ounce of focus, dedication, and discipline I had in my body. When I walked across that stage, I breathed a sigh of relief and put all that behind me. Now I had to get all that energy and focus back. Nothing doing. I was a mess! My body and my mind were in celebration mode, and I still had four papers and a team assignment due. It was the equivalent of pushing a marble uphill with my nose. I hated those last four weeks. I just kept telling myself, *just XXX more days.*

By June 5th, I was completely ready to embrace life without school. No more evenings sitting at the computer. No more weekends doing research, rather than talking to family. No more isolation. I was *so* ready to enjoy fresh air. I indulged myself doing all the things I had wanted to do—I lay out in the sun, I bought plants and did gardening, I watched television. I had my life back!

Then, with almost no time passing, I began to explore the possibility of a Master's degree. The idea seemed absurd. But my childhood friend Lizzy had one. She got hers right after she completed her Bachelor's degree, many years ago. Lizzy has consistently had good jobs, good opportunities. I wanted some of that!

I elected to participate in a company PDP session (Performance

Development Panel), where an employee can go before the leadership team of the site and map out his or her career plan, soliciting
feedback and advice on how to proceed. The main topic for me was
undertaking the Master's program, which I wanted the company to
pay for as they had my Bachelor's. With little discussion, the room
gave me a resounding "No!" stating as their reason, "We don't think
you will use it."

"What?"

I thought to myself, *OK, by show of hands, how many of* you *have
a Master's?*

I decided that the blessing of the leadership team was inconsequential to my pursuit. I wanted it, and I intended to get it. I inquired
about pursuing a Master's degree with an academic counselor at the
University. He advised me, "Don't put it off. Do it now!"

"What do you mean?"

"The longer you take a break, the harder it will be for you to get
back into the swing of things. It's best to go back right away."

"But I planned to take the summer off."

"I wouldn't. I'd go back as soon as possible. Just take a few weeks.
I'm telling you—you'll be sorry if you don't go back now."

So seldom do I listen to anyone once my mind is made up. But
I listened this time. I remembered how each year the workload got
harder and increased in magnitude. This was not going to be any
different. If anything, it would be worse. Best to jump right back in.
Worst case scenario—the counselor would be wrong, and I would
simply sail through it!

But the counselor was correct. The workload and level of difficulty increased exponentially. It was unreal! I immediately found myself
unable to conform to my former practice of coming home and mud-
dling through the participation from 7-10 pm. My household was too
noisy. Instead, I began to address all my participation in my office after hours, embracing the silence that the emptiness afforded me. The
work was demanding, very difficult and time consuming like nothing
before it. I was exhausted more days than not. With the workload at

the office increasing along with my responsibility, I began to feel as if I were running on the treadmill and barely able to keep up.

By the middle of the course, my body and mind were both beginning to wear out. I found myself sitting at my desk barely able to focus on the subject matter. My head would jump from daytime responsibilities and action items to class work, and the two would blend without my consent!

One evening very late, I found myself head in hand with no strength left. Tears began to flow, more as a physical response to the exhaustion than anything. I had nothing left. I was collapsing. As I sat in desperation, the office phone rang: "Hey, what are you doing out here?" It was an operator from one of the units who had seen my vehicle in the parking lot.

"Oh, um—homework."

"You're supposed to go home and get some sleep, you know?"

"Yeah." That really did it. I began to cry harder.

"You want something to eat? We have some fruit and stuff here."

"Oh. Yeah. That might be good. I'll be out in a few minutes."

I pushed my chair back from the desk and got up to go out. As I got in my car, I began to feel a bit better. Maybe I had needed a good cry. Maybe I just needed to get up and walk around. But I really think it was more the phone call—the knowledge that while I sat at my office desk alone, caving from the pressure, *somebody out there was wondering if I was OK.*

After just a few more minutes I went back and finished the assignment. Then I was free to go home and get my four hours of sleep before the next day's work.

From that evening forward, when I reached those points of desperation, I would think of that phone call. And I knew I was going to be OK!

74. What's the Buzz?

RIGHT ABOUT THIS time, I was advised that my mother was suffering with a condition that required surgery to correct, but had put it off for the better part of 18 months. She felt badly, and so was waiting until she felt better or stronger before she would consider agreeing to this. When I heard this, my first reaction was, "Don't you realize you're not going to feel better until you have the surgery to correct this?" It seemed so logical to me that I couldn't understand what about this she didn't get. After several conversations, Mom agreed that she needed to have the surgery.

Now, scheduling this at the earliest convenience for her and everyone involved in the surgery meant that my mother would be "going under the knife" two days before my 50th birthday. *DAMN!* was all that went through my head. I don't remember thinking about doing anything special for my birthday; somehow I had thought that right about now would be the time to plan it. Now that was off, because It was my duty to care for my mother. I knew I was going to be the one who would have to assume the role of caregiver throughout my mother's recovery period.

I booked a flight, gave Mom the information so that she would know I was all set to come, and made arrangements at work to set up the continuation of everything I was doing remotely from her house in Tampa. About 4 days before I was to depart, while I was visiting one of the control rooms in the plant, my cell phone rang. Without even thinking (typically, I looked at the caller ID first), I grabbed it and answered it. "Hello, this is Ellen."

"Hey, it's me (my brother). Mom told me you were coming down to take care of her after her surgery. Gee, that's great! She gave me your itinerary, so I will pick you up at the airport."

SHIT! "Oh, you don't have to bother with that. I can just take a taxi."

"Don't be silly. Of course I'll pick you up. See you in a few days."

In seconds, I was dialing my mother. "What are you doing giving him my itinerary? I told you not to even mention that I was coming down there! What's wrong with you?"

"You carry on so. Just let him pick you up."

"I didn't *want* him picking me up. I wanted peace and quiet. Was that too much to ask? Don't you listen to me when I speak?"

"I'm sorry. I didn't even think about it."

That was the truest thing she had said to me—she didn't even think about it. I had spent the better part of my adult life determined to avoid this type of negativity, and yet my mother had put that completely out of her head and did what she wanted. It was making me crazy.

Trapped, once again, I let the plan alone and flew in to Tampa. Outside the baggage claim area was my brother, smoking a cigarette and standing by his recent acquisition—a Crown Victoria (former police car). Now, this wasn't just the kind of car that *resembles* a police car. This thing used to actually *be* a police car, complete with the locks controlled from the driver's door, missing door handles on every other door, etc.

"Hey, you look great!" he said.

OK, I thought to myself.

"Why are you smoking? I thought you quit after you had the heart attack?"

"Oh, don't worry—I'm fine."

All I could think to say was, "I'm *not* worried. *I* can breathe fine. Just don't smoke in the car with me in it!"

We embarked on the drive from the airport to the hospital to see my mother, who was recuperating from her surgery—which had been two days before. Not five minutes into the journey, my brother began yelling at the traffic, "Can't these idiots see that this is a police car *(referring to the used Crown Victoria he had recently purchased from the police departments overstock)*? What the hell are they doing getting in my way like this?"

I was as incapable of shutting up as he obviously was! "No," I said. "The idiots don't realize that this is a police car. The idiots think that a police car typically has a police officer driving it!"

"They don't know I'm not a cop! Hell, if I jump out and put my gun in their face, they'll think twice.

"Swell—now I'm riding with Dirty Harry!" I mumbled under my breath. I rolled my eyes, looked out the passenger window and told myself, *It's going to be a short ride! Please, God—make it a short ride!*

When we arrived at the hospital, Mom looked frail. She was, after all, 79 years old. *She* should *look somewhat frail,* I thought. But surgery clearly had taken a toll on her. She was sitting up and able to speak, but obviously tired out.

"The doctor may want me to stay another day."

I thought to myself, *Oh, hell no—you're coming home today! I'm not going to listen to my brother carry on about society not recognizing him as the cop on the beat all day and night.*

But, all I said was, "Oh, no—let's ask the doctor."

God was watching and in total agreement with my wishes. Mom ended up discharged and we were able to drive her home. My brother did not stay long once we arrived at her house. The one thing he was good at was retreating when someone was ill. It's just as they say—everyone has a skill!

Mom and I remained in her house for three weeks while I nursed her through her convalescing. She spent the better part of the first week on Vicodin. She was in bed, I in the living room on the floor, as I worked on my computer, made telephone calls to the office, and scheduled teleconferences. I was getting a great deal of work done, even though I wasn't actually in the office.

As Mom began to regain her strength and the pain subsided, we had conversation after conversation about many things, the main one being family. She insisted that we have a "get- together" to celebrate my birthday. My birthday—which was officially over, which I had spent on the floor of her house by myself working. Now—*Let's celebrate?* Let's have another reason to put me through enduring the Dirty Harry rantings of my brother about how people don't respect him?

This was totally not what I wanted. *CAN ANYBODY HEAR ME??????*

"Tell me—what is it about my saying I don't want to be around my brother that you find so completely unacceptable?"

"Well, I know he gets wound up every now and then; but he is still your brother."

"No, 'wound up' doesn't even begin to cover it! It's ridiculous. I *hate* being around him. Worse, you always told me when I was growing up that once I was an adult, I could do what I wanted. Just when is that supposed to kick in exactly? I mean, I'm 50!"

"Oh—you always let this get to you. I just flip a switch in my head every time he starts to carry on. I don't even hear it."

For the first time in my life, I understood my mother. At least, I understood what the difference between her and me was. "That's it! You just said it! Oh my God! All these years, I never understood you. You've got this switch in your head, and when you're around something or someone that bothers you, you just flip that switch and poof!—it's gone! Well, guess what? I don't have one of those switches. So while you're shutting it off, I'm taking it on the chin and hating every minute of it. And I'm doing so because you're dragging me into these situations. I don't like this. I've never liked this!"

"I can't believe you're making such a big deal about this," she said with a look of surprise on her face.

"I know you can't. And that really makes me more sad than crazy. But here it is: *If you continue to do this to me, I will never set foot down here again.* I can't take it anymore! Do you get it now?"

She all but said, "All you had to do was say so"—but I knew that wasn't true!

So on the actual day of my 50th birthday, I sat on the living room floor of my mother's home, limited to the offerings of my laptop computer and network television. At the very pinnacle of my life, I was alone. It was a reminder of everything in my life that I wanted to forget—not being *alone* so much as being *lonely*. So many times throughout my life, I had felt completely isolated, alone in an apartment after school, unable to talk about things that really bothered me. After fifty years, with all my attempts to lift myself out of the rut, here I was again. Like a boomerang—thrown out in a different direction only to circle back to exactly the same spot!

Desperate for some sort of release, I took the remote control and began flipping through channels on the television. No matter how bad my life is on any given day, the offerings of daytime TV are far worse—programs about Who is your baby's daddy?, Divorce Judges, Small Claims Courts. Geez!

On a PBS (Public Broadcasting System) channel, there was a panel of comedians discussing aging. I caught it quickly and thought to myself; *and on my 50th birthday!* Surely this would be funny! The panel, although comprised of what I was certain were comedians, consisted of no one I recognized by name. A woman on the panel began speaking about an occasion on which she found herself walking through the streets of New York City on a hot summer's day, when she noticed a very handsome young man walking down the street. She referred to him as strapping and built. "This guy was a stone fox," she declared. "And as he walked past me, I waited to feel something—anything. But I didn't. I felt nothing. And I thought to myself, 'When did that stop? When did I stop feeling anything stimulating?'"

WHAT? Just when thought it could not get any worse! Now I have to listen to this stuff? UGH!!!! In an instant, I turned off the set and returned to jotting off an e-mail or two to a coworker/friend back at the plant.

It was at that moment that it hit me: Turning 50 didn't bother me. *What bothered me was struggling to get what I wanted my life to be—and negative wasn't it!* I wanted what I wanted my life to be – MINE! I wanted to be happy. *I wanted my life back!*

The remaining time in my mother's house was much more

enjoyable. We had no visits from anyone—which I loved! When she was given a clean bill of health on her recovery from the surgeon, I made my arrangements to return to work.

The day of my departure, we had breakfast at the table.

"Did you find your surprise on the night table?"

"No, I didn't notice anything."

"Well, go look."

On the very far side of the table away from the bed towards the wall was a white box. As I picked it up and examined it, I was stunned. "Mom, what the hell is this?"

"Oh, I think you know what it is."

"Are you kidding?"

My 79-year-old mother had bestowed a pocket vibrator on me as a gift.

"I'm not taking this," I told her.

As usual, she missed the point entirely. "Oh, it's just a little something—I have lots of them."

"Oh, God help me!"

Upon my return to work, I could hardly wait to enter my realm for the security of the normal day-to-day interaction I had with the staff. I picked up lunch for the entire group and brought it out as a sort of celebration. In the midst of lunch, I couldn't help myself. I just had to share the story of my crazy mother giving me this vibrator - forgetting, of course, that I was in the South with a room filled with Southern men!

"You guys are not going to believe what my mother gave me as a going away present. Go ahead—guess!"

A few shrugs of "I don't know" and they conceded that they had no idea.

"A damn vibrator!"

The entire table went silent, with the exception of one poor soul who was choking on his lunch. Although I was laughing, they were positively stunned. The silence was one of those deafening pregnant pauses that go on longer than normal. Finally the man sitting opposite me, trying not to flinch, leaned over towards his coworker and said, "Hey, remember this morning we were talking about those little pearl handled pocket pistols and how they are handed down from father to son? Is this the same sort of thing?"

Ahhh—I was back!

75. Chute

DEATH IMPACTS YOU in a surreal fashion. The air actually feels different. The whole environment changes around you. Never was this as profound as the day I learned that the fateful "house guest" from days past had left the earth.

I had been working all morning in the house—doing laundry, straightening up. I was planning errands that had to be run that afternoon. Typically, in spare moments away from work, I would try to place a phone call to my mother, just to touch base with her and let her know what was going on. It was, more or less, a weekly thing.

In the midst of our conversation about very mundane happenings, Mom blurted out, "Guess who died?" My mother is now elderly. As most of her acquaintances, friends and neighbors are also elderly, this could be anyone.

"Who?" I asked, meaning, *who now?* When she told me, I was stopped dead in my conversation. I couldn't believe it!

I am unable to count the number of times in my life that I have been told of someone's passing. Suffice to say, it has been many. From every single experience I have had with this, I have yet to feel the way I felt upon hearing this news. I felt free! Now, I have had altercations with this one or that one, have not particularly liked someone, or really detested a few. But I have never once wished harm on any of them—ever. I must say, sincerely, though that I was thrilled at this particular news. Now, from that moment forward in my own life, I was never to be bothered by that individual—ever again! I could go anywhere, do anything, knowing full well that there was absolutely no chance I would even see him—never mind having him try anything. *Free at last, Free at last. Thank God Almighty, I'm free at last!*

My demeanor took on an entirely different complexion—one of calm, contentment. At long last I had found peace. The air looked just a shade brighter. Flowers smelled just a bit sweeter. Food even tasted better. It was as if a cloud had been lifted. Everything improved. At work the following Monday, I remember thinking, "No matter what happens, it's all good!" I had never felt that way before. My life was coming full circle. I had faced my past, returned to school, and earned my degree. And now, after facing my demons head on, I had lived long enough to survive them. I was the victor!

There was about to be a rather rigorous "Turn-around" (TAR) at the plant beginning in a few weeks. Turn-arounds are scheduled maintenance outages for the purpose of making extensive repairs and upgrades to unit equipment. They require many more work hours than a normal run schedule and encompass everyone. My new lease on life assisted me in making this a "party"—as much as it could be a party! I was planning little surprises of food, rewards and brain teasers to break the monotony of the work schedule. My creative juices were flowing like rapids.

The days and nights blended together. It was the kind of schedule that spawned the expression, "Meeting yourself coming in and going out the door." Everyone was exhausted. Still, there was a certain camaraderie that accompanied the rigor, which made it appealing. Everyone sharpened their tongues, and humor flowed freely in an effort to lighten the load. We were constantly trying to make each other laugh—successfully.

In the midst of the madness, several engineers began talking about skydiving. "Oh, man, I've always wanted to sky dive—ever since I can remember!"

"You guys planning to go?"

"There's a few of us talking about it—after the TAR is over."

"I'm in! If you guys jump—I'm in!"

"Seriously?"

"Absolutely!" Talk of this trip was on again, off again, day after day—depending upon the mood, the workload and the level of exhaustion. One minute everyone was interested; the next, they were backing out. The idea of jumping terrified me. Why I wanted to do this even I couldn't figure out. I was not a lover of extreme sports. In fact, you could hardly classify me as a thrill seeker.

I remember telling my husband about this group from work talking about going skydiving, testing the waters to see if he would mind my going along with them.

"You? Skydive? Are you serious? Why would you want to do this?"

"I've always wanted to do this. Always!"

"You don't even ride roller coasters. What the hell?"

"I know. But I really want to do this."

"Hey, if you want to do it, that's fine. *I'm* not jumping out of a perfectly good airplane."

Knowing there was a consensus out there of people who were interested, I didn't want to leave the topic alone, risking that people would back away. I had had brushes with the possibility of doing this throughout my life and knew first hand that this could easily fall apart. I wanted to do it—once and for all. I would approach different colleagues who had expressed an interest in going. "Are you still interested? The TAR is over. Let's book it before we can't do it anymore. You don't want to jump when it's really cold out. It's already September. Let's make arrangements."

After much insisting, I managed to get one engineer to keep true to his word and book a reservation. The skydiving business required a $50 deposit, which was non-refundable unless they canceled due to weather or something unforeseen. The appointment was set for three weeks out. So far, it was just the two of us. (Originally there were to be five or six). If the other person backed out, I would be alone. I didn't want to do this alone, that was for sure! I needed the encouragement of someone doing it with me in order to actually go through with it.

Between my nervousness and my excitement, I could not stop talking about my reservation to jump. Day by day, as the time grew near, I found myself talking about it non-stop. When I wasn't talking, I was thinking. Even in my sleep, I had thoughts of jumping. As the countdown grew short, I was becoming nothing short of a nervous wreck. It was absolutely all I could think about. I was committed!

In fact, I had told virtually everyone I knew. In the event that I were to back out now, I would be talking about having backed out for the rest of my life—and I knew it. Now I had pushed myself into a sort of fear-filled paralysis.

By the night before the jump, I was terrified. My ability to sleep had been severely impacted to the point where I was running on only a few hours per night. As this, my last night, was a Friday, my husband was home from working out of town and was there for the weekend. As we went to bed that night, I tried everything I knew to relax. Nothing worked. Bobby fell asleep quickly, but was disturbed by my tossing and turning. Throughout the night, I tried to just lie and rest, but was unable to put the thoughts of the jump out of my head.

That night I learned what it must be like to be on death row. Decisions of stopping the appeal process made perfect sense to me. Who could take this? I just wanted it to be over. As I rolled frantically from side to side, Bobby reached out and with both arms, scooped me up and pulled me close.

"Settle down now," he whispered to me. "Come on."

Even if it was going to be the last night of my life, I felt comfortable and happy in his arms.

Morning came quickly. I had barely slept. Rather, I was in a sort of twilight state ready to surrender and get ready. I had now decided. Rain, snow, clouds—nothing was going to prevent me from jumping; I couldn't go through the waiting again. In retrospect, I think I should have just jumped—just gotten up and gone to the airport and put my money down. No waiting, no planning—and certainly no sweating!

The engineer who had made the reservations with me backed out at the last moment. "My wife has been crying all week; I just can't do it."

"Are you NUTS? Why'd you tell her? You should have just jumped and then told her afterwards."

That was crazy advice for me to be telling him. He had two small children, whereas my children were grown. In fact, my youngest was to turn 21 that day. He made a point of telling me, "I can't believe you're gonna do this on my birthday. What if you die? I'll always re-member that you died on my 21st birthday!"

"I'm not gonna die!" I had repeatedly assured him. Now all I had to do was to assure myself!

With the engineer backing out, there was only one other person going. Quite frankly, Luke was the one I had thought would certainly *not* jump. Now it was just the two of us. Rather than take off with him, I asked Bobby to join us.

"I'm not jumping," he kept insisting.

"I know. But you could come with us—for moral support."

There we were, the three of us, departing in Luke's truck and headed for the airport in Cullman, Alabama. The drive took about 25 minutes. Not long enough! Upon arrival, I looked for the tandem instructor who had been so highly recommended to me by another coworker who jumps regularly. "I would like to jump with Hank," I told the woman. I was hoping she cared.

Without confirming or denying that Hank was available, she gave me three pages of disclaimers to sign—all of which repeated, "THIS IS A DANGEROUS SPORT. THIS CAN RESULT IN DEATH." Everywhere it stated something to that affect. I had to initial acknowledging that I understood.

As I signed my life away—literally—a friend telephoned. It was Victoria, the plant manager's wife. With her very Welsh accent, she said, "I realized it was 10 o'clock and thought surely I should ring you to wish you good luck and happy landings for your jump. Are you still jumping, dear?"

"Yes, I was just signing all the papers and paying as you called."

"Well, I won't keep you—but I do want to say, be sure to yell 'Geronimo!' as you exit the plane."

"What?"

"Yes, that is the proper etiquette for parachuting."

As I hung up the phone, I thought to myself, only someone from the UK would be concerned with the proper etiquette as I plummet 10,000 feet to my death!

As it turned out, I would be plummeting 14,000 feet. We were given instruction on what to do as we dressed in jumpsuits and gear—a process that took approximately 15 minutes. That was it, the extent of my training. Hank was my tandem instructor, which was the only thing that kept me from being incapable of speaking at all. He was a very confident, mature man, who had jumped more times than I could imagine. His training began in the military in the '60's and then continued on since then. If I was going to die in this jump, it would be because my time was up—not because Hank didn't know what to do!

On the other hand, the plane was a flying gas can! Had I not been more preoccupied with the jump, I would have been terrified to board this plane. What a piece of junk! It had no seats. There was a platform in the rear, which turned out to be Hank's and my seat. Everyone else was squatting on the floor of the plane. On either side wall was a steel grab bar which everyone used to balance themselves as they approached the door, which was opened at 10,000 feet. Because Hank and I boarded the plane first, we were the last out. That meant that I had to watch everyone else go out the door. The only sound I heard besides the sound of the tremendous wind force was the clipping of equipment being secured and checked. One by one, jumpers and their tandem instructors approached the door and then DISAPPEARED. You don't go out the door and away—you go *down*. Whoosh—and you're gone!

Hank had instructed me, "When I say 'Ready!' you cross your arms in front of your chest with one hand on each shoulder." As I got closer to the door, I could feel myself becoming overwhelmed with incomprehensible fear.

"Ready!" yelled Hank.

Instantly I crossed my arms. At that moment, I thought, "SHIT—that's why!" Now my hands had let go of the side rails, so I was free to be pushed out the door. We both rocked back and forth, counting down "1, 2 . . . ." and on "3" we were to jump. It was too late now—I was going out the door. I decided I had only one choice—to jump like my childhood friend Lizzy told me to jump when I was learning to swim in the city pool. Just throw your arms out like superman and dive in!

"THREE!" Out we went.

My first reaction was to look back. As I did, I saw the plane disappearing to my right. "Oh crap—I'm really out here!" The next second, I looked around and saw the world all around me. I could see for miles and miles. There was no sensation of my stomach churning like it did going over the big hills in roller coasters. There was no sensation of fear either. At this point, I was out the door and flying—like a bird. Well, not exactly; birds can steer!

Before I could think, the photographer was about 6 feet in front of us, grabbing my hand, telling me to wave to the camera. As I tried to wave, I realized I couldn't breathe. The wind was rushing into my face with such velocity; my breath was being taken away. I tried with one hand to cover my nose and mouth to block the wind. Hank reached down and grabbed my hand, pulling it back out into the proper formation. I then reached for my face with the other hand. Hank again pulled it back. Finally I said to the camera man, "I can't breathe!"

This crazy man yelled back at me, "You're OK—just smile!"

As my picture was captured for posterity (as well as evidence), I felt a tug from the harness, almost as if I were being pulled up. That wasn't exactly it—I was being slowed down. The chute had been deployed. "Oh hell, yeah! I am going to live through this!"

Seconds later, I realized that I had what can only be described as searing pain in my legs. I tried to assess what was wrong. I looked down. *Damn, it's the harness; it must be too tight.* My first reaction was to loosen it, but as I looked down to release the buckle, I saw my feet dangling thousands of feet above ground and thought, *bad idea.*

As we drifted downward, the pain became more severe, and my body became weakened—so much so that I felt I would faint. We were getting closer to the ground. Hank was now alerting me to the fact that I would need to lift my legs for the landing.

"I can't."

"Get 'em up!" he yelled in my ear.

"I can't—I'm weak."

"Now! Do it!"

I grabbed for the handles on the side of the suit legs and willed them up just enough so that Hank could land us both. As my feet touched down, I had no strength what-so-ever. I went down on my knees first, then my hands. I couldn't even decide if I was sick to my stomach and going to vomit, or if I was simply going to faint. The thought going through my head was, "I so totally get why the Pope kisses the ground when he lands!"

It took a few moments for me to regain my composure. I was experiencing what can only be described as system overload. Every ounce of adrenalin racing through my body had my system on full alert. But—I had jumped! I had jumped out of a plane at 14,000 feet—and lived!

As I walked with my husband, Hank, and Luke across the runway back to the hanger, I felt a confidence I had never known. From that moment on, I knew I could face anything with no fear. My life had been changed forever!

76. Silencing the Roar

MY EXCITEMENT AFTER jumping was difficult to contain. While I felt I couldn't stop talking about it, I was exhausted from the lack of sleep prior to the jump. For several weeks prior, I had not rested—not really. Immediately upon getting in the truck to go home, I passed out. How Luke drove, I will never know. He and Bobby talked the rest of the way, but I could not tell anyone what they talked about. I was at peace, curled up on the back seat.

When I got to our house, I pulled out the DVD recording that had been made preserving the memory of the jump. Quickly I made copies to share with friends. I remember watching the video again with Dani and Cyrus—our grandchildren. Dani was seated next to me on the couch and Cyrus across the room on the recliner. As the video showed me going out the door of the plane, Dani pulled her legs up to her chest and covered her mouth as if to say, "No, Nannie—don't do it!" She was visibly frightened. Cyrus, on the other hand, had a big smile on his face, "Neat! Can I do it?"

"Dani—Nannie is right here next to you. This already happened. I'm fine!"

That viewing launched a celebration of sorts, with family members all coming in and out of the living room, replaying the video at will. No matter how many times I watched it, I was still thrilled. I drove out to the plant that very day to drop off a copy of the DVD for some operators on the night shift to watch when they came in.

The following evening, I actually put in a personal appearance at the plant. Upon my entering the control room, a few of the workers applauded. It was great fun talking about the experience with them—and living to do it!

The day I jumped, everything changed for me. Cartoons of parachutes adorned my office door, and comments poured in via e-mail, telephone and text. It was difficult to focus on work. My adrenalin was still pumping from the experience.

But try as I did, I could not stay at this level of excitement. The responsibilities of my job were looming, and I was forced to return both my physical being and my psyche to the duties at hand. The demands of the project were increasing. There were 25 tasks to be done on any given day, and those 25 tasks would generate 10 action items each. It was like juggling pebbles. Needs were arising everywhere.

With the day-to-day responsibilities of life pulling me back to reality, the distance between me and the jump grew. "Normal life" was returning in full force, as was exhaustion. The rigors of the job were demanding, and at the end of the day, I was left welcoming sleep.

My dreams were peaceful—as always. I dreamed of my childhood, returning to the apartment where I grew up, on Sedgwick Avenue. The window sill beckoned, and I sat there, as I had hundreds of times before, staring out the window, looking at the activity in the street below and longing to be a part of it all. There was an abundance of life going on outside—traffic, neighbors visible from their apartment windows, children playing in the street, passersby walking on the sidewalks.

The window that I frequented was really three windows together. The one center window was more of a picture window—much larger in size than the two flanking it, which were regular-sized windows that opened from the bottom or top. The three windows were surrounded on the outside by a fire escape. In this dream, however, I could not help but notice that the fire escape did not extend to the window on the far left. It only covered the center window and the far right. I sat on the left windowsill looking down for the longest time. I wanted to go out where the activity was. I wanted *out*—period.

I got down from the window sill standing firmly on the floor. With both hands I lifted the window bottom up so that the window was wide open, both panes of glass together as one. Then, carefully, I placed my hands on either side of the window molding, bracing myself to balance as I stepped up on the window sill—first one foot, then the other. With my feet supporting my body, my knees pressed tightly to my chest, I scrunched my head down to be able to clear my way past the window edge. Then, with a very strong push similar to that with which you would propel yourself from the edge of a pool, I jumped out the window!

I awoke, startled beyond belief. "Oh, God," I thought. I sat up and looked around. There I was, in my bed. My room was exactly as it should be. It was early morning. My alarm had not gone off. The dream had awakened me. I sat in silence, trying to regain my composure, thinking about the experience of the dream. *I had jumped—I had jumped out my bedroom window!*

My entire life, I had wanted to jump, but I had never realized why: The yelling, the stress, the tension of being around my father, the fear of the "house guest" entering the room uninvited. In the back of my mind, I had wanted out of that apartment.

I REMEMBERED IT all vividly. I remembered thinking back on the actual apartment fondly. I had *liked* it—at least, I thought I did.

WHAT I DIDN'T like were the events that took place in that apartment. I wanted to get away from them. I wanted to put them behind me. Jumping symbolized freedom—escaping from the bad, from the memories of bad things that happened there. If I got out, I could get away. I would be free! It had taken me over 40 years to get up the nerve to jump away from all that hurt me.

I had feared the jump would kill me. I was wrong. The jump saved my life.

One of the earliest gifts I recall from my Nana was a children's book signed by the author. The book was entitled, *Clyde of Africa*, written by Ken Heyman and Michael Mason. It was a wonderful story of a young lion cub that accidentally discovered his ability to roar. This skill took him quite by surprise. Thus, he ran around roaring at everything! He roared and roared and roared some more, until he roared once too often! He roared at a wildebeest—which caused him to be chased. After a while, the lion met a giraffe. Rather than roaring at the giraffe, he licked his face. The giraffe licked him back. Then he realized that he *could* roar—but he didn't always have to.

This was a sweet children's book, with many wonderful photos of actual animals in Africa. The book, while a favorite of mine (partly because I liked it and mostly because it was a gift from Nana), sat on my bookshelf the duration of my life. Nana passed away right after my dad stopped coming to visit, before my mother allowed the house guest to stay.

As a child, I was hurt and frightened. Bad things happened. They remained with me much in the same way I kept that book. No one knew. At times, I didn't even think about it. But there it was - always with me. I used to think people could see the pain.

What everyone *did* see was the difference in the way I acted—the way I roared all the time, simply because I could. The more differently I behaved, the more differently I was perceived. It became a vicious cycle. I would gravitate towards hurt, because that was what I was used to. We seek out what we are familiar with—good or bad. As a result, I was hurt more and more. I *expected* to be hurt—all the time; and when I was, I concluded that I was right to have expected that result.

I can't tell you exactly how many times I roared, but it was often. I roared for years! Now I roar less often. I see that there are more giraffes in the world than there are wildebeests—or things to roar about. And that's a good thing!

Acknowledgements

SIMPLY PUT; I am grateful to every single person I ever met. Good, bad, or ugly; our acquaintance left an impression and subsequently molded me into the person I am today – someone I am happy to be.

But for those who were truly my friends; those who listened when I ranted, made me laugh when I wanted to cry and gave me hope when I thought I had nothing left - to each of you, I owe my sanity if not my life itself. I thank you from the deepest part of myself.

CPSIA information can be obtained at www.ICGtesting.com
Printed in the USA
BVOW071324010812

296805BV00002B/5/P

9 781432 791001